Teacher Skills and Strategies

For Teachers

In recognition of their 'impossible task'

> Teaching is not to be regarded as a static accomplishment like riding a bicycle or keeping a ledger; it is, like all arts of high ambition, a strategy in the face of an impossible task. (**Lawrence Stenhouse**, 1985, p. 124)

Teacher Skills and Strategies

Peter Woods

 The Falmer Press
(A member of the Taylor & Francis Group)
London ● New York ● Philadelphia

UK   The Falmer Press, Rankine Road, Basingstoke, Hampshire
                RG24 0PR.

USA   The Falmer Press, Taylor & Francis Inc., 1900 Frost Road,
                Suite 101, Bristol PA 19007

© 1990 Peter Woods

First published 1990

Library of Congress Cataloging in Publication Data

Woods, Peter.
  Teacher skills and strategies/Peter Woods.
  Includes bibliographical references.
  ISBN 1–85000–732–2: ISBN 1–85000–7330–0 (pbk.):
  1. Teaching. 2. Teachers — Great Britain. I. Title.
  LB1025.2.W67 1990
  371.1'02 — dc20

British Library Cataloguing in Publication Data
Woods, Peter, *1934–*
  Teacher skills and strategies
  1. Teaching
  I. Title
  371.102
  ISBN 1–85000–732–2
  ISBN 1–85000–733–0 pbk

Jacket design by Caroline Archer
Based on an illustration by Sharon Keightley

Typeset in 10½/13 point Bembo by
Bramley Typesetting Limited, 12 Campbell Court, Bramley,
Basingstoke, Hants.

Printed in Great Britain by
Taylor & Francis (Printers) Ltd, Basingstoke

Contents

Acknowledgments

Over the years many colleagues have contributed to the thought that has gone into this book. They include Martyn Hammersley, Andy Hargreaves, Andrew Pollard, Jennifer Nias, Lynda Measor, Pat Sikes, Stephen Ball, David Hargreaves, Martyn Denscombe, Ivor Goodson and Elizabeth Grugeon. Not all of them would agree with everything I have written, but the book would have been the poorer but for their input. A special word of thanks to Jimmie, Clive, Sue and Kath. Sheila Gilks has again provided expert secretarial assistance.

For permission to reproduce material previously published, my thanks to the Open University for parts of the Introduction (which originally appear in 'Teaching', Unit 11 of Course E208 (1988) *Exploring Educational Issues*, Milton Keynes); to the Falmer Press for Chapter 2 (from Delamont, S. (Ed.) (1987) *The Primary School Teacher*); Chapter 5 (from Barton, L. and Walker, S. (Eds) (1981) *Schools, Teacher and Teaching*, 1981); and Chapter 6 (from Goodson, I.F. and Ball, S.J. (Eds) (1984) *Defining the Curriculum*); to Manchester University Press, and to Lynda Measor, who co-authored the article, for Chapter 3 (from *Research in Education*, 31, May 1984); to the Open University Press for Chapter 7 (from Cole, M. and Walker, S. (Eds) (1989) *Teaching and Stress*, Milton Keynes); to Routledge for Chapter 4 (from *The Divided School*, 1979); and to James for the poem in Chapter 8.

Introduction: Opportunities to Teach and Learn

This book illustrates a wide range of teacher's craft from some highly successful aspects to less successful. In doing so, it leans towards a certain model of teaching wherein personal qualities are certainly important but have to be seen within the prevailing structure of 'opportunities to teach'. Where opportunities are plentiful, teachers will be freer to address the purer problems of teaching, that is how to promote pupil learning of relevant and worthwhile skills and knowledge. Where they are less plentiful, teachers' energies might be directed toward increasing them, to adjusting means to ends, or even adjusting the ends themselves. Where opportunities are not seen to exist at all, and indeed on occasions when conditions appear to be suppressing and running counter to their appearance, teaching can be said to be in crisis. This, then, represents a continuum. Some teachers may be at a particular point on it for much of the time. Most will experience several aspects of it at different points of their careers or different times of the school year or week. In sum, the quality of teaching cannot be assessed independently of the opportunities to teach. Personal, cognitive and social factors are all important. This can be substantiated by examining some recent reports and research in the area.

An Official View of Teaching Quality

A spate of government reports during the 1980s conveyed what we might term the 'official' view of good teaching and what promotes it (DES, 1983, 1985a and 1985b). A report by HM Inspectorate, *The New Teacher in School* (DES, 1982) set the scene. They reported that 'nearly a quarter of the teachers in the present sample (were) poorly or very poorly equipped for the task they are given to do'. The criteria they used for making this judgment were those they would use for 'assessing any work in schools' and were 'implicit in the evaluation of work seen' (p. 3). Thus, successful lessons would involve good relationships between teachers and pupils, teacher characteristics here showing

> a quiet, calm, relaxed, good-humoured attitude . . . combined with firmness and a sense of purpose; a demonstration of interest in and knowledge of the pupils individually and an appropriate level of expectation of them; and mutual respect . . . the teachers being sensitive to the needs of the pupils and respecting their contributions whatever their limitations. Where these qualities were shown, pupils were confident enough to play a full part in the lessons, to offer their own ideas and ask questions, or seek help when unsure, while the teacher could blend praise and encouragement with an occasional reprimand, the latter without arousing resentment. (pp. 6–7)

Good classroom management is associated with 'a crisp, orderly, punctual start to the lessons . . . a planned and tidy ending, an assured manner, good use of the eye and voice and the giving, where necessary, of clear instructions' (p. 7). In primary classrooms, where pupils may be working in a variety of tasks and subjects, 'the teachers should move purposefully around the classroom anticipating needs, checking and extending the pupils' work' (*ibid*). There should be appropriate aims and objectives, taking account of the age and abilities of the class, their previous experience and the nature of the subject being studied. Where inappropriate, it was often because they were too limited, being based on 'the recording or memorising of facts or the practice of techniques without any attempt to develop a depth of understanding or to maintain a progression' (p. 9). Pupils' work should be 'thoroughly and constructively marked'. Appropriate books, materials and equipment for the range of pupils present should be selected. HMI recognized here possible problems of resource in the school, but were concerned about 'lessons in which teachers had resigned themselves to using the inadequate or unsuitable materials available in their schools and had made no attempt to supplement or adapt them' (p. 10).

Work should be matched to pupils' capabilities and needs. In primary schools, lessons which did this 'called on a number of teaching techniques: assignments at different levels after a class exposition, well-differentiated work-cards, skilfully varied oral questioning which maintained a good pace and individual and group work with well organized intervention by the teacher' (p. 12). Older pupils did not become bored, nor the less able frustrated. Opportunities were provided for pupils to take 'increasing responsibility for organizing some parts of their own work' giving them a 'sense of purpose in their work' increasing motivation, and developing 'self-reliance and cooperation' (p. 13). In secondary schools, such lessons showed 'a good choice of teaching materials which made demands on the pupils, well planned purposeful tasks which allowed for contributions from pupils of different ability, good well paced oral work with differentiated levels of questioning, and a variety of learning styles combining class exposition with group or individual work' (p. 14). Mastery of subject is clearly very important. Without it, teaching approaches 'maintained an often slavish adherence to the textbook reliance on narrow questions often requiring monosyllabic answers, an inability to follow up and extend pupils' answers and an over-prescriptive method whereby the teacher was able to remain within a constricted, safe pattern of work' (pp. 14–15).

Language in the classroom was seen as an important area. There should be opportunities for useful dialogue between teachers and pupils, for pupils to express their own thoughts and ideas and to have their language extended. Teachers should vary their style of questioning to suit the occasions, and 'make good use of the pupils' responses to carry the work forward' (p. 18). In good lessons, questions were carefully balanced between those addressed to the whole class and those to named individuals. Some teachers 'were skilled at breaking down a problem into stages so that, by posing supplementary questions, they could narrow or broaden the scope of the enquiry helpfully for the pupils' (p. 19).

HMI point out that all these factors were 'clearly interdependent and it was rare to find work of high quality in respect of some but not of others. This, perhaps, reinforces their point that 'the personal qualities of the teachers were in many cases the decisive factor in their effectiveness' (p. 80). Some, in their opinion, were clearly unsuited to teaching and the training institutions were taken to task for passing them as fitted for teaching.

It would be difficult to imagine such a conclusion in the 1940s and 1950s when there was a desperate shortage of teachers; or indeed in the early 1990s. Standards of adequacy are almost inevitably affected by social, economic and political climate, which, amongst other things, affects the supply of teachers. As for the 'deficit model' that accounted for the perceived inadequacy within the teachers themselves, the inspectors themselves refer from time to time to 'other factors'. The more these are brought into focus the weaker the deficit model becomes. Much of what the inspectors criticize in lessons, such as too much direction by teachers, failure to distinguish among pupils in mixed-ability classes, boring tasks, the dictating of notes, appears to be fairly common in schools. The scale of the inadequacy is almost certainly too vast to be all put down to teachers' deficiency.

As for 'personal quality' being the decisive factor in effective teaching, McNamara (1986) has pointed out that there is no indication that this arose during the research as a key variable that required definition, close observation and analysis. 'The notion of "personal quality" is merely invoked ex post facto after the research has been completed in order to account for the so called findings' (p. 32). Further, it is not related to the extensive literature on teacher personality, which shows the problems in relating it to effective teaching. For example, we might approve of qualities a teacher possesses, but that teacher may not be able to employ them in such a way as to bring about pupil learning. There are other problems about the question of teachers' personal qualities. Can we all agree whether a particular teacher has good ones or not? Do all teachers require the same kind of qualities? Should not the teaching staff of a school reflect a variety of views, personalities, qualities . . .?

The New Teacher in School put the issue of teaching 'quality' on the agenda, whatever the problems surrounding it, presented an outline model of HMI's conception of it, and evaluated a number of teachers in terms of it. The emphasis on 'quality' and how to secure it has grown with further publications. If the *New Teacher* had its sights on training institutions, *Teaching Quality* (1983) was aimed at LEAs, discussing how they could help 'improve the match between teacher expertise and subject taught' and 'raise professional standards by retaining and encouraging the best and most committed teachers . . . making full use of management tools such as premature retirement, redeployment and if necessary, compulsory redundancy in the interests of achieving a good match between their teachers' qualifications and skills and the need of teachers in the school' (para. 8). *Better Schools* (1985) continued with the related quests to 'expose the heart of good teaching' (para. 135) and to manage the teaching force to ultimate efficiency, better teachers being promoted, those 'encountering professional difficulties' being identified and counselled, and where that did not work, being considered for early retirement or dismissal (para. 180).

These reports have to be seen within the context of growing central control of the educational system. The criteria are centrally determined (as opposed, for example, to being determined by the teachers themselves), rating systems set up against which to measure teachers, and strong suggestions made about how they can be met. This must be done within the prevailing system and with existing resources. Interestingly, *The New Teacher in School* carries a disclaimer inside its front cover to the effect that 'Nothing said in this discussion paper it to be construed as implying Government commitment to the provision of additional resources'. As for the system, DES Circular 3/84 stated 'In assessing the personal qualities of candidates, institutions should look in particular for a sense of responsibility, a robust but balanced outlook, awareness, sensitivity, enthusiasm and facility in communication' (para. 14). As McNamara (1986) points out, an educational argument could easily be advanced for replacing what might be seen as the conservative 'robust but balanced' with the radical 'critical and reformist' (p. 36).

As for an explanation of teacher effectiveness, Broadhead feels that not enough consideration has been given to factors that impinge on 'all teachers' work which lie outside their control' (DES 1985b, para. 3). Broadhead points particularly to the enormous disparity between different age-groups of children, their different needs and consequently different demands from teachers. Yet even though HMI draw a distinction between primary and secondary teaching occasionally, the assumption seems to be that one model, by and large, fits all of them. They have missed, too, Broadhead argues, the complexities of relationships within the classroom. 'Real life' has been reduced to a 'plethora of prescriptive descriptions' (1987, p. 68). What we have, then, is not a theory of successful teaching, but a check list of points that might be useful in a teacher appraisal process where that is conducted by somebody else observing the teacher. It does not contain guidance on how a teacher might improve his/her personal effectiveness beyond the implication that 'weeding-out' and behaviour modification will enhance effectiveness. There is no consideration of what lies behind teacher behaviour. If the latter is 'inadequate', it is considered to be redeemable at source, and if not, to be dispensed with. This reflects, perhaps, the new managerial ethos that pervades the environment in which teacher quality is being discussed.

There is also a problem in placing teachers in categories. It might be a useful 'sorting' device, but in terms of professional development it might prove counter-productive. A lesson might be drawn here from the literature pointing to the dangers of labelling pupils. We may shape our behaviour towards them in accordance with the label, and they may come to respond in line with that; that is they come to act out, and hence confirm, the behaviour expected of them. Broadhead concludes that 'perhaps the issues to which those concerned with developing a theory of educational effectiveness should be addressing themselves are not "What is the ideal state and how many have made it?" but "What is happening along the way?"' (p. 70). I turn to this next.

Opportunities to Learn

Prominent among social scientists' attempts to identify effective teacher behaviour have been the 'teaching styles' and 'classroom tasks' researches associated with Maurice Galton (1980a and 1980b), Neville Bennett (1976 and 1987) and their colleagues. The 'teaching styles' research developed from the debate over 'traditional' and 'progressive' styles of teaching, brought to the fore by the Plowden Report of 1967. The research yielded a mass of useful information about teaching in primary schools and about teacher–pupil interactions. Yet, though initially the quest might have been to identify the effectiveness of various styles, the research showed, in the end, the problems of conceptualizing teaching in terms such as 'traditional' and 'progressive', and relating these to the realities of classroom life. Most teachers use both to varying degrees (Bell, 1981); and though a wider range of styles was identified it was always difficult isolating what parts of teachers' behaviour were responsible for which learning outcomes. Further, as far as successful teaching was concerned, there appeared to be more important factors running across the styles.

As far as implementing the terms of the Plowden Report are concerned, the research illustrated the considerable difficulties primary school teachers face. Further, it showed the need to probe deeper on more specific behaviours if 'successful teaching' was to be identified sufficiently to be of use to teachers and to teacher-trainers, or to advance our understanding of teacher-learning processes. One of the most prominent attempts to get to grips with this kind of detail was that by Bennett and his colleagues in their work on 'classroom tasks' published in *The Quality of Pupil Learning Experiences* (1984).

For Bennett, the key to the new line of research lay in the observational data of the 'Teacher Styles' project — a good illustration of research development when one line of enquiry has become exhausted. It was noticed that the more successful 'formal' teachers gave a greater proportion of their curriculum time to mathematics and language activities, and that within these classrooms the pupils spent much more time involved in their work. These findings appeared in line with Carroll's (1963) model of school learning, which held that, all else being equal, mastery of a task was determined by the opportunities provided by the teacher for a pupil to study a given content, and the use made of that opportunity by the pupil. This 'opportunity to learn' model yielded a number of interesting studies relating to (i) the amount of schooling made available to pupils (length of school day, for example, can vary as much as six hours per week in Britain); (ii) the allocation of time to various curriculum activities (which can vary considerably both between and within schools, though the National Curriculum in the 1988 Education Reform Act is designed to reduce this); (iii) the use pupils made of opportunities provided i.e. the amount of time they spend on tasks (in Bennett's 1980 study of Open Plan schools, it was found that involvement varied from nearly 90 per cent in some classes to less than 50 per cent in others).

However, the provision of time is an organizational, rather than pedagogical matter. It counts for little if the children do not understand what they are required to do, or if the pacing or sequence is faulty, or the work too hard or too easy. It is necessary, therefore, also to consider the nature and quality of tasks. This in fact was the focus of the Bennett project reported in 1984. Central to it was the notion of 'match' or appropriateness, a concern that had run through HMI reports from 1978 to several of those mentioned earlier. For example, in the 8–12 Middle School survey, they found that 'overall, the content, level of demand and pace of work were most often directed toward children of average ability in the class. In many classes there was insufficient differentiation to cater for the full range of children's capabilities' (HMI, 1983 and 1985). In other words, there was inadequate matching of tasks to children's abilities.

As well as a theory of learning, to help them characterize tasks Bennett *et al.* also needed a wider view of the teaching–learning process of which tasks are a part. Bennett (1987, p. 59) saw this as a circular process. The teacher decides on the choice of tasks. This is then presented to pupils. They do it, the teacher assesses the results, diagnoses any problems, and this informs the next intention or purpose. Much teaching proceeds in this circular way. Mismatches can occur at any stage of this process. The teacher may choose an inappropriate task for the pupil concerned (ability of pupil, stage of development etc); it may be presented in ways that are not clear to the pupil, or in a situation or with resources that make it difficult to do; the teacher may make a faulty diagnosis, and so on. We should also note that, like most models of educational processes, things are not as neat and tidy as they may appear in this model. As the author points out, these are processes, not discrete events, there is a large measure of overlap between them, and not all of the processes appear in every task.

The authors found some interesting differences in the nature of tasks teachers set pupils, reflecting, they thought, important differences in the quality of learning. Thus 60 per cent were practice tasks, and only 25 per cent 'incremental' (accumulating and consolidating new knowledge and/or skills), and 7 per cent 'restructuring' (discovery and invention) and 'enrichment' (problem solving). Surprising here, perhaps, in the continuing aftermath of Plowden, was the low incidence of discovery or invention demands.

As for mismatching, there was a significant discrepancy between the tasks teachers intended and the actual ones that children faced. Thirty per cent of number tasks and 20 per cent of language tasks did not carry the teachers' intended demand. This was mainly due to diagnostic errors and to problems in designing tasks. The central question was the degree of match between a task and a child who performed it, or, in other words, the contribution the task made to the child's learning. Taking into account the results of the child's work, the observation of the child's strategy and the interview with the child afterwards, it was found that in language, only 40 per cent (43 per cent in maths) of all tasks matched in this respect, with 29 per cent (28 per cent) being too difficult, and 26 per cent (26 per cent) too easy. In both areas, high attainers were underestimated on 41 per cent of tasks assigned to them and low attainers overestimated on 44 per cent of tasks. While the teachers sometimes recognized that a child was in difficulty, the problem of underestimation did not arise with them.

This high level of mismatching came about, in Bennett *et al's.* opinion, through teachers' emphasis on procedures (layout, neatness etc), quantity, and judging pupils by their own standards ('It's good for Steven'). Teachers recognized some of the signs of overestimation (though less often underestimation) but they rarely planned to go back to diagnose children's problems. In nearly all cases, the response to the perceived overestimation was to plan more practice on difficulties in procedure using similar examples, or to go on to the next task in the scheme. This, then, was a mismatch between the child's task performance and the teacher's diagnosis of it.

For achieving better matching, Bennett *et al.* recommend things like rationalization of the queuing system at the teacher's desk; deciding whether they want error-free work, or imaginative, expressive writing; exploring further possibilities in teaching to groups; employing more teachers' aides, such as parents or suitable unemployed school leavers (pp. 219–21). These remedies might help to create more time for teachers, but, the authors argue, teachers also need to develop their skills in diagnosis and time should be allocated on training courses for this. During in-service work, provision for teachers from different schools to share their knowledge and experiences might help break down their sense of isolation, which itself helps perpetuate existing practices. The creation of specialist posts to promote work in this area would give it a boost. The authors recognize, however, that there are no easy solutions. Desforges (1985) concludes: 'Indeed, it might be that the classroom as presently conceived has reached levels of productivity, in terms of learning outcomes and happy relationships, consistent with its design limitations. Improvements might require radical reconceptions of teaching and learning situations' (p. 102).

As for questions about the research, it might be asked if, despite the polish of its design, it has done justice to the complexities of classroom activity, to teachers' decision-making and to pupils' learning. In the first place, it might be argued that a wider conception of 'matching' is needed to embrace the social and the affective as well as the cognitive. It is well known, for example, that background cultures, such as those of social class, gender and 'race' have considerable influence not only on children's disposition toward school and learning, but also upon thought processes themselves (Schostak and Logan, 1984). Learning is a process, which takes place within a context and a history. To achieve cognitive matching we would need knowledge of pupils' interests, values, concerns, and the influences operating on them. The match might be more dependent on the treatment of the influences than repair of tasks. For example, a girl's difficulties with a scientific task may be due more to the influence of gender codes upon her and her teachers than to her 'natural' abilities (Kelly, 1981; Whyte *et al.*, 1985). Simply to repair the task in such a situation to match her *apparent* abilities would be to minister to a state of affairs which forecloses on educational opportunities for large numbers of children.

Teachers subjectivities also need to be taken into account. One of the major problems in the Bennett *et al.* research is whether their approach keeps faith with the teacher's approach. Teachers were consulted in the research, but only within the framework and theories of the researchers. In other words, very little is known about these teachers, *their* theories of teaching and learning (though some are inferred — again within the framework of the research), or the general pedagogical context within which the tasks occurred. There is no 'longitudinal' dimension, that is to say, teachers were not observed over a period of time. The tasks are extracted from the complex reality of classroom life and held up for analysis as fairly discrete items, despite the researchers' recognition of them as processes operating within a wider context. Teachers' and pupils' work is ongoing and, arguably, has to be studied in the round to do it justice. For example, tasks can be, and most probably are, multi-functional. A teacher's approach, typically, would be to ensure a fair range of tasks over a given period of time with any particular child according to the child's perceived needs and the teacher's own theory of learning. To examine one or two tasks given to a child in that period, therefore, possibly misrepresents the teacher. A practical solution to this would have been to include one or two in-depth, longitudinal studies of teachers.

Teachers might also query some of the assumptions behind the diagnoses of mismatching. For example, judgments of 'overestimation' and 'underestimation' are based on *observers'* perceptions of discrepancies between task performance and pupils' abilities. There are clear indications in the study that teachers considered there to be less discrepancy. Where there was some, it could be within what we might call the 'margin of error' given the difficult circumstances in which teachers have to work; or it might not necessarily be a mismatch, since difficult and easy tasks can be functional for learning. A difficult task can inspire or challenge, push to the limits, or restore an appropriate sense of one's own abilities. An easy task can boost confidence. You have to ask, therefore, too difficult or too easy for what? Again, if the answer is the pupil's cognitive abilities, the teacher may reply that there are other considerations, such as personal and social development, and motivation. A significant feature here is that the pupils were generally happy and content and industrious. Rather than interpreting this as a factor blinding the teachers to mismatching, they might argue that it makes a splendid climate for learning among 6- to 7-year-olds and that it was produced in large part by a judicious selection of tasks.

Teachers might disagree also with some of the distinctions made: for example, those between 'procedural' aspects of tasks and their product. To the teachers, some of these procedural aspects may well be part, and a very important part, of the product. For example, neatness, layout, punctuation, 'good writing' are, arguably, crucially important matters, especially at this particular age when, possibly, the work habits of a whole school career or even a lifetime are being formed. Procedural aspects may also be deemed important by teachers when some of the basic skills that hold the key to later learning opportunities and accomplishments are being fashioned. If we accept, however, that there was a certain amount of mismatching and that it retarded pupil progress, it is important to identify the reasons. Even though the teachers were experienced and generally recognized as able, Bennett *et al*. felt the problems lay with them and various kinds of misjudgment that they made. This was not, however, a matter of lack of 'personal qualities' as in the DES reports. These teachers were rated highly in this respect by the researchers. This is more a matter of research and teaching combining to pinpoint problem areas. Attention can then be given to those areas to yield an even more advanced professionalism, and thus to increase the pupil's opportunities to learn.

The Oracle project, the 'quality of pupil learning' research, and the DES reports all reveal much useful information about classroom teaching. They are all, too, aware of the problems of dealing with classes of thirty or more children and other pressures on teachers. The question is whether awareness is enough; whether, in other words, we can single out aspects of the teacher's work and study them in isolation, or whether they relate together in some way. As it is, these studies tend to take for granted what teaching means, and what it means to teachers. Also, teaching has been considered as if teachers are free to decide which style they wish to adopt, how they will monitor tasks, whether they will choose to diagnose instances of mismatching and so on. In other words, it has been studied as a technical process employed by teachers for effective learning. Thus, improving teaching is a rational business of, either identifying people with the appropriate personal qualities and selecting accordingly or attempting to train people up to them, discarding those who do not reach the mark; or teachers improving their skills of matching tasks to children. Both site the point of improvement within the teacher. As the DES document *Teaching Quality* put it, 'The teaching force, some 440,000 strong, is the major single determinant of the quality of education' (1983, paragraph 1). This, however, neglects two related influences upon teaching which have a critical and integral bearing upon the product, one internal, and one external to the teacher. Together, they amount to 'opportunities to teach'. Without some understanding of these, the use of the 'opportunities to learn' model is severely restricted.

Opportunities to Teach

The factors internal to the teacher are to do with commitment and interests; those external are to do with constraints. They interact upon each other. Thus the constraints upon teaching may affect the teachers' commitment to the job and how and where they perceive the realization of their interests and indeed the 'personal qualities' they choose to exhibit. Doubtless, too, 'personal qualities' will play a part in the perception of constraints and how they are tackled. It is dubious, however, as to whether they can deal with them to the extent of justifying regarding them as the single most important factor in the quality of education. Personal qualities are part of the overall holistic activity of teaching. They can be made, or broken, by other factors. They should not, therefore, be considered independently of them. I shall consider teachers' commitment and interests, and constraints upon teacher activity in turn.

Teachers' Commitment

It is often argued that one of the most important factors in successful teaching is pupils' motivation. Less attention has been paid to *teachers'* motivation. This tends to be taken for granted. However not all teachers are as committed to teaching as each other, or in the same way (Lortie, 1975; Lacey, 1977). Some are thoroughly dedicated, others less so. Some of the former teach because they love to do so and love children (what might be termed 'vocational commitment'); some because they consider it a good professional job in which they can excel and advance (what might be termed 'professional commitment'). Some might be in teaching for what they can get out of it materially ('instrumental commitment'). The concept of commitment has become topical in the late 1980s when there is a crisis of morale throughout the profession and some teachers have been found to re-examine their involvement with the job. It must inevitably affect teaching efficiency.

Sikes *et al.* (1985) have summarized the various studies of commitment as follows:

> . . . In Figure 1, we have put together analyses from other recent work on this (Lacey, 1977; Woods, 1979; Nias, 1981), with our own indications from this study to provide a composite model.

Figure 1: Forms of Teacher Commitment

	Vocational	Professional			Instrumental
	Education	Subject	Teaching	Institution	Career
Core					
Mixed					
Peripheral					

This shows a vocational 'calling' to teach or dedication to a set of ideals about education; a professional commitment to subject-based teaching, to teaching as an art or craft, and to the institution, such as the school; and an instrumental commitment to a teaching career purely as a useful career to be in. An individual teacher may show one, some, or all, of these types, may vary them from time to time, or at certain ages . . . , and may also vary in intensity of commitment from core to peripheral. We might hypothesize that the teacher career generally sees a shift from left to right as it progresses, with a corresponding switch between core and peripheral. The initial phase of the teacher's career in our sample marks a progression from vocational to professional commitment, and it is not unreasonable to assume an increase in instrumental commitment during the 'settling down' phase of the life cycle, when many teachers acquire or extend their familiar responsibilities. But shifts may be more fluid than this, depending on certain critical incidents. These need not necessarily all be in the same direction. A good crop of examination results, an unexpected piece of good work from a particular child, a generous pay award, an increase in in-service provision, a lowering of the teacher-pupil ratio — such events might induce a shift from right to left [in Figure 1]. Others — for example, a bad experience with some disruptive pupils, an unsatisfactory pay award, a piece of educational policy of which they disapproved, being 'passed over' for promotion — may promote a shift to the right.

During the current critical period, with the profession under contraction, the schools underresourced by comparison with the 1970s and deep dissatisfaction about salary levels, we might expect a left-right, and a top-bottom shift, or a combination of the two. This might be accompanied by the development of alternative careers outside teaching, in some other occupation or business, in the family, or in a hobby. (pp. 237–8)

This illustrates some possible variability in commitment depending on the matching of self to job. It points to possible changes in the view of the self over time; and to the influence of other factors on the job which have serious implications for the self, and consequently, for the quality of one's work. More will be said about commitment in Chapters 4 and 5.

Teachers' Interests

Pollard (1985) provides some details of how considerations of self bear on teachers' actions. In an analysis based on his experiences as a classroom teacher and a researcher, he identified certain interests associated with maintaining a sense of self in the classroom. These were: maximizing enjoyment; controlling the workload; maintaining one's health and avoiding stress; retaining automony; maintaining one's self-image.

Maximizing enjoyment

Personal fulfilment could come from teaching and/or relationships. It could include serious accomplishment and a certain amount of humour and laughter.

Controlling workload

As one of Pollard's teachers remarked 'the job is endless', so some control has to be exerted individually. Those with 'vocational' commitment might work all hours of the day and night and enjoy it. Others might show more of a drift through 'professional' to 'instrumental' commitment. Whatever the approach, getting through the work, term, school year, is a prominent interest for all teachers and, to do that, they must control their workload.

Maintaining health and avoiding stress

Frequent references were made to health and the need to adapt work patterns in its interests. Stress, in fact, has become a prominent issue as teachers have acquired more responsibilities and greater accountability, but with fewer resources and less control (see Chapter 7). When stress appears, its treatment has to be the prime issue.

Retaining autonomy

It is important to Pollard's teachers that they retain their independence and control of their own classrooms.

Maintaining self-image

Pollard (pp. 28–9) states that

> Every individual, and thus every teacher, is different. He or she has a unique personality and a unique biographical background. Upbringing, social class, background, age, sex, race, work experience, professional training: these and many other personal factors influence 'the person they are' and lead towards the construction of their particular self-image. When teachers enter a classroom it is fundamentally this self-image that they draw on when they project their personality and take action decisions. Self-image is thus a classroom concern which is drawn on, is fostered and has to be protected . . .

Teachers have their own way of working and some would find it difficult to change. Teachers frequently related these feelings to their upbringing and to role models provided by their parents and their own former teachers (see also Lortie, 1975; Hanson and Herrington, 1976; Mardle and Walker, 1980).

These, then, are elements of what Pollard calls 'primary self-interest', by which the personal survival of the teacher is defined. 'Order' and 'instruction', which are often regarded as the main constituents of the teacher's role, are, in fact, secondary 'enabling' interests. Their importance lies in the extent to which they can advance the primary interests.

Consideration of teacher interests and commitment provides another dimension to the issue of the quality of teachers. As one teacher told Riseborough (1981), following a forced demotion after a school merger, 'You know, if you take this [status] away, not all the money in the world will make him feel content with his job, and this is what teaching is all about. You've got to feel right' (p. 15). If you do not feel right, for whatever reason (demotion, depressed salary, troublesome, oppositional head or colleagues, disruptive pupils, crowded timetable, problematic home life, etc., etc.), you would be unlikely to deploy personal skills and qualities to best effect, and you would be unlikely to improve on your rate of 'matching'. The implications for policy are possibly to shift the burden of responsibility for good teaching, in part, from the teachers to the circumstances that bear on them. Teachers themselves are clearly a major determinant of the quality of work that they do, but if they 'do not feel right' because of factors beyond their control, such factors (school, LEA, or government policy) may bear a heavier responsibility. A different conclusion is therefore possible from those placing emphasis upon personal qualities or professional skill, important though these are.

Constraints on Teachers

As well as influences such as commitment and interests bearing on teachers from within themselves, as it were, there are forces from without, over which the teacher may have little control. These are termed constraints because they delimit a teacher's field of activity. They do not stand apart from the teacher, but rather the two interact. Thus teachers might try to do something about the constraints, either by removing or modifying them or by removing themselves to another situation, or by adapting their 'selves'. An example of one such adaptation was given in the discussion of commitment earlier. There are two broad kinds of constraint, those deriving from inside the school and those form the wider society outside the school, though the two are often interconnected.

Societal constraints

Andy Hargreaves (1984) points to three broad areas of constraints at this level:

(a) Two major goals of our education system which are fundamentally contradictory. One of these is to educate all children to their maximum potential and to give individuals their due. At the same time, schools have to select and socialize children for society. Examinations are a major device for this in secondary schools and their whole organization and pedagogy might be geared towards them. They reflect both diagnostic and differentiation functions, but insofar as they 'sort children out' they set them on career paths within the school and beyond, which become increasingly difficult to change. Pupils thus become 'channelled' into 'appropriate' career lines, which for some may not be in their best interests.

(b) Material constraints which curtail teaching policy. The level of funding determines the number of teachers employed, the kind and state of school buildings, the provision of books and other teaching aids, the amount of in-service training. Government policy fixes the pupils' length of schooling, the length of the school day and year, teachers, terms and conditions of service, and general policy about kinds of schools (tripartite, comprehensive) and curriculum. This is increasingly so following the Education Reform Act of 1988. Thus matters like the pupil-teacher ratio, the teacher's timetable, and the contexts and aids for teaching are largely determined by forces external to the school. Some schools try to alleviate these constraints by fund-raising activities and/or appealing to parents — but these are localized solutions.

(c) Hargreaves argues that from time to time certain educational ideologies appear (such as 'progressivism'), which come to be defined as 'correct practice', and upon which career advancement depends. Teachers are then presented with the problem of meeting the terms of the ideology and the other goals of the system (as in (a) above) which might be in tension with the ideology, within the material constraints (as in (b) above). How they meet this problem is a matter of current study and debate. One explanation is advanced by Sharp and Green (1975). In the 'progressive' primary school of their research they found the teacher's major working concept was the emphasis to 'be busy', to 'get on on your own', or 'find something to do'. Does this offer pupils more initiative in and control over the teaching and learning process as progressive ideology would have it? Not according to Sharp and Green. They argue that 'normal pupils' for the most part settle down to routine activity and form a 'bedrock of busyness' (p. 177). These are pupils who 'can be accounted for generally within the framework of the teacher's commonsense perceptual structures and rationales' (*ibid*). The ethos of progressivism, however, allows the teacher to integrate the 'problem' children (i.e. the ones not in tune with the teacher's framework) within usual practice, for they can be encouraged to work on their own and to pursue their own interests and needs. The management problem thrown up by the circumstances in which teachers have to work (see (b) above) is reduced and ideologically justified by the doctrine of progressivism, as all pupils become part of the 'bedrock of busyness'. Sharp and Green claim, however, that, far from meeting the essential point of child-centred philosophy that it should apply equally to *all* children, in practice it means the teacher is freed to spend even more time with the 'bright' teacher-directed children. Thus a 'progressive' appearance masks a 'selection' reality. Sharp and Green have been criticized for not taking the teachers' perspectives into account and their case also rests on the study of three classes in only one infant school. Their work did, however, reveal the problems that confront teachers in this regard, even if their explanation has to be rather more tentative. (p. 67)

Recently there has been a great emphasis in primary teaching on group work, which involves breaking down a class into smaller groups of five or six children, which might then each be engaged on different activities. The thinking behind this is clearly influenced by similar 'child–centred' and 'constructivist' ideas of learning. It is clear, however, that this has enormous managerial problems and questionable educational outcomes (see Bennett, 1987; Galton, 1987). Yet it is the vogue and there are great pressures on teachers to conform.

It will be noted that such work addresses a different question from the reports addressed earlier, namely why do teachers act as they do rather than what is the ideal state and how can teachers individually be brought up to it. In a later article, Hargreaves (1988) discusses other factors, which he argues, constrain teachers to use traditional, routinized methods, and which hold back reform. These include having to deal with large cohorts of children, which makes it difficult to give individual children attention; pressures and limitations caused by examinations; situational constraints, such as class size, school buildings, level of resource; the isolation of individual teachers; the emphasis on subject-related pedagogies; and status and career factors.

In combination, it might be argued, these exert very much heightened pressure. Experienced singly, they might be much better managed. Thus it is easier to cope with large cohorts if you have the time and resources to do it. Similarly, it is easier to counter the anti-educational effects of examinations if you have a small, well-motivated cohort. Loss of status in one area of one's work might be compensated by an increase in another . . . and so on. If all factors bear on a teacher one might argue that the pressure is more than just their sum. The fewer that apply, or the less strongly that they apply, the more the degree for manoeuvre.

In addition, there are other factors that need to be entered on the list, at least for teachers in the UK. These include demands for greater accountability, teacher appraisal, and a general diminution of their share of control over the curriculum, examinations, and school processes in general. Thus their power-base is weakened at the same time as they are being urged to implement far-reaching reforms, notably through the 1988 Education Reform Act. The government reports discussed earlier might be seen as part of this kind of pressure. Thus considerations of teacher quality that leave constraints out of account can be a constraint in themselves. Similarly, research studies that omit teachers' views also contribute (May and Rudduck, 1983).

It will be seen that many of the components of teaching quality listed in the DES and HMI reports mentioned earlier are dependent to a large extent on these factors. Thus the ability to 'demonstrate interest in and knowledge of the pupils individually' is severely limited by the large cohorts with which the teacher has to deal and the amount of work she has to do with them. The 'recording or memorizing of facts' may not be so much a matter of choice by an inadequate teacher as a strategy by a 'good' teacher to manage a difficult situation. Having pupils 'organize some parts of their own work' may sound fine in principle but may make for serious classroom management difficulties.

As for teachers showing 'a quiet, calm, relaxed, good–humoured attitude
. . .', the curious thing is that many of them who do not do so within the
classroom, do so *outside* it. These teachers clearly then have the relevant
personal qualities. The question needs to be asked what happens to them
during teaching and why.

Institutional constraints

Societal demands are mediated through the school. Prominent among studies
here is the notion of the school 'ethos'. As yet, this is an ill–defined concept,
but nonetheless one considered crucial to the effectiveness of a school (Rutter
et al., 1979). The ethos is manifested in things like the system of rewards
and punishments, the nature of the relationships between teachers and pupils,
the nature of pupils' participation in the school, the relative emphasis on
academic or pastoral goals, the prevailing pedagogical orientation, the
decision-making processes among the staff.

Rutter *et al.* found that schools with better behaviour and academic
performance tended to have more teaching time (as opposed to other
activities), planned their teaching on a group basis and had teachers who
taught more than one subject. In lessons, teachers in such schools spent more
time on the subject matter and less time on setting up equipment or handing
out materials. They also included periods of quiet work in their lessons and
started and finished lessons promptly. There was better behaviour where
schools were neat and tidy, where there was more teacher continuity and
adequate clerical help, and where children remained in the same group. It
was, however, the *combined* effect of such variables that was much more
powerful than any single item. This supports the view of such as Lawton
(1987, p. 4), who argues that individual teachers are important, but limited
in their effects, and that the question of the quality of teaching should also
be seen in terms of the whole school.

The ethos may be informed by a particular educational philosophy and
promoted by the headteacher through judicious appointments to staff as well
as by direction of everyday activity, but schools are also affected by material
and social factors, which might influence the view of possible and desirable
goals. For example, schools that are situated in deprived inner–city areas
with poor housing and high levels of unemployment may feel forced to
elevate pastoral care and classroom control to the top priority over academic
instruction. Such schools can become imbued with what Denscombe (1985,
p. 59) calls a 'low-achievement orientation', which 'results from mutually
reinforcing expectations held by teachers and pupils where teachers, looking
at factors like the social class, ethnic mix and material environment of the

school, come to hold low expectations about the pupils' academic performance, while the pupils, reflecting such expectations and bringing relatively low academic aspirations from their social background, combine to produce a school ethos in which academic attainment gets written off as irrelevant'. 'Effective teaching' in such a context may amount to 'keeping 'em quiet'. In his research in three London comprehensive schools, Denscombe (1980) actually found that the status of a teacher was judged by colleagues by the amount of noise issuing from a classroom and the number of times he/she referred difficult pupils to another teacher. This orientation, Denscombe argues, is aided by the organization of our schools into 'closed' classrooms. This all helps to promote 'a hidden pedagogy' that is, a tacit set of assumptions based on managing constraints rather than on teaching principles.

The notion of 'ethos' may also assume a degree of consensus within the school. This may be true of some schools, but others are more marked by conflict and a diversity of goals. Schools are divided into separate units (subject departments, year groups, houses, special groups) that develop their own agendas and loyalties, and may frequently come into conflict with each other. Such conflict may be about the provision of resources, status (particularly the status of one's subject) or about ideology. The latter is particularly salient for notions of 'effective teaching'. Sharp and Green (1975, p. 68) have defined a teaching ideology as:

> A connected set of systematically related beliefs and ideas about what are felt to be the essential features of teaching. A teaching ideology involves both cognitive and evaluative aspects, it will include general ideas and assumptions about the nature of knowledge and of human nature — the latter entailing beliefs about motivation, learning and educability. It will include some characterization of society and the role and functions of education in the wider social context. (p. 68)

As noted earlier, 'progressivism' is one such ideology, as are 'multiculturalism', and 'anti-racism' and 'vocationalism'. Teachers within the same department might have profound differences on this score. In consequence, Ball (1987) has gone so far as to describe schools as 'arenas of struggle . . . riven with actual or potential conflict between members . . . poorly coordinated . . . ideologically diverse' (p. 19).

It will be seen that studying isolated and discrete activities of teachers and pupils in the classroom has limited uses, for such activities only gather meaning from the historical, political, social, institutional and personal contexts within which they take place. A knowledge of such contexts would appear necessary for views of what is both possible and desirable teaching activity.

Summary

In this introduction I have examined three broad approaches to the issues of teachers' quality and teaching efficiency. Official reports do not question the social and political systems within which teaching takes place, nor the level of resource. They assume that the components of what constitutes good teaching are already known and see the main tasks as finding out how many measure up to it and devising policies about what to do with those they consider do not. The components of this ideal state of good teaching are never made explicit in the reports. While some of these may be unremarkable and non-controversial, problems might arise in the connotations that might be put on some of them ('co-operation', for example, as contrasted with 'reformist'); on how they might be identified in practice; on their linkages with pupils' learning and, consequently, on their usefulness as an encouragement to good practice. Some might argue that they are more likely to induce stress among teachers, threatening to expose them to external forms of evaluation over which they have no control and through which they might experience what they see as unjustified sanctions. The DES might argue that they are mounting a responsible and determined drive to improve the quality of teaching in our schools. The analysis shows, however, that that cannot be divorced from political considerations and the socio-economic context. That would help explain the emphasis on personal qualities and the demoting of other factors, such as headteachers' views and resource problems.

Notwithstanding this, some of the same features appeared in the research studies considered. However, they do show the problems of getting to grips with the complexities of teaching. The 'teaching styles' approach followed the line of development established by the Plowden report, but it has become clear that there are problems in classifying teachers in this way. Differences within teaching styles appeared greater than those between styles, but in any event the results were not conclusive. The research on the quality of pupils' learning experiences (Bennett *et al.*, 1984) broke new ground and raised important points about 'matching' in the tasks that pupils were asked to perform. One may, however, query whether teaching and learning can be reduced to a series of tasks; and teachers' and pupils' subjectivities and motivation were left out of account, as were social factors and constraints surrounding the tasks.

It was argued that in any consideration of the quality of teachers, teachers' motivation and the factors influencing it have to be taken into consideration. It cannot be taken for granted. Similarly, the constraints within which teachers work might open up some lines of activity, but close down others. While there might be opportunities for teachers to exert some influences themselves on some of these factors (e.g. those connected within the institution), they have little control over some of the others, particularly those that arise from outside the school. Teachers cope with these typically through devising 'strategies'.

The three broad areas discussed here, therefore, have had markedly different emphases, the first concentrating on teachers' personal qualities, the second on cognitive processes and the third on social factors. While these at times are represented as competing explanations involving markedly different policy implications, I would argue that they do not have to be seen in that way and that all these elements are necessary for a comprehensive understanding of effective teaching, or indeed any sort of teaching. 'Opportunities to learn' are contingent upon 'opportunities to teach'. Cognitive matching needs to be seen within the context of social interaction and personal development. How teachers handle the complex issues raised within such a scenario very much depends on their personal knowledge, abilities, dispositions and skills. Better teaching would therefore involve both improved initial and in-service training of teachers, and some material and situational changes, especially the allocation of improved resources. This, arguably, would help promote a higher rate of matching within tasks on cognitive and on other dimensions.

Content of the Book

This book is firmly within the 'opportunities to teach' mould, though it recognizes the interconnections among the areas discussed. Of course personal factors are important in teaching. So, too, are the conceptualization of tasks, their design and adequacy, how they are operationalized and the results diagnosed. But they have to take into account the teachers' perspectives, and the prevailing social, political and economic circumstances. If these were constant and unchanging and affording a broad range of opportunities, personal factors would be the most important differentiator. Teachers do differ in abilities and teaching skill. Similarly it is useful for teachers to consider the analysis of learning tasks, for this brings into focus the connecting parts of one kind of teaching–learning process, and raises the questions about matching that otherwise might have been overlooked. However, the impact of both is lessened if the social circumstances do not afford the opportunities to practise personal teaching skills and to reflect on one's teaching. The impact is likely to be counter-productive if social factors are omitted from explanations which, in truth, require their strong representation.

The book therefore conveys a model of teaching and learning based on 'opportunities to teach and learn', which recognizes the importance of motivation, subjectivities and social factors for both teachers and pupils. It is informed by symbolic interactionism, with its emphasis on the self, process, construction of meanings and social interaction; and its focus on perspectives, cultures, strategies and contexts (Woods, 1983); and by 'social constructivism', which emphasizes the progressive construction of cognitive representations through experience and action in the world. This learning theory stresses the appropriation of knowledge by the child, who thus comes to 'control' and 'own' it, with the teacher as stimulator and enabler (Donaldson, 1978; Bruner, 1986; Edwards and Mercer, 1987). The theory will be applied here also to the teacher as learner, and there are links here with the 'teacher development' and 'teacher thinking' movements which have gathered pace in recent years (Schon, 1983; Todd, 1984; Ben Peretz *et al.*, 1986; Smyth, 1987; Woods, 1989).

This emphasis on the teacher as agent is tempered by a consideration of the circumstances in which teachers teach. The interplay between all these forces makes for a wide range of possibilities in teaching on a number of continua, from, for example, continuing professional development to deskilling and alienation; from freedom to initiate and enact teaching policy to externally determined activity; from golden opportunity to leaden constraint; from the heights of satisfaction that come from successful teaching to the depths of despair that come from failure. Such is the reality of teaching, which for teachers as a body may lean in one direction or the other depending on the trends of the moment; and which for individual teachers within that body may differ depending on their own personal qualities and circumstances.

To assess this, it is necessary to take the teachers' perspective. This is true of estimating what constitutes teaching quality also. Rather than invoking criteria from some external, and unidentified, source, and measuring teacher activity against that, the approach here is to identify what works and what does not, and in what circumstances. Thus in featuring some of these circumstances that give rise to concerns for 'survival' rather than teaching, and to 'stress', but also examining some of the essentials of the teacher's skill which bring about the highest accomplishments, the book makes a statement about what constitutes teaching quality and what conditions are necessary to promote it. Since this is a matter of political as well as educational debate, the book to some extent makes a political intervention, as well as attempting a theoretical advance and providing a practical and therapeutic aid for teachers engaged in the struggle for professional development.

The book is organized in three sections along a broad continuum of skills, strategies and stress that relate to the balance of opportunity and constraints. Thus, in the first section, teachers are afforded opportunities to exercise their skills; in the second, opportunities are more limited, and the activity turns to coping with constraints; in the third, opportunities are non-existent or under threat, and even running counter to aspirations, giving rise to stress; finally, I consider what teaching opportunities there are likely to be in the age of the 1988 Education Reform Act.

In the first section, three prominent skills are identified involving creativity, orchestration, and generating an educational climate. These are not the only skills, of course, but they do seem essential and they do complement other studies. For example, Bennett *et al.* (1984) might have found pupils doing few creative tasks and teachers apparently misreading the appropriateness of a large number of routine ones. Effectiveness consists in the repair of these mismatches. This may be so, but in the schools of my research, particularly primary schools, the best teacher work, that is the work that yielded most pupil advance or learning, was marked by a noticeable spirit of invention and innovation that seems to be a distinctive hallmark of teaching in British primary schools. A wider area of teacher activity than 'tasks' was under examination, though there are tasks embedded within it. Inventiveness, adaptability, flexibility, a willingness to experiment and, at times, take risks figure among the personal qualities associated with this; but these flourish in some conditions, and languish in others. I consider this teacher creativity in Chapter 1.

The teacher skill of orchestration (Chapter 2) is a professional rather than a personal skill. Indeed, such is its nature of combining basically conflictual elements into a harmonious whole, that it runs against the personal grain. We cannot teach large classes of children by instinct. There is an art, therefore, in how the skilled teacher handles conflictual elements in the role, cultivating warm personal relationships with children and a caring ethos in the school on the one hand, while managing some problems of control with more authoritarian techniques on the other; all the time exhibiting a seamless web of activity that flows productively in the face of all exigencies. Since these skills were common to all teacher styles observed, they are possibly some of the factors running across the styles noted, but not identified, in the Galton and Bennett studies.

The third chapter in this section focuses more upon the collective teacher skill of generating a productive school climate; and, since it is an elusive concept, a way of examining it. The ethos described is represented as a 'middle-ground culture', it being the result of an attempt by teachers to interlock key communicative elements in pupils' background culture into their own concerns (see also Howard, 1989). It is bounded by teacher aims as indeed was the activity described in Chapter 2, and is nowhere near a complete merger. Separate cultures of teachers and pupils as Pollard (1985) argues in his school do exist. But on the middle ground, teachers and pupils reach out toward each other and construct a basis on which the official business of the school can be negotiated. Such an ethos does not just happen — it has to be worked for, constructed and maintained. It is another example of teacher creativity, in this case a collective accomplishment. It shows that, if the teachers of a school can agree, they can exercise considerable influence on institutional constraints and opportunities by acting together and contributing towards the environment in which their individual teaching takes place. Personal qualities of teachers are important in the maintenance of an ethos, once established (see also Yeomans, 1989; Nias *et al.*, 1989). Appointments, therefore, do matter. But there is a two-way process between ethos and individual — each can contribute to the other.

The second section examines aspects of teaching which are more circumscribed, where basic aims are delimited, giving rise to strategies aimed at re-fashioning the means to the desired ends, and even on occasions the ends themselves. There may be a great deal of creativity, but it is directed toward the managing of constraints rather than the furtherance of teaching. This is the case in Chapter 4, where, such are the pressures in the school in question, teachers, in some aspects of their work, are more concerned with 'survival' than 'teaching'. As Hargreaves (1988) points out, all teaching is a mixture of opportunity and constraint. Where the constraints begin to bite, teachers develop 'coping strategies', the action that resolves the tension between agency and structure, between individual freedom and creativity and external determination. This has, been a popular subject in interactionist literature in recent years (Hargreaves, 1977, 1978, 1979 and 1980; Pollard, 1982; Denscombe, 1985; Woods, 1979 and 1980). All these studies might be seen as being situated on a 'management' dimension with 'coping' at its fulcrum. Towards one end, the constraints diminish and teaching interests take precedence, as, for example, in the aspects considered in Chapters 1–3. At the other extreme, constraints obliterate teaching interests to the extent of forcing attention on a more basic need (Maslow, 1943). Taken by itself, the chapter might appear to offer a cynical view of teaching. It is certainly the darker side of it, but one that has to be seen within the general context of the model presented here.

In an attempt to provide some conceptual unity to these predominantly empirical studies Pollard (1982) devised a comprehensive model of classroom coping strategies. This has three analytical layers, consisting of social structure, institution and classroom; and factors running through these layers classified as to how they relate to three crucial issues — the physical and material structure of the classroom setting, the biography and self of pupils and teachers, and the role or decision-making problems they face. Chapters 5 and 6 explore aspects of the teacher 'biography and self' part of this model. If Chapter 4 depicts a kind of 'survival ethos', perhaps in association with a 'low achievement orientation' as discussed earlier, which seems to influence the whole of the school, Chapter 5 returns to the point that teachers may be the same in some respects but differ in others, and they do have choices.

I am concerned here to locate the reasons why, of two teachers with similar educational interests, aims and dedication, one succeeds, and the other does not. 'Personal qualities' are not sufficient to account for this, at least as conceived in the DES reports discussed earlier. The answer lies, I argue, within the self and the identity that each has constructed and seeks to promote, which in turn affects how they seek to realize their interests, namely the coping strategies that they devise.

Chapter 6 continues the exploration of self in the biographical arm of the model outlined by Pollard. It takes a life history approach to enquire deep into the past of the 'successful' teacher of the previous chapter with a view to identifying the formative influences on his teaching. It shows the impact of significant others at various stages, but also the effects of socioeconomic trends and events. How the individual steers a path through this maze of factors is basic to the model of person underlying this book. It includes the impact of the individual on the teaching situation. It is not a question, therefore, of teachers operating within constraints which they have no opportunity to influence. Here, I was interested to see how the teacher's self interacted with curriculum, and how, to some extent at least, he/she made the subject that he/she taught.

It might be argued that the role management depicted in Chapter 2 is another illustration of the Pollard model in respect of another of the three key issues he lists. This would be quite correct, for it shows how teachers cope with contradictions in the role. These contradictions can be traced through the various levels, from for example, the general educational policy that fixes sizes of cohorts and classes, through the expectations of the LEA, parents, governors and pupils, through the mediation of the headteacher to the manifestation of the problem in the moment-to-moment action in the classroom and the teacher decision-making concerned. This is an indication of the basic interrelatedness of all the chapters. I have chosen to place it in the section on 'skills' because it can more easily be identified as a productive teaching skill. The 'strategies' in the second section are concerned with more general attitudes and behaviour and usually require the modification of teaching aims. The skill involved in the role-management described in Chapter 2 is also a first-order skill, that is, it is a skill that most teachers have to learn in order to teach in any situation. The strategies considered in section two involve second-order skills, that is adjustments that are made when situations become more complex. Most teachers' work will require a combination of teaching skills and coping strategies as their situation undergoes change from area to area, school to school, year to year, day to day, lesson to lesson.

Most teachers, too, will have experienced some of the problems and reactions considered in the third section, though perhaps not to the extent depicted in Chapter 7. If the first section illustrates some of the better aspects of teaching quality, and the second section how teachers cope and survive the numerous difficulties that assail them, the third section is about non-coping and 'death'. I am speaking about stress and burnout, resignation and early retirement, and other ways in which a teacher can experience a 'spoiled career' (Goffman, 1968). In these situations the problems are of such an order that they outweigh a teacher's coping resources. In Chapter 7, I am concerned to identify some of the factors that cause teacher stress, both with regard to external factors, and to biographical ones to do with teacher interests and commitment. Some of these are the other side of the coin to those considered in the first section which can yield such high rewards. Thus, one can experience debilitating frustration from blocked freedom and creativity; profound distress from some manifestations of role-conflict that are beyond the bounds of 'normal teaching'; and despair from being enveloped in a school ethos that permeates all aspects of one's work and is impervious to change. Interestingly, too, those at greatest risk appear to be those who might be considered as having some of the best personal qualities for teaching and certainly the purest form of commitment. These find it hard to cope by altering their teaching aims. For them there is no 'coping' or 'survival' half-way house; it is either 'teaching' or nothing. In general, personal qualities are not considered to be the major factor in what appears to be a growing incidence of stress in the profession (Cole and Walker, 1989). Those unable to cope find out and act accordingly at an early stage. But stress is becoming more common at all age- and career-stages, and factors external to teachers are almost certainly responsible.

Among external factors bearing on teachers the 1988 Education Reform Act looms large. To some, this represents an educational crisis of the first magnitude, threatening the death of education as we know it, reintroducing selection and setting up constraints and control and delimited curricula which, it is argued, will stifle teacher initiative and inspiration such as appear here especially in Chapters 1–3 (Simon, 1988; Haviland, 1988). The supporters of the Act argue that, on the contrary, it will improve educational standards and extend opportunities for pupils and parents. Within the guidelines formulated by these considerations, there will be just as many opportunities for teachers to practise their skills, and, indeed, more need of them. This debate shows the difficulties of separating educational matters such as the quality of pupil learning and what are thought to be desirable teacher personal qualities from political considerations. I consider these arguments in Chapter 8, and reflect on the impact of the Act on classroom processes as I see it. I do this in the light of the 'opportunities to teach and learn' model expounded in this introduction. The actual outcomes will not be known for some considerable while. Certainly specifying the ends without providing the means (i.e. increased resources) can only add massively to the list of things teachers have to cope with. However, there may be things within the Act that do offer teachers opportunities to teach. They have long experience in turning political intervention to educational advantage. And it is a long way from governmental offices to classrooms. When the dust settles, things may not be all that different, at least in terms of teaching skills and coping strategies, though the latter may need to become even more refined.

While this account of the structure of the book so far draws attention to the interrelatedness of the chapters in terms of the model of teaching outlined earlier, there are some discontinuities among them. They are, for example, the product of different research studies, carried out at different times over the last twelve years, in different schools at different levels. Thus Chapters 1 and 2 are derived from research carried out in primary schools between 1986 and 1989; Chapter 3 from research in the early 1980s in a comprehensive school (Measor and Woods, 1984); Chapters 4–6 from research in a secondary modern school in the late 1970s (Woods, 1979); while Chapters 7 and 8 are more generally based. However, in some ways these differences help to delineate the various features of the model in bold relief. For example, it could be argued that there are fewer constraints at primary level. In general, there are fewer examination pressures, less teacher isolation, fewer subject-related pedagogies, less problematic pupil motivation (though how all this will be affected by the Education Reform Act of 1988 remains to be seen). It would not be surprising therefore if the kind of teaching skills under examination here in Chapters 1–3 were more evident in primary schools; and the survival and coping strategies described in Chapters 4–6 more characteristic of the more severely constrained secondary school. This is not to say that these schools show one type of behaviour and not the other; nor that there are not skills and strategies that are more common and indeed perhaps specific at one level rather than the other; but that they do offer the best illustration found in these various researches of the feature of the model described. All the chapters, therefore, are guided by the same theory and the same ethnographic methodology (Woods, 1986) and they describe aspects of the same general model. They are not, by any means, the whole picture, but are intended, rather, as a contribution towards it which does nonetheless encompass some of the range of success and failure, joys and terrors, hopes and despairs, rewards and penalties that are all part of the complex activity of teaching.

Chapter 1

Teacher Creativity

Teaching: Dead or Alive?

Creativity has more often in the past been conceived of in relation to pupils, the prime question being how teachers might induce more of it in their charges' thinking. The assumption is that teachers, almost by definition, are themselves creative. It is not an issue as far as they are concerned. In one of the standard texts of the 1960s, for example, only half a page out of ninety-seven was devoted to 'the creative teacher' (Cropley, 1967). However, against this we have an opposing view, that teachers, almost by definition, are uncreative. This is not a judgment on them as persons. It is what teaching does to them. The classic analyst in this tradition, Waller (1932) puts it thus:

> One is puzzled to explain that peculiar blight which affects the teacher mind, which creeps over it gradually, and, possessing it bit by bit, devours its creative resources. Some there are who escape this disease endemic in the profession, but the wonder is that they are so few . . . Those who have known young teachers well, and have observed the course of their personal development as they became set in the teaching pattern, have often been grieved by the progressive deterioration in their general adaptability. (p. 391)

This 'deadening of the intellect' (*ibid*) in teachers has been noted by others. Lortie (1973 and 1975) and Mardle and Walker (1980) have pointed to the effects of long-term socialization as pupils. MacDiarmid (1969) comments on how the creative urge does not go well with teaching. Elbaz (1981 and 1983) points out that because of emphases in curriculum research and study, there has been 'little encouragement for teachers to view themselves as originators of knowledge'. Even in higher education, we distinguish quite strictly between research (discovery) and teaching (putting across what you have discovered).

As well as these studies directed toward the intrinsic nature of teaching, others argue that political and economic developments are progressively de-skilling teachers and proletarianizing the profession (Lawn and Ozga, 1981; Apple, 1982; Apple and Teitelbaum, 1986; Ball, 1987). It is argued that, inasmuch as they accept matters such as appraisal, profiling, records of achievement, and evaluation as a 'good thing', they are contributing to the system, and losing control of their own labour. If they were not before, they certainly are now becoming mere technicians in the service of the ideas of others. What invention and spontaneity there used to be is, some claim, being driven out. Thus Brighouse (1987) gives the (typical) example of an innovative teacher forced to leave the profession, who told him:

> The profession will need 'systems people' in future — all schemes of work, work cards and rigidly sticking to the syllabus. I quite often don't know what will happen in spite of a lesson plan until I'm half way through the lesson you know? Is that bad? Oh, I have a broad map but sometimes the youngsters — they're so damned interesting — we get carried away along some exciting by-road. (p. 11)

Similarly, Barker (1987) thinks 'Visions are off the agenda'. As a young teacher he was a 'missionary', seeking to 'liberate the latent talent of ordinary people'. As a headteacher he was an 'agitator', trying to convert his school from a 'lesson factory into a community school, a focus for the culture and vitality' of the area. Now 'schools are being strangled by externally directed, far-reaching changes which seem out of control'.

While not denying the threat in these developments and the potentially constraining nature of the teacher's job, it is possible to construct another argument, one that points to their developing professionalism, growing self-awareness, increasing skills and control, and more opportunity for personal innovation. The considerable 'action research' movement has shown that many teachers can and do investigate their own practice, submitting their teaching to critical scrutiny, and experiencing a sense of improving their craft (Nixon, 1981; Carr and Kemmis, 1986; Hustler *et al.*, 1986). The associated 'Continuing Professional Development' movement is also becoming something of an industry (Todd, 1984 and 1987). Much of this is underpinned by the conception of teacher knowledge advanced by Schon (1983), Eisner (1979), Zeichner (1983) and others. Schon argues that a technical-rationality model has been influential in the past. According to this, the practitioner utilizes technical skills based on systematic and standardized knowledge that is then applied. The implications for training and evaluation are clear — competence is a matter of building up to preconceived norms, and it can be judged by the degree to which a teacher's behaviour measures up to them. By contrast, Schön's 'reflective practitioner' is altogether more innovatory and creative, discovering problems and issues, inventing and experimenting in the search for solutions, and continuously adapting. As Clark and Yinger (1987) argue, many of the teacher's problems are 'uncertain practical problems which require unique and idiosyncratic approaches to solution because of their strong ties to specific contextual factors, the uncertainty and competition among goals and the grounds for decision, and the unpredictability of uniquely configured events' (p. 98). Consequently, 'the skill required is that of intelligent and artful orchestration of knowledge and technique' (*ibid*). This is similar to Connelly's (1972) conception of the teacher as 'user-developer', which recognizes the autonomous decision-making function of the teacher in adapting and developing materials to particular situations. It is not far removed, also, from the view of 'teaching as an art', associated with, for example, Eisner (1979 and 1985). For Eisner (1985, p. 104), educational improvement comes not from the discovery of scientific methods that can be applied universally, but from 'enabling teachers and others engaged in education to improve their ability to see and think about what they do. Educational practice as it occurs in schools is an inordinately complicated affair filled with contingencies that are difficult to predict, let alone control. Connoisseurship in education, as in other areas, is that art of perception that makes the appreciation of that complexity possible.'

Two other theoretical positions have a bearing on this. One is constructivist learning theory. The emphasis here is on the construction of general representations from real actions and experience, on joint, social learning (since human action is cooperative), and on intrinsic motivation, that is learning for its own sake in the search for constructions that will enable us to cope with the world (Donaldson, 1978; Bruner, 1986). Meaning is negotiated and recreated between teacher and learners in the cultural 'forum' of the classroom, a view that contrasts strongly with transmission conceptions of education. The teacher in such a scenario becomes an enabler, a facilitator, one who has to be alive to the shifts and turns in pupils' thinking and to its cultural supports, and to encourage the pupil to build on his or her relevances. This requires adaptability, flexibility and experimentation. It also means a certain autonomy for the teacher — ownership of the various pedagogical and cultural forms of knowledge involved, control of the educational processes, and freedom to manoeuvre and negotiate.

Not out of sympathy with this is the symbolic interactionism deriving from the work of G.H. Mead (1934). At the heart of this is the social construction of the self, and the ongoing dialectic between the 'I' and the 'me'. The self is a process, not a solid entity, continually created and recreated in each social situation one enters (Berger, 1963). As Mead has it (1934), 'The "I" is the response of the organism to the attitudes of the others; the "me" is the organized set of attitudes of others which one himself assumes. The attitudes of the others constitute the organized "me", and then one reacts towards that as an "I" ' (p. 175). There is a certain impulsiveness and spontaneity in the 'I'. This is why, Mead argues, we are never fully aware of what we are or what we are to become. Certainly we are subject to certain influences in varying degrees, but these can never be fully deterministic. 'The possibilities of the "I" belong to that which is actually going on, and it is in some sense the most fascinating part of our experience. It is there that novelty arises and it is there that our most important values are located. It is the realization in some sense of this self that we are continually seeking' (*ibid*, p. 104).

Ames (1973), describes the self thus:

The 'I' is spontaneous, impulsive, ceaselessly venturing, not only out into the world, but confronting the 'me' in dialogue. The 'me' is the result of dealing with other people. It is an internalization of the community, with its institutions, whereas the 'I' remains more isolated, more untamed, though cautioned and controlled by the 'me'. On the other hand, the 'me' is constantly prodded by the 'I' which breaks away to say and do more or less unexpected things in society: while society in turn is constantly being stirred up and tested by fresh impetus from the 'I' of each of its members. The plunging and daring 'I' is civilized and guided, also given opportunities, incentives and support, by society. But there is always an unstable equilibrium between society, representing what has been achieved or bungled in the past, and the exploring, reforming, revolutionary 'I'. This sets the problem and promise of education confronting parents, teachers and statesmen. (pp. 51–2)

All this lends itself to the notion of person as 'constructive coper' (Davis, 1972), one who struggles within situations always to adapt, seeking to maximize interests but frequently adjusting these in order to realize achievement in a continual dialectic with the situation. Out of this, too, has come the work on coping strategies (Hargreaves, 1978; Pollard, 1982). The concept of 'coping strategy', it has been argued, promises a synthesis of micro and micro. It is the meeting point of external constraint — among them the political developments discussed earlier — and individual creativity. Recently, Scarth (1987) has demanded clearer conceptual analysis of 'strategies' and 'constraints'. He might have included 'creativity', and in some ways this may seem the more urgent task since it is the more surprising notion. For how can one be 'creative' when one is 'coping'? The latter carries connotations of struggle, backs to the wall, making do, with little scope for invention. Pollard (1982) has developed a conceptual model which embodies both notions. But how does it work in practice?

These, then, are the theoretical considerations that lie behind this discussion of teacher creativity, though the immediate catalyst was my observations of teachers at work and consequent discussions with them during some recent field research. Before I give some examples of these, however, we need a little more idea of what I am intending by the term 'creativity'.

Creativity

Creativity involves innovation, ownership, control and relevance.

Innovation may, as Pribram (1964) argues, extend the boundaries of the conventional, involving first a thorough knowledge of the relevant field (see also Bruner, 1962). It can result from a new combination of known factors, or from the introduction of a new factor into a prevailing situation. Yet, as Clark and Yinger (1987) note, each teaching situation is unique, and thus teachers might be said to be always creating to resolve the problems thrown up by the complexity, uncertainty, instability, and value conflict of the classroom. Occasionally a breakthrough may be achieved in what has been called the 'Aha!' syndrome — the sudden realization of the solution to a problem. It may be planned in the sense that it is the product of deliberate experimentation; or it may be unusual, unexpected, serendipitous. Miracles do happen (Jackson, 1977). But they must be grasped, apprehended, and the opportunity seized. More often the level of novelty is less dramatic, and less perceptible, especially the more sophisticated the teacher is in his or her craft.

The innovation belongs to the teacher concerned. It may be the teacher's own idea, or it may be an adaptation, perhaps in new circumstances, of someone else's idea. Some novel aspect of the process is produced by the teacher concerned. The teacher is at the centre of activities here, as catalyst, a position overlooked by curriculum studies that focus purely on intended outcomes (Reid and Walker, 1975). The teacher has a certain autonomy here, and control of the process. It is a situation where the more spontaneous 'I' can flourish in interaction with the socialized 'me', where the 'self' is fully reflexive. In routinized situations, the 'I' is suppressed, perhaps to emerge triumphantly elsewhere. Others are dictating the agenda. There is an affective element involved here. Nias (1988, pp. 203–4) illustrates the personal satisfaction of teachers who reported 'you're the one who is making it happen at first hand', or 'it's you who's instigating things in the classroom'. The end result of this, Nias reports, was that such teachers felt 'more intuitive, relaxed and spontaneous', more able to be 'adaptive and flexible'. There are two points here. One is that teachers need to be in control and not, for example, being dictated to by higher authority or by pupils. The other is that they also need this for their own realization of self as teachers. As Eisner (1979) notes, 'it is easy to neglect the fact that teachers have needs that must be met through teaching' and he refers to 'the human need for pride in craftsmanship and being able to put something of oneself into work' (p. 166).

If the 'I' is important, so is the 'other'. In 'taking the role of the other', teachers must perceive accurately the attitudes and meanings brought to the situation, the personal and social resources that underpin them, and the possibilities for future action. The 'other' is both a validator and motive-spring (Perinbanayagam, 1975). There are situations where a teacher's ideas do not bear fruit. A brilliant and original programme of work cultivated over a weekend might fall on stony ground on Monday morning, forcing a fall-back on to routines. The situation in its complexity cannot always be predicted. It depends in large part on pupils, and their collective and individual attitudes do differ (Riseborough, 1985; Sikes *et al.*, 1985). The others here must be receptive, though the creative act may make them receptive. The teacher, thus, must be culturally attuned to his or her pupils, and to other aspects of the situation, some of which may be beyond the teacher's immediate control — school policy, parental background, the weather . . . Creative acts bring change. They change pupils, teachers and situations. But the teacher's perceptions of the situation must be as accurate and complete as possible, though it can never be grasped in full.

Similarly, the 'gestures' the teacher makes in the process Mead describes as 'the conversation of gestures' must be appropriate in the given context. They must convey the meanings intended and be apprehended by the other as intended. A teacher of my acquaintance who might have been considered extremely creative along the 'innovative' dimension, was not successful on the 'relevance' criterion. He was not culturally attuned, and the pupils wrote him off as 'not a proper teacher' (see Chapter 5). In this case the 'I' was predominant, out of control one might say. It would not be difficult to produce other, less altruistic, examples of teachers who felt they were being creative, but not having that effect. They might appropriately be said to be self–indulgent. In some instances what a teacher regards as a creative act might lead to destruction. A creative act leads to results, not blockage. Something is transformed in consequence. It creates a product, in this case pupil learning. In Sprecher's (1959) words, 'A truly creative product has the characteristic of being itself creative in the sense that it generates additional creative activity' (p. 294). The teacher casts a new light and pupils 'have their eyes opened,' or helps to unify a great deal of information and expressing it in a highly condensed form reveals essences which lead to new lines of thought (Jackson and Messick, 1965); or introduces a new activity and stimulates pupils' inspiration. Feedback, therefore, is necessary. The 'conversation of gestures' is a two–way process; joint action is negotiated in the cultural forum of the classroom.

These criteria are advanced by the ability to take the role of the other, and to rehearse potential interactions in advance of the event. This process is accompanied by adaptability, flexibility, and a willingness and facility for improvization and experimentation. One is reminded of Mead's emphasis on the importance of 'play' in the socialization of the child. Considering the pupils, the time of day, the classroom context, previous and surrounding activities and so on, the teacher will interpose a new factor, or arrange a new conjunction several times over, envisaging the possible consequences. This is a 'playing with ideas', an exploiting of opportunities as they occur with an end in view which nevertheless might be altered in the working out of the ideas in practice. A range of scenarios needs to be rehearsed, numerous options envisaged. Whether they will work in practice remains to be seen. Mistakes may be made, and successes, when they come, may appear to happen almost by accident. A teacher told me, 'you don't know what's going to work, that's the point, so you must be prepared for failure, but when it does work, it's marvellous'.

Mackinnon (1975) notes that 'there can be little doubt that the "chance" occurrence of an event at the appropriate time during the creative process may be signally important in providing the cue or material necessary for the creative act' (p. 73). This might seem to defy analysis. Some of these occurrences, teachers would claim, cannot be described in rational terms, preferring to attribute their actions to intuition — 'it just felt right to do it that way' (Jackson, 1977). However, though the intricacies of the situation are such that a measure of luck or an extraneous variable might act as a trigger, all else has been arranged and made highly conducive to such an outcome. The chance element would not work in any situation, for example, one that encourages conformity and getting the one 'right' answer, and that discourages guessing.

Since the unusual and unexpected might happen, creative acts are often accompanied by feelings of anticipation before and excitement afterwards. The thrill of discovery and of breakthrough is integral — it is part of the product for both pupil and teacher. A feature of the creative act, therefore, is a certain holism, one characteristic of which is the combination of cognitive, cultural, social and affective factors. Another characteristic is the combining in thought of public and private, formal and informal, school and out-of-school. Teachers and pupils are not encased within their formal roles, nor their activities compartmentalized into discrete sections of time and subject nor certain of their characteristics isolated from others (Elbaz, 1981). Holistic thinking is necessary for a number of reasons. It establishes the widest possible 'play-base,' and also the most valid one. In order to know and negotiate with the other, knowledge is required of the other's construction of self, much of which has taken place outside the school's orbit, and which has a considerable history.

Some psychologists contrast holistic with algorithmic thinking, the one being creative or autistic, the other rational. Both are necessary. McKellar (1975), for example, sees the first as author of the creative act, with rational thinking being the editor. Thus a teacher might have a profusion of ideas, some of which work, some of which do not, with a fair degree of unexpectancy and accident. The application of those ideas, and certainly their evaluation, will require more systematized, step-by-step working-out and analysis.

These characteristics are typical of art forms, and might appear to contribute toward the conception of teaching as an art. Certainly when all goes right, when a teacher's initiative works well, when a new combination of events falls into place, when a sequence runs smoothly there is a certain elegance and beauty in such patterns which provides aesthetic satisfaction, as in solving a complex mathematical problem by the nearest route or in generating particularly apposite theory to explain particularly problematic events. This does not mean that teaching is solely or even primarily an art form and not scientifically based or susceptible to scientific analysis; merely that it shows these characteristics on occasions, and particularly during creative moments.

Creative teaching

I turn now to examples of 'creative teaching' that I observed during some recent research in primary schools. They are intended to convey the flavour of the activity rather than represent an exhaustive list. I shall consider 'creative coping' in Chapter 6.

Creative Teaching Around a Structured Base

Sue was charged with the task of assisting two pupils adjudged to be in need of special teaching, a boy and a girl, both aged 7. She worked under the direction of an external supervisor, who provided a heavily structured programme for Sue's use. Sue wove a series of creative activities around this programme, converting it into a live, experimental, relevant scheme which teacher and pupils could engage with and regard as their own. They had 'Crown Readers', graded reading books which aim to build up vocabulary and idiom through repetition of words and association with pictures, while holding the child's interest through a simple but imaginative story with clearly defined characters with whose activities the child can identify. After reading each book, the child completes a workbook, designed to test and consolidate. Book 1 begins:

THE CASTLE
This is the castle
It is big
It is old
It is big and old

THE KING
I am the king
I live in the castle
The castle is big
It is big and old

There is also a 'big guard' and a 'little guard' and a baby, always appealing to young children and useful for repetition.

'Big and old' the baby said
'Big and old'

The Crown Readers are typical of reading schemes designed as a complete exercise which a teacher could 'take pupils through', and from which they would no doubt learn something. But they have their limitations. The associationist learning principles are at odds with those of teachers preferring a more constructivist approach. And some of the associations are distinctly anti-educational, the books being replete with gender stereotypes. Consider this poor maid in Book 3 *The Maid and the Mouse*, which has a picture of the maid on a shelf, a guard chasing a mouse, and the baby laughing on the floor:

I am the maid
I live in the castle
I brush in the castle
It is a big castle
I brush and brush and brush
I brush the walls
I brush the doors
I brush the windows.

Sue was not happy to work *within* this scheme, preferring to see it as a resource which required considerable modification. She therefore adapted it to a new learning form by encouraging Sarah and Robert to make and perform a play of their own, based on some of the stories. They each had a crown and a cloak, and they 'loved it'. Sue asked Sarah if she would like to make the props and she eagerly accepted, making the crowns, pots of paint etc. Sarah insisted on wearing the crown and cloak whenever she had to say anything. When another girl was drafted in to take Robert's part when he was away, Sarah insisted she put on the crown and cloak. She even wore them when sitting down and reading. The end product was a playlet 'We will mend the castle', based on the Crown Readers' vocabulary up to and including Book 4, which could be recorded as a radio play, or acted out. Sarah and Robert did give a performance before an audience of their class. They had chosen and written the words and made the props, with help, of course. The play now began:

Queen: Look at the castle
King Robert
Look at the doors, the windows, and the walls

King: The doors are broken, Queen Sarah.
The walls and the windows are broken

Baby: Broken, broken, broken

Stephanie, another 'slow learner' had to be drafted in to play the baby, which was regarded as a star role. Later, they were inspired to make up another play of their own based on Robert's suggestion of 'The Three Bears'.

Let us make some porridge
Yes, we will make some porridge
Let us go down to breakfast . . .!

The framework is still that of the Crown Reader, but this time the words are theirs. The play, it will be noted, contains another star role, that of Baby Bear, and there were squabbles over who was to play this. Robert seemed to think he had author's rights. Sarah just felt she would do it better. The matter was resolved by the toss of a coin which Sarah lost, but accepted.

This shows how the project provided some forms of learning, in this case to do with social behaviour and rules of conduct. Sue's part in all this was to mediate, arbitrate, enable. The play was theirs, but she prompted and made suggestions: 'What's the story, what would you do there, what would you say . . .' The project shows an interesting combination of associationist and constructivist principles, and of transmissional and pupil-centred teaching. The adaptation established ownership, control and relevance, conveyed excitement and novelty, and provided opportunities for play wherein the teacher participated as facilitator. It thus became part of the pupil's world. This is particularly important, it might be argued, for pupils from some working-class homes. Sue reported that middle-class parents were very supportive of traditional forms. They would reinforce the teacher's work by faithfully taking their children through the Crown Readers again. But Sarah, for example, had no such culture of support.

Teaching as Discovery

The need to attune to a pupil's culture is illustrated in another episode with Sarah, where Sue was trying to teach her how to count money. This proved difficult to begin with, for Sarah could not recognize coins. Then the teacher was provided with a clue, which she pursued like a true investigator. The clue was Sarah's recognition of a 50p coin — the only one she identified. How did she know that?

'Because we put them in the tele, of course.'
'How long does it last?'
'About 8 minutes.'

'What happens when it runs out and you haven't any more 50ps?'
'My dad goes down the pub and asks the pub man.'
'All right. I'll be the pub man and you be your dad coming for some 50ps.
There you are, there's a pound, how many 50ps do you want?'

Occasionally they switch roles, and Sarah is the 'pub man'. And Sue rings
other changes. What programmes does Sarah like to watch?

'Oh, it's run out. This time you've only got 10ps. How many are you going
to give the pub-man for one 50p' etc etc.

Sue says you have to experiment. 'You try all sorts of things. Some work,
some don't. You have to have a stream of things to do, a great variety, with
plenty of props. It's no use just presenting formal activities. You have to
improvise.'

So Sue devises her own aids, attuned to the perceived needs, abilities,
and background of her pupils. She plays to Sarah's strengths, capturing her
wish to make a kite, having read about it, which then inspired her to write
about it; suggesting that she make a full size policeman, with 'Stop!' coming
out of his mouth, like one of the classes did. Sarah loves doing things like
this, and even volunteered to write about her trip to the park. This was a
significant step. Sue devises games for Sarah to play. One, for example, was
based on a spelling activity of 'Study-Cover-Write-Check' ('sacawac'). Sue
devised a particular checking system for Sarah, whereby she awarded herself
ticks and crosses. They agreed on the rules — 'a tick if right, if a cross then
you have to get two ticks, each day you get a blank and have to start from
memory; this goes on for ten days, collecting a tick on the back for each
time right; when Sarah has ten ticks she can tear it up. She loves that —
her moment of triumph.'

> Now she has a reservoir of words to choose from to write.
> Sometimes she will sit and say she doesn't know how to write a
> word she has ripped up. Sue will say, "Come on now, Sarah, you've
> had ten ticks for that, you know it, think!" This is really hard
> concentration for her. You can hear her brain ticking over. It's
> marvellous how it works — it comes eventually.

Sue was always making up cards to support her teaching. Cards with a word
on one side and its picture on the other, cards you could do things with,
fold, mark, match with others, cut, shape. She played Sarah at pelmanism,

snap and dominoes (and lost). She invented a bingo game to teach Sarah number recognition; and she made up a device with circular cards of different sizes fastened together that you could revolve to make up different words beginning and ending with 'ch' and 'th'. This proved a huge success with a number of pupils.

Even so, Sue was always 'looking for a bit of new blood' with Sarah. On one occasion she appropriated an idea from television and suggested a treasure hunt ('Goody! I can be Anneka and Robert can be the man behind the desk!') Sarah and Robert would devise it and write the instructions, and their classmates would do it. The aim was not only to provide a new activity to aid their writing, but to help build up her relations with other children. She was not held in high regard and 'it was not something she can help herself'.

Breakthroughs

At times in teaching a pupil's learning achieves a quantum leap; a particularly intransigent blockage is freed; or a transformation in attitude and motivation undergone. While many factors contribute towards these, not all of them understood, creative teaching can be one of the motive forces.

At another school, Sue was assisting with some ethnic minority children who spoke English as a second language. One of them, Gita, was an elective mute. She spoke fluent Bengali at home and was said to be competent at English, but had not been perceived to utter a word at school to anyone during her 18 months there. Gita did her work for Sue competently enough, showing herself to be very capable, but would not communicate, other than writing her name for Sue when asked. In small group work, Gita would not talk, other pupils telling Sue 'Gita can't talk!' She kept her head down at first, but as tensions eased and laughs came, she smiled. She also nodded at some questions, and shook her head for 'No'.

The following week, Sue took Gita into the library where other people were working silently. She showed her the 'What's Wrong' cards. Gita wouldn't look at them to begin with.

> Then I put one in her hand and watched. She looked up from under her eyebrows. I fingered the cards, pointing out the mistakes. Soon she did this herself and showed me what was wrong. We did not speak. Once she smiled broadly. After this I played a 'copy me' game. Gita copied me and soon was obviously enjoying the game. Touch

my head, eyes, shoulder, floor. I got quicker and she copied. Then I touched my mouth, and opened it wide. Gita would not do this. I left the mouth and went back to other areas but I had lost her completely . . . In class I discovered that Gita does talk with Rufin in the playground. I asked her to ask Gita what we were doing in the library . . .

(Teacher's notes)

The next week:

With Gita, we played copycat game, then Gita did it and I copied her. When I asked her how old she was, she indicated she was 5-years-old, and her baby brother 3-years-old. At break, I went in the playground. Gita and Monwara came and held my hand firmly.

One week later

I took Gita in the library for five minutes. Played the copycat game. I started and once begun she was happy to follow. I got quicker. Then I asked Gita to lead. She did so very confidently and smiled and laughed. After play, Mrs Jones asked why the elephant children must look after their masks and Gita put her hand up to volunteer an answer. When asked, she couldn't say anything, but it was the first time she has done this. During the acting of the play Mrs Carr came in to collect Gita to 'read' (the attempt was regularly made). At 3.30 pm she brought her back and said Gita had *read* five books aloud (in a whisper).

   Great breakthrough! Jill over the moon, lifted Gita up high in the air. Yellow table allowed to go first because of a 'special reason'. Mrs Carr said she had assumed, as always, that Gita would read. Her lips began to move, then out came a whisper . . .

From then on, Gita behaved normally, seemingly enjoying school, relating well to her peers and teachers, and talking.

   Not enough is known to provide a full analysis of what led up to this breakthrough. But Sue's contribution almost certainly helped. What she achieved, it might be argued, by trial and error was a means of communicating with Gita, and by which Gita could communicate with her with confidence and enjoyment. What we see illustrated is a 'conversation of gestures'. From a position of former isolation, Gita reaches out and happily engages in meaning construction. This, we might argue, is an important step for Gita's construction of self. We could say that in Gita's case the 'me' — the self as object was underdeveloped at least in the school area. She found it difficult to 'take the role of other' (not uncommon among 5- to 6-year-olds). The lack of interaction between the 'I' and the 'me' was reflected in her lack of communication with others. The case was complicated by Gita being an ESL child. The indications were that she behaved normally at home, but could not transfer that self to school. Once she had found a way of conveying her own meanings and confidently predicting the other's response, she achieved a certain equilibrium. Sue thus acted her part here as 'significant other' (Kuhn, 1964). Possibly the real breakthrough occurred when Gita began to participate in this 'conversation', for language is only one form of gesture, and arguably a natural sequel to what occurred. Sue's insight was to locate communication with Gita on a broader range of gestures than simply language. This led to not only the conveying of information, but to enjoyment and reward on Gita's part and a close relationship with the teacher concerned. Once the communicating and relationships had been established with one teacher, the development of that communication might be expected to follow with another teacher in whom she felt similar confidence.

The accident factor and the unexpected breakthrough is well illustrated in the case of 'normal Jonathan', another of Sue's special pupils, bright, but exhibiting behavioural problems:

> One Monday 6-year-old Jonathan came in like a tornado, shouting, pushing, hitting. Mrs Ross says he is always like this on Mondays, but Sue has never known him so disturbed. Sue walked him out of school and in again twice, but everything she said received a negative 'No!' 'Don't care!' 'Shan't!' etc. Sue persuaded him to go and tell Mrs Ross 'Good morning, you look nice' but he wouldn't do it for Mrs Robertson (he'd said it to Sue). Then, as she always did, she told him about her weekend and a competition she had entered. If she won she would get a fluffy animal. Who would she give it to? Perhaps Sarah or Jonathan?
>
> At this, Jonathan jumped off his chair with a smile and said 'Wait a minute, I'm going to be *normal* Jonathan now,' and off he went outside and came in quickly, sat down, even said 'Good morning' to Mrs Robertson. All was positive after this. He even volunteered to give up his sack race for another boy.
> (Teacher's notes)

Jonathan is clearly able to assume a different self at will. He obviously knows what is expected of a normal pupil. The teacher's problem is to find the cues and construct the situation that will tempt the 'normal Jonathan' to prevail. He had failed to respond to all the usual blandishments, but there was clearly something about the fluffy toy, and perhaps the competition with Sarah for the toy and/or Sue's favours that got through to him. Sue had not really expected it after the earlier failure and was pleasantly surprised. It was simply one gambit in her repertoire of 'trying anything', with only equal, possibly less, chances of success than others previously made. It illustrates the possibilities. If only one can go on experimenting, a chord might be struck, an emotion appealed to, an interest aroused, sufficient to establish communication, and cause a disturbed child like Jonathan to enter the society of the school. Had it not occurred, he could have gone on all day, and all week, fighting against it. This is not to suggest, however, that Jonathan's problems could be completely met at school. Teachers are often called on to treat the symptoms of disorder when the basic causes lie elsewhere.

Creative Projects

Here I refer to compilations of teaching activity on a broader front involving groups or classes of pupils, and possibly more than one teacher. The first example is the creation of an integrated wall display based on the story of Bhindoo, Bhadoo and Bhidoo. Briefly, these travelling Indian musicians visited a palace, entertained the King and Queen and their guests, but received no payment. The musicians then put a spell on the castle occupants, sending them to sleep, and for good measure, over a period of ten days, caused all the surrounding trees and shrubbery to grow to such a height and thickness that the palace disappeared from view.

Each member of the class of 7-year-olds selected an aspect of the story to illustrate. Alpesh was intrigued with the shape of the gate, a keyhole, so he drew that, and put his little story in it; Joanna loved music, so illustrated the three musicians with their instruments, with music notes going round the outside of the paper; Saheel insisted they were apple trees, so drew some. The individual contributions were done to such a scale that they could all be put together to make up the whole, some making extra contributions to make sure all the important detail was covered. In addition, the picture provided different perspectives of time and space. The trees, for example, were small at first, gradually growing larger over the ten days. As for space, two perspectives were provided, the outside, among the trees, and inside the palace, looking out through the window.

This was a novel way of portraying the story. The basic idea came from a one-off television programme, but contained several refinements. The exercise combined many areas of curriculum — language, art, perspective, music, social relations and mores, multiculturalism. Its holistic and relevance features are also fairly clear. Another aspect of its novelty was that it was the only wall picture in the school hall that was 'non-Christmassy' (it being mid-December). The teachers concerned had felt under great pressure to produce 'cribs' and other appropriate decorative material, that they had felt like making a point (without being anti-Christmas) by keeping it up.

The same television programme ('Watch') provided the germ of an idea for a puppet show for one class to do for its assembly stint for the whole school. They built on and developed this idea. The puppets acted out the tape-recorded nativity play, with carols. There was Joseph, Mary, Jesus, donkey, shepherds, sheep, angels. The pupils had made these, and presented them on long needles behind a screen. As the tape played, the relevant puppets popped up and down, moved, and addressed each other. There was great fun at the dance. The jazzy music made even the sheep and donkey dance, and one shepherd to flap his arms, another to twizzle round, and another to fall off his needle. The audience's rapturous reception of this novel twist to a familiar theme clearly showed that they considered it a great success.

A creative piece of team teaching was the school exchange that I have discussed elsewhere as a good example of 'matching' along all aspects of a 'teaching and learning opportunities model', that is one where teacher intentions match practice, where task matches pupils' abilities, where context and relationships match social relevancies, where teacher and pupil motivation are taken into account, and so on (Woods, 1989a). One aspect of this is teacher initiation and involvement. Much of the idea, or if not that, its implementation, is theirs, and such is its novelty they, as well as the pupils, are not left untouched by it. They learn with the pupils; creativity builds on creativity.

How did this project originate? Two teachers were involved, and one described the beginnings thus:

Miss B: I was at my dad's. Julie came round to see my dad, and we got talking about children and schools and what we all did in our schools. And we said wouldn't it be a good idea if we joined forces and your class wrote to my class and so on and that was how it began.

PW: That was purely your idea?

Miss B: It was our idea.

PW: It hadn't been recommended in any sort of official places?

Miss B: Oh no. I'd done a little one before but that was at Cotley and we just made letters and wrote books about the school. But I'd never done where you actually . . . where the children actually met.

PW: Stanley (the other school) have had?

Miss B: They've done one before but I've never done one.

PW: Had Julie?

Miss B: Well it had been . . . *thrust* on them . . . (!)

PW: I see. So it hadn't been their own?

Miss B: No. This one came from us. So we all said, well we'll go and ask our head. So I went and asked David (her headteacher): And David said 'oh that was fine' and then she did the same. And then we started planning what we wanted and she thought she'd like children to see the village because that is a completely different environment to what they are used to. And I said well it would be nice if our children could see the Hindu Temple because that would come in part of their sort of religious syllabus apart from anything else. To see other religions. And then we thought about well what else could we do if we exchanged and I sort of tentatively said well wouldn't it be nice if our children could use your apparatus, because we haven't got any . . . And we were talking about it, and we decided that we had this week when we had a minibus so that week we would be able to get over to see them. Then we had a meeting with Mr. Jones (headteacher) at which we all discussed it all and sort of well I'd already told David what the programme was and persuaded everybody around to our idea of the programme, what we wanted. By sort of making it seem as if it was somebody else's idea. . .

The other teacher (Julie), interviewed later, confirmed this, and made this significant comment:

It came from a spontaneous meeting between myself and Deirdre. This was a spark between two teachers and two different schools that had been missing from the previous thing. So we built it up outside school first in every aspect. And that was the difference in the preparation — that you got the teachers sparking each other off.

This notion of 'spark' is clearly important in this kind of creative endeavour and draws attention to the chemistry of the interrelationship and the circumstances in which it occurred. Cleary all this has to be got right. The final remark of Miss B's indicates how, in the power relationships of a school, a creative strategy is sometimes required to implement creative teaching. A measure of teacher autonomy in the classroom is one matter. Where teacher initiative spills over beyond the classroom and then beyond the school, other factors come into play — school reputation, headteacher's mediation, school policy vis-a-vis other schools, implications for colleagues, and so on. All have to be coped with if the project is to prosper. The transcript gives some examples of this.

The contrast is also drawn between a similar project which they feel to have had 'thrust' on them, and this one, which they feel to be their own invention. I say 'feel to be' since, though in many respects it was clearly theirs, drawing on knowledge that only they possessed and utilizing ideas that they generated as they went along, we do not know if the headteachers concerned were not also engaged in the strategy of 'idea-displacement'.

The other feature here is how the generation of the initial idea took place almost by accident when one teacher was visiting the other's father on a different matter. This was a social occasion, out of school, where the conversation of like-minded individuals was allowed to pursue the possibilities and generate the initial impulse, unfettered by the constraints that attend schools and classrooms.

There are, of course, 'whole school' projects, where all the staff combine in the planning and development. One such was noted in a small multi-ethnic lower school (Grugeon and Woods, 1990). The staff here spent half a term developing a practical mathematics project which became a focal point for cross-curricula activities for the whole school. The teacher who first initiated it was keen on practical, everyday mathematics, and it occurred to her that if the children made houses that formed a street it could provide a rich learning experience. Gradually, a street was built up with houses and shops on either side, which the children could walk down. Their houses were there. All had windows, doors, and numbers. The two travellers were helped to make a trailer site. There were cardboard figures, some with authentic turbans. There were numbered squares for a dice game which involved progressing down the street. Over the weeks more detail was added — a church, drawings, writing and a community with which they could identify. In the street, every child in the class could find a point of reference: Michelle's pub, The Foresters Arms, the sweet shop, even the dentist. Among other things, it was a good example of multicultural mathematics in action. Everything could be handled and moved, as this was essentially a game inviting participation. Their own physical presence in the street helped develop their sense of progression and of probability, as well as their conceptualization of number. The teacher concerned had been strongly influenced by the constructivist principles enshrined in a course she had attended. 'I just thought, well, start off with something that's very meaningful to them really . . . I didn't think it was going to be quite so big as it is, then gradually I sort of adapted it to meet the mathematical needs of children . . . they all seemed to like their little families . . . I didn't really force it on them, they enjoyed doing it'.

During the project a number of worksheets were devised for particular purposes, and only used when the related experience became meaningful to the child. The advantage of this approach particularly with the very youngest children, is the freedom and flexibility this gives teachers to try out and to adapt worksheets to suit individual needs.

The prominent characteristics of this project were the explicit constructivism, the space within which it was allowed to develop, the collaborative spirit of the staff (they were 'of a mind'), under the leadership of the head, holism, and the sense of excitement in accomplishment that attends many such experiences.

Creative Teaching Performance

The skills involved in role performance are considerable. The sheer range of roles a teacher has to play demands a great number of abilities, an alert awareness to cues, and fine tuning in response to them. Harris (1976) in arguing the case for teaching as an art, includes these points:

> At times the teacher is orator, with all that this involves for quality of voice, pitch and modulation. In close vein he(sic) is an actor, literally having to 'perform' the novel or poem he is reading, or to bring life and clarity to textbook language. In the broader sense of 'actor' he has to communicate, most effectively, his feelings of approval or disapproval, sympathy or rage. Many a well-intentioned teacher flounders because of the vast differences between demonstrating concern for one's own family on the one hand, and demonstrating it to three dozen comparative strangers in a classroom. Sometimes the teacher needs to be preacher. There are times when pupils simply have to be told what they ought to do. Preaching is an art in itself, and requires considerable tact and subtlety . . . The teacher as comedian is a much neglected study . . . (p. 94)

Eisner (1979) helps out with the last point, in arguing for a similar 'practical judgement based on ineffable (but not necessarily irrational) forms of understanding'. He writes:

> For the standup comedian to function effectively, he must be able to 'read' the qualities emanating from an audience. These qualities change as he proceeds with this act. The tone of the laughter, the tempo of his own words, the timing from line to line; all of these must be grasped immediately. Indeed, it is almost as though acting becomes second nature; no time to formulate hypotheses, no time to consult and compare theory, no time to seek substantiating evidence or data, and certainly no time to administer tests to determine the level of interest. Out of the flux of interacting the comedian must blend his own; a line one second late falls flat. And the configurations change. Automaticity and reflectivity must go hand in hand. The act must reach a crescendo and finally, when the audience has nearly had enough, be brought to closure ... What we are seeing when we see artists work is not the absence of rationality and intelligence but the ultimate manifestations of its realization. Such individuals work with the creation and organization of qualities, they act with the qualities of speech and gesture ... the teacher with words, timing, and the creation of educational environments. What these artists have in common is the aspiration to confer a unique, personal order on the materials with which they work. And most work in contexts that are in a state of continual flux. No recipe will do. No routine will be adequate, even if routines must be acquired as part of one's repertoire. (p. 272)

Clark and Yinger (1987) argue that the skill required is that of 'intelligent and artful orchestration of knowledge and technique' (p. 93). I also use the term 'orchestration' in discussing various conflicting aspects of the primary teacher's role (Chapter 2). The skilful teacher must be instructor, facilitator, critic, friend, parent, controller almost all at the same time, and present a persona to pupils that is one and indivisible, where the seams do not show. Handling these conflicting elements in a constructive way is another example of turning what looks like disadvantage to good account — typical of creative acts. The inexperienced or uncreative teacher gets stuck, experiences what Wagner (1987) calls a 'knot' in their thinking and a reverse trend of emotion can set in, like one of the teachers Wagner interviewed:

> It always make me so angry that I don't make such a presentation

more lively and exciting; one could make this much more interesting, and I always talk so boringly and always in the same flat tone of voice, it's just horrible ... sometimes I think I am going to train myself and practice being more stimulating. I have seen very active teachers who do this really well but I would feel like a complete fool doing this. I would feel like a phoney! (p. 163)

This teacher appears to be stuck within a routinized conception of self, any deviation from which represents an act of bad faith towards the 'real self'. Yet she perceives fairly accurately what is required, setting up conflict that causes anger. Is this a matter of personal qualities or situation? I would argue for the latter.

Social Factors Affecting Creative Teaching

The creativity literature tells us that creative people are independent, curious, alert, inventive, enthusiastic, determined, industrious, intuitive, introverted, imaginative, flexible, adaptable. The teacher above appears to be inflexible, unimaginative, unadaptable, dull, unexciting. But are these invariant traits? Her anger suggests not, for it shows a disturbance in the self between the realization of what is required and how she will appear to others if she attempts it. Had she not felt such or any emotions, one might have concluded that such complacency was not a good teaching attribute. As it is, this teacher might have been encouraged to experiment, to role-play perhaps, in order to help see herself in a different light and not 'as a fool' when attempting something different. The self is an ongoing process, subject to adjustment. In this case, the teacher appears to have become 'self'-conscious to a counter-productive degree. This is not unusual given the 'public-performance' nature of the teacher's job. Unfortunately much teacher training seems designed to eliminate creativity rather than to encourage it; and in-service training is usually directed toward specific tasks.

Certainly, as outlined in the introduction, there are many factors constraining teachers to act in conservative and routinized ways. One of these is the demands of controlling cohorts rather than individuals. It is not insignificant that some of my examples — those concerning Sue — are to do with one-to-one relationships. Two of the projects mentioned — the 'exchange' and the 'mathematics' street — had the effect of disbanding or scrambling the cohorts concerned. They also neutralized another common problem, that of teacher isolation. The 'exchange' would not have been such an exciting event without the 'spark' between the two teachers; and the mathematics project was a whole-school collaboration effort. This does not mean that one cannot be creative with a cohort, as, for example, 'orator' or 'instructor'. But opportunities to ring the changes would be an advantage.

Similarly, some argue that public examinations induce transmission style teaching (though there is some dispute about this — see, for example, Hammersley and Scarth, 1986). While subject specialism gives rise to subject-based pedagogies, subject commitment, and subject fragmentation — all clearly at odds with the holistic nature of creativity discussed earlier. Another of the constraints mentioned by Hargreaves (1988), status and career factors, might run against the more altruistic motives in teaching. The creativity becomes displaced towards one's own advancement and can result in the dullest teaching. Thus the apparently exciting wall display, the initiation of a field course, a prepared play, can disguise the heavily transmissional elements that went into their making with an eye to public accountability and personal performance. The public record is all. One teacher told me that when he was a pupil it was part of pupil folklore when on a school trip 'not to look out of the window or you'll be asked to write about it'. At one primary school where I was working, all personal projects and activities were put to one side in favour of more heavily formal activities in preparation for a visit from the Senior Adviser.

If these are 'constraints', that is restrictions that more or less impel teachers to act in certain ways, what factors aid creativity, and give them scope? It might be inferred that their opposites — more individual, non-examination, inter-subject teaching etc. — might be called for. But it is not quite so simple. Examinations, for example, can sometimes be a resource (see Nuttall, 1988) and we have yet to see the effects of the GCSE, which has been designed in part to tackle some of these problems. As for 'subjects', subject-identities are bound up with status and career. For many teachers they are one of the principal means of self-realization. This is clear from the recent cut-backs, which forced many teachers to re-deploy or take on different or additional subjects or change their level of teaching. Far from opening up new opportunities, such moves were generally perceived as retrogressive (Sikes *et al.*, 1985; but note Anon, 1988).

These factors, therefore, are debatable. They are the means through which more basic requirements may or may not be met. These requirements I would suggest, at least as far as creativity is concerned, are fourfold, and they reflect the criteria discussed earlier. First, for ideas to be produced and take root, inspiration and incubation is needed. The prime element here is time — not just hours or days, but subjective time involving ownership and control. This yields time to reflect on what is needed, on countless interactions of past experience, on the composition of the likely situation, and to play with various permutations and combinations, experimenting with interjecting various extraneous factors, and setting up hypothetical programmes, which are then tried out in practice. They might not always work, so latitude is needed in which a few mistakes are accepted as part of the enterprise. This is not simply, or even necessarily, a matter of more free periods and fewer duties, though that would no doubt help. In creative activities, time is often created where formally none was suspected to exist — outside school hours, in-between lessons, a snatched moment in the course of a lesson. Even whilst one is teaching, in the maelstrom of activity something might occur that creates the germ of an idea at the back of the mind, to be held there until further reflection could be brought to bear. More important here than actual time, perhaps, is the amount that is the teacher's own time, and the freedom he or she has to exercise the mind in spontaneous and innovative ways.

Secondly, resources are needed. The more money that is put into teaching, the better the buildings and equipment, the greater the range of opportunities. Again, however, this is not simply a matter of money. Indeed, on occasions hardship can promote creativity. Primary school teachers avail themselves of all manner of materials, from toilet roll cardboard cylinders to milk bottle tops and cornflake packets. 'This snakes and ladders board will help my children to count'; 'with a few adaptations this method of making Christmas trees on "Blue Peter" can be employed by my pupils — all they need is some coloured paper'; 'I'll take these old photos in of my forefathers, and ask the children to bring in theirs as a basis for discussion about life earlier this century'; 'you need a stream of things to do'. The teacher who made this comment seemed to be in a state of continual awareness about what she could appropriate to aid her teaching. 'Don't throw that away, I can use that'. Having said this, such initiative can be blunted if inadequate official resource is put into the school, if, for example, the supply of basic materials is depleted, or if conditions affect pupils and teachers working normally. It can be considerably enhanced if an LEA, for example, is particularly supportive of teacher-centred activities. Aspinwall (1989), for example, describes how an LEA helped to give teachers a sense of empowerment through sponsoring them to revitalize their curricula.

Thirdly, a teacher requires a supportive school ethos, one wherein teacher creativity is valued and encouraged. Authoritarian regimes do not do so, and to these, creative teachers are a nuisance. Fontana (1986) notes that 'creativity involves an independent and original approach to life and sometimes the creative person has to show a touch of ruthlessness in giving his (sic) creative work precedence over the social demands made upon him by others' (p. 10). The hierarchy will be no less ruthless, with the result that creativity becomes displaced into strategical thinking. Creative teaching favours a participatory-democratic environment, a 'bottom-up' management structure to match the 'bottom-up' model of teacher knowledge discussed earlier (Sikes *et al.*, 1985; Hunter and Heighway, 1980). Such models have the teacher's self at their centre. It is allowed to flourish within them. In this sense, this is teacher-centred teaching. The principles of ownership and control discussed earlier are intrinsic to it.

There is more to school ethos than management structure. Teacher culture is clearly important — relationships with one's peers and the 'way of doing things' that most schools seem to develop. Ideally it is one that both contributes to, and takes from individuals in balanced interaction which allows for the growth of both. Thus individuals are neither fully determined by school cultures, nor are they permitted to run wild. A good example of such an enhancing environment is provided by Gates (1989) who describes how the staff of his comprehensive school engaged in long-term, systematic 'mutual support and observation'. For them, teacher isolationism was not a problem. The teacher self gained another perspective on performance which aided self evaluation. By contrast, in heavily constrained circumstances like 'Black School' (Webb, 1962), 'Lumley' (Hargreaves, 1967) and 'Lowfield' (Woods, 1979), creative teaching is difficult. One's ingenuities are diverted towards coping and survival (see Chapter 4).

Pupil culture is also important and herein lies the fourth factor. For, as noted earlier, teacher creativity must bring a response. Brilliant ideas are of no avail if they fall on stony ground. Certainly a teacher's skill in negotiation may affect pupil motivation. But there are factors beyond the teacher's control also exerting influence. Social class, 'race', gender, age, neighbourhood factors, employment prospects, and a pupil culture that may have grown up in response to these and many more, including situational variables such as school organization, and which may be fairly impervious to change — all these help guide the nature of the pupil response. If creative teaching is aimed at generating creative learning, then it has to be noted that this does not occur in a social vacuum — that creativity, or at least our perceptions of it, is not a single, absolute quality. An example may clarify: a sixth form group studying French are required to listen to a radio programme (in French) each week, which is then discussed (in French); and then for homework, asked to compose an essay recounting the subject matter. One week, one of the pupils had a bad headache during the radio transmission and was unable to make any notes or take part in the discussion. Rather than not do the exercise or copy from someone else, the pupil composed an essay in French describing the onset of the headache, the way it affected his perspective during the programme, and the consequences. The pupil thought this an individual and original way of meeting the problem, but his effort was struck through with heavy red pen and he was referred to the Principal, presumably for insubordination.

This reminds us that creative pupils can be a problem for teachers. They make unexpected responses, do strange things, create diversions, ask embarrassing questions (Cropley, 1967). A pupil's creativity may not match a teacher's. It might draw on different social class or ethnic, perhaps, referents and not be recognized for what it is. It might be displaced, like teachers' on occasions, into strategical thinking (for example, Willis, 1977). It may lie dormant, conditioned by years of socialization, and untapped by teachers' overtures, as perhaps in the case of girls' approach to science (Kelly, 1985). Thus teacher creativity requires a response, but that response needs to be correctly identified.

A Concluding Comment

The literature abounds with examples of the sheer tedium and ineffectiveness of unrelieved, systematic transmission teaching, of routinized teachers regimented 'like horses, all running on the same track at the same speed' (Elbaz, 1981, p. 64). We know, too, that there are so many different, emergent, changing and conflicting factors in teaching that they require either that kind of treatment, or a divergent cast of mind. As one teacher records, 'we fly by the seat of our pants most of the time' (Abbott *et al.*, 1989).

As noted at the beginning, there seem to be conflicting trends in motion at the moment, some of which appear increasingly to direct, others to free the teacher. After periods of 'black box' teaching (before the 1970s, when the teacher did not appear to exist as a factor), 'bashing' the teacher in the 1970s; and 'directing' the teacher in the later 1980s, perhaps we are due for a period of 'freeing' the teacher in the 1990s, when they might be allowed and encouraged to use their own considerable inspiration. Many current manifestations of this are so much part of minute-to-minute activity, so integral to a stream of events, and in an ironical way a taken-for-granted element in the teacher's day-to-day job, that it is in danger of being overlooked. A resurrection of interest in creativity, but this time directed more toward the teacher, and situating such studies within their appropriate social referents might give a boost to a new prevailing trend which seeks to display the educational promise of teacher innovation and experiment.

Chapter 2

Managing the Teacher's Role

Stand up, stand up, shout thank you Lord,
Thank you for the world I'm in.
Stand up, stand up, shout thank you Lord,
For happiness and peace within. (Assembly Hymn)

Introduction

Why do teachers carry on teaching? Material rewards are not great, unlike the risk of stress, so there must be other factors. Prominent among these, according to Pollard (1985) is 'enjoyment' deriving from the pleasure of working with children (see also Nias, 1981), but curiously this has been largely left out of account in consideration of the teacher role — probably as a legacy of the tendency to see the world largely through official interpretations. These would tend to see such matters as part of the informal interaction occurring in gaps in the important business during the school day, and therefore of lesser importance. Others might view any emphasis upon them as indulging in the romantic, idealized, sentimental outlook that primary teachers are often alleged to be subject to (Jackson, 1977). Hoyle (1969) could consequently write, 'Any undue familiarity with pupils on the part of a teacher is seen as a threat to the general esteem of teachers'.

Riseborough (1985), however, has shown how pupils can act as 'critical reality definers' for teachers, and Nias (1984) their importance as significant others. Interestingly, on the actual effects of pupils, these draw diametrically opposite conclusions from the samples they studied. For Riseborough's teachers, pupils, while not being simply reactors to teacher practice, used their originality and creativity to 'give their teachers hell' and 'strike at "the heart" (the sacred self) of the teacher as a person in such schools' (p. 261). Nias' (1981 and 1988) teachers, by contrast, tell how pupils can confirm them in their own eyes as teachers, make them feel loved, needed and successful. One of the distinguishing features of these samples is that one was from secondary schools, the other primary. This is not to say that all secondary school teachers would respond as Riseborough's did (see, for example, Connell, 1985; Sikes *et al.*, 1985), but in general terms, it would seem to be a salient factor. There are, for example, no similar accounts to Riseborough's that I know of from primary school teachers, while there are from secondary (for example, Woods, 1979); and there is support for Nias' point from other primary school studies (for example, King, 1978; Hartley, 1985).

There are at least three interrelated reasons why this is so. The first is to do with stage of pupil development. In the one, they are still undergoing primary socialization (Berger and Luckmann, 1967). This consists of creating 'in the child's consciousness a progressive abstraction from the roles and attitudes of specific others to role and attitudes *in general*' (p. 152).

> It takes place under circumstances that are highly charged emotionally. Indeed, there is good reason to believe that without such emotional attachment to the significant others the learning process would be difficult if not impossible. The child identifies with the significant others in a variety of emotional ways . . . (p. 151).

These feelings are to some extent reciprocated. As Jackson (1977) argues, 'Like parents, teachers develop possessive feelings about their students, who become a source of worry, annoyance and pride'.

There is still a measure of dependence on the teacher. Teacher as parent, therefore, is a prominent aspect of the primary school teacher's role. Secondary teachers also act 'in loco parentis', but this is more a legal–bureaucratic matter. At primary school there is more affective attachment as an essential component of the role. At secondary level, a distinguishing feature of pupil development is adolescence, the drive for independence and secondary socialization. The 'sustained and warm relations' that colleges of education recommend may need to be balanced more at this stage by the 'affective neutrality' as recommended more typically by university departments (Taylor, 1969; Grace, 1972).

A second reason is to do with the organization and ethos of schools which reflects this primary–secondary socialization pattern. Primary schools are much smaller than secondary, more locally centred, community-related, 'warm and caring', family-oriented. Teachers and pupils all come to know each other very well as individuals. As one teacher told me 'I think it important that you know the kids and you all grow up together' (something which is almost impossible in large secondary schools). There can be then, also, a strong degree of group cohesiveness in primary schools where 'affective ties bind members to the community and gratification stems from involvement with all the members of the group' (Kanter, 1974).

A third reason is to do with teaching approaches. While so-called 'pupil-centred' approaches are by no means exclusive to primary schools, there has been a heavy emphasis on these within them especially since the Plowden Report (1967), to a degree which secondary schools, given their commitments to external public examinations have not, as yet, been able to match. While some versions of these are not perhaps as far removed from so-called 'traditional' approaches as is sometimes claimed (Sharp and Green, 1975; Galton, 1983; Gracey, 1972), some do have a strong quality of democratic pupil involvement. For Rowland (1984 p. 4), for example, 'the process of teaching and learning is two-way. It involves not only the child's attempt to interpret and assimilate the knowledge and skills offered by a teacher, but also the teacher's attempt to understand the child's growing understandings of the world'. Pupil and teachers learn together in a collaborative venture, pupils reinterpreting what is taught to relate to their existing knowledge, coming to recognize the need for new skills, the teacher acting as facilitator, watching for appropriate moments to guide and instruct, practising the art of 'conversation' with them as one of the chief techniques. Rowland (p. 59) describes informal discussion he had with some of his pupils, how they often appeared 'to be grappling at the very frontiers of their knowledge and reasoning ability', how 'children are able to organize their thinking in such spontaneous discussions, how they take account of differing views expressed by their friends and what this can show us of their ability to reason in what is often called an "abstract" manner' (p. 60). By these means, it is claimed, pupils control their own learning and knowledge.

These factors — the need to provide for primary socialization, the organization of primary schooling, and teacher approach — have implications for the teacher role. Inasmuch as the teacher-pupil relationship involves a certain degree of intimacy and emotional attachment, mutual interest and help, equality, and steadfastness, it is one of friendship. The notion of 'teacher as friend', however, would appear alien to some approaches, except, perhaps, as a teaching strategy. The reciprocality here involves friendliness in exchange for good order and work on a sliding proportional scale — rather than friendship for friendship's sake. The principles involved here seem to require more affective neutrality (Wilson, 1962) and social distance. Even here, however, the requirements of 'teachers as parent' call for some affective relationship. More importantly, in my experience, many teachers who would subscribe to certain principles of teacher-directed learning (involving teacher ownership of knowledge and transmission forms of pedagogy) would also subscribe to forming strong, friendly, relationships with their pupils informally, which cannot help but overrun into the formal area. Few teachers, in consequence, if any, are able to regard their clients as just 'cases', as doctors and lawyers might do (*ibid*). In a sense, friendship cuts across 'teacher as teacher', that is, the need to instruct and to control, and becomes a potential source of role conflict and strain for both sorts of teacher.

The potential conflict can be heightened by the pressures operating on teachers to be (a) 'teacherly' — the emphasis on measurable objectives, evaluation, results — from parents, inspectors, central government; also by the lack of resources to mount a learner-centred approach entirely adequately (the system is very much geared to transmission modes); (b) 'friendly' — their own need for enjoyment and pleasure in the company of their pupils, as already noted. Pollard (1985), in fact, rates this kind of enjoyment as one of teachers' primary interests, while 'instruction', and 'control' are only enabling interests — a means to enjoyment and a satisfactory self-image. Pollard points to teachers' liking for humour and jokes which 'seemed to provide opportunities for the relaxation of roles, and clearly teachers enjoyed relating closely with the children on these occasions, provided of course that they controlled the humour rather than becoming its butt' (p. 24). This neatly points the contrast between different teachers — for some, the humour is part of the role, an essential element in the way they conceptualize it. For others, it is 'time out', to be indulged in 'back regions' (Goffman, 1968). For both, however, it has a key importance. Here again, overindulgence in friendliness can mean that it is difficult to break free when the situation demands one to be teacherly. This is turn can undermine the basis of the friendship, for this has to include a mutual respect. The relationship, thus, fails in all respects.

If the role strain is unresolved, it may promote stress, which the teacher will seek to relieve in one or more ways — for example cultivating split personalities (Lacey, 1976), compromising their ideal classroom organization (Gracey, 1972), modifying their attitudes (Morrison and McIntyre, 1969), revising their commitment (Sikes *et al.*, 1985). If, however, the role strain is resolved, it can lead to effective and enjoyable teaching for all concerned.

To illustrate this proposition, I describe some aspects of primary school teachers' role-management, focusing on the apparently conflicting elements already discussed. I draw on some approach conducted in an urban multi-ethnic junior school, which I shall call Albert Road. The school was in a largely working-class area, with some 200 pupils in total (with 56 per cent from ethnic minority groups, the largest of which was Asians — mainly Hindus) and eleven teachers (two of whom were Section 11). For some eighteen months from the spring term of 1985 to the summer term of 1986 I spent a day (sometimes half-a-day) a week observing pupils and teachers in the school in communal gatherings like assemblies, festivals, outings, but mainly in two classes, one of 7/8-year-olds, the other of 11-year-olds. I was impressed by a certain quality in teacher–pupil relationships, which I can best represent as deriving from the successful combination of basically conflicting roles, and which applied to all the teachers, however differently one would want to categorize their 'styles'.

I shall look, therefore, first at some distinctive affective elements in teacher–pupil relationships, and secondly at certain aspects of pedagogy which derive from those.

Relationships

Prominent among these are (i) the ties of friendship that develop between individual teachers and children; and (ii) the 'family spirit' within the school as a whole. I shall examine each in turn.

Friendship

> What did the policeman say to his tummy?
> You're under a vest! (Pupil joke)

Relationships between pupils and teachers seem to meet several of the criteria of friendship. In these pupils' own terms friends spend time together, help and care about each other, give each other things, find each other attractive, and play and have fun together (Woods, 1987). Teachers can meet all these requirements with pupils to some degree, while not fulfilling them in their entirety since the other aspects of their role pull against them. In an exercise on friends, for example, Kamlesh, an isolate in the form, claimed the teacher for her friend:

> My friend's name is Mrs Brown. She is very kind. She looks nice as well. She helps me with words all the time. I cannot play with her because she is an adult. Well, she is a teacher as well. She can make me laugh all the time. She taught me about tadpoles as well.

This meets several of the criteria, and although she cannot play with her, she 'makes her laugh', which is perhaps the next best thing for an adult. Further, in being her friend, the teacher does not forsake her formal role — she teaches as well. Friendship, in fact, makes an excellent basis for learning (see Woods, 1989a).

The teacher befriended many of the children. Farida, for example, a Bengali Muslim, was ostracized by the rest of the class, and clung to the teacher in the playground. She was so serious, never smiled, had considerable domestic difficulties as well (the oldest of five children so was often 'mum'). By November the teacher felt she 'was getting through to her . . . was getting a smile out of her — and thought that Farida now trusted her'.

The teacher also, for her part, can see pupils as her friends. Seema, for example, a very mature girl, was regarded as an equal and as an ally in the classroom. If the teacher was struggling with another pupil who couldn't understand, she would look up and Seema would catch her eye and smile, and make a knowing shake of the head in sympathy. Kamlesh and Seema might be special cases, but they do illustrate the possibilities and terms which most of the pupils in class 1 availed themselves of to some degree at some time or other. This is not to say that the teacher could fulfil all the same services as contemporaries. But the teacher can perform some important functions for pupils, while pupils provide the teacher with moral and emotional support. A great deal of the pleasure of these relationships is manifested in laughter:

> Two older girls came into the staffroom to ask Mr Morris for the computer. 'Don't forget to kneel' says one to the other. They kneel and bow down 'Oh Lord and Master, may we have the computer please sir, oh great one'. (Teacher laughs. When they are gone he tells me 'They're a great bunch, this lot. You never know what to expect next!')

Teachers are bombarded with jokes and riddles:

> Why don't you play cards in the jungle? Because there are too many cheetahs there.

> What do you get if you cross an elephant with a fish? Swimming trunks!

Teachers are quite good at jokes too:

> Wash it in the toilet. Well, not in the toilet, in the basin in the toilet.

Teachers play tricks on pupils: in a 'senses' lesson, two of the 'tastes' (which they sampled blind) are lemon curd and mustard. There was much running out to the sink after the mustard! There were similar booby traps in the bag they had to dip into to 'feel'. Pupils play tricks on teachers:

> Robert plays a trick on Mrs Coe. He puts the practice clock at 10 and tells her it's 10 o'clock. She says 'Oh dear!' then looks at the real clock. 'That's tricked you' says Robert in triumph. 'Gosh, Robert' she says.

> Dipak plays a joke on Mrs Brown. 'Hold out your hands'. She does so. He then chants something, slaps her hands, and then her face with both hands. She blinks and staggers back. 'More gently next time!' she said in astonishment. She told me later 'I didn't know what to say! It hurt!'.

Pupils share intimate confidences with teachers: Richard was ecstatically excited one day to find a china doll in the oddments box. It had no clothes on, and he showed me its rear aspect with great relish. With a glint in his eye, he said 'This is alive', so heightening the rudery.
Teachers show a certain vulnerability:

> Angela teases Mrs Brown with a joke spider. She jumps and shudders 'Ugh!' Angela squeals with delight.

59

Teachers play tricks on each other:

> Mr Morris comes into the room with one of his boys. 'Go and stand next to Tracey' (a student teacher) he says. Tracey is talking to some of her pupils at her desk, but the boy stands beside her so that they are touching. 'Yes? what do you want?' He says nothing, just looks ahead non-committally. She moves slightly, and he moves with her. They begin to realize something funny is happening, and Mrs Brown caps the joke by putting a paper hat with 'Dunce' written on it (a stage prop) on the boy's head. Mr Morris said he was experimenting with 'invading people's space'.

> Mrs Durrant teased Mrs Brown with a large spider in the hall. She pretended it was in her tissue and brought the whole class in to witness Mrs Brown's reaction. Mrs Brown told this to her own class, to their great amusement.

The affection between teacher and pupil is illustrated in so many ways in the course of a day:

> 'Mrs Brown, my hands are cold'. (Mrs Brown takes his hands, rubs them and warms them up.)

> 'That's all you wanted, isn't it?'

> Kamlesh tries to step into a leotard, but gets in a muddle. Mrs Brown helps her out of it, with some difficulty, laughs with her, wraps the leotard round her face like a blindfold, and smacks her bottom in friendly fashion to send her on her way. Kamlesh sits pleased, slowly blinking her big eyes and long lashes in her way.

Many of these children the teacher felt did not have a great deal of parental interaction, and she felt like a mother to them. She tends to physical and emotional injury. Even the time-honoured activity of inspecting heads, which used to be done by a nurse, is now done by the teachers.

The primary school teacher has her pupils for a year, and comes to form strong affective relationships with them, marked on the one hand by her own regret at losing them at the end of the year, and their frequent visits back to her room the following year. They come to ask 'if she has any jobs', to tell her things or just to talk to her — or they just come and stand. Those of her present year often gather round her at playtime if she is on duty, and she has a laugh and joke with them.

The question might be raised as to *which* children the teachers related to in this way, and whether this showed any connection with structural factors, (such as social class, gender, race) as a number of studies have suggested (see for example, Camilleri, 1986). At Albert Road, the offer and taking of friendship appeared to be open to all. No 'deficit' judgments are made about pupils. The teacher seeks to identify good and strong points to draw them out further, and the weak to improve them. Problem pupils are regarded positively. Even Herol, the 'problem of the infants' was going to be given 'a chance', by his new teacher. 'We'll start from the beginning. Perhaps when he gets in this school he'll be different'. The model is to be one of 'consociates' that will be put on offer in so many ways. 'Naughtiness' thus is not always something to be punished. Mrs Brown felt that with Warish, for example, it was a case of lack of social skills. She was even pleased to see Warish becoming a little naughty at times as that indicated a developing personality from an originally withdrawn and nervous state.

The Family Spirit

I belong to a family, the biggest on the earth, 10,000 every day are coming to birth . . . (Assembly Song)

School ethos contributes towards the sense of community and caring and the notion of the school as a family. Family events themselves reinforced this sense. A birth, for example, was a matter for communal joy and celebration. The way the latter was stage-managed on one occasion well illustrates the spirit involved. Mr Thompson had recently become a father. Towards the end of one assembly, the teacher in charge, Mrs Durrant, who, with her pupils, had been illustrating movement and energy, selected twenty pupils from the audience to dance to some music. Somehow or other Mr Thompson got dragged in to this by some of the senior girls, and ended up dancing with Mrs Durrant, to the delight of the audience. At the end he was asked to 'stay where he was' while the other dancers returned to their places. He was then presented with a gift for which there had been a school collection, for his baby from senior girls. There was a small speech and an enthusiastic clap from the audience. He thanked them, expressed his surprise and pleasure at the event and the gift and then asked 'Do you want me to open it?' There was a massive 'YE-E-E-S!'. He unravelled the paper to discover a giant panda. Everybody was delighted. Later, as the concluding music was played, Mr Thompson, now seated with the panda on his lap, waved its paw at departing classes.

Babies always aroused special interest. When 'Baby Lucy' came to visit, class 1 were fascinated to hear about activities and development, likes and dislikes. They formed a 'welfare club' when a supply teacher brought her poorly young son in with her one day. A high point of the year was a visit from two lambs. Similar interest, care and concern was shown however for other members of society with special needs, notably the aged, and those with disabilities (see Woods, 1987).

Major school festivals reinforced the 'caring and sharing' ethos. The most important of these were Diwali and Christmas, which between them occupied much time and attention in the autumn term. At Diwali, the Festival of Lights, 'we shared in everyone's happiness'. Pupils enact the story of Ram and Sita, their struggles with wickedness and hardship, and the eventual triumph of goodness and truth. 'Our good wishes go to everyone in this room, outside and throughout the world . . . Diwali is also a festival of sharing. Part of that is a gift for everyone here. As you receive your gift, think how you can share what you have to offer'. The sharing went down to individual class level. Gita, for example, brought in some toffee for her class that her mother had made specially. (There were other occasions for sharing — on Angela's birthday, for example, she brought liquorice allsorts in. She stood at the front giving them out as names were called, popping every other one into her own mouth).

How to treat others was a recurring message in assemblies. Friendship and relationships among pupils in general was a popular topic. For the most part, the message was straightforward — the need to think of and care for others, help them, treat them properly, share things with them. Sometimes it took a surprising twist (to me, at least). In one assembly, for example, teachers narrated and pupils enacted (with audience participation) the story of Glencoe. Important here is not only the message but the way it was put across.

> In our story there are some nasty people. They steal things, murder people, set fire to houses. Let me have my naughty people (some pupils go to the front, looking nasty). Not nice are they? (no-o-o-o-!).

The story unfolded with much hatred, wickedness, and duplicity. The class promised to behave themselves. 'Put your hands up if you've ever promised to behave yourself' (All do!). 'However, Dalrimple hated the McDonalds and was a very wicked man. He wanted them all killed. So he made a plot. So let's have our soldiers' (a whole gang of them go out). 'They stayed with the McDonalds as friends for twelve days, then as the day arrived, they began to give them little messages'. The pupils enacted these in little scenarios: 'That's a very nice blanket you've got — I would take care of that tonight'. 'You have a very handsome son, take good care of him *tonight*'. The teacher continued: 'At 5 a.m., the massacre began. An old man of 70, a little boy of 4, and a woman, were the first to be killed. Over thirty McDonalds were killed by people who had been living with them as friends. But 150 escaped! Some soldiers had said "what we're doing is wicked, so we must give some warnings". So though murder was done, the soldiers were not all bad . . . Now where are my singers . . .'

This assembly also contained announcements about a 'conker competition' and a competition for the 'best dressed and cuddliest teddy' ('plus an extra prize which I'll tell you about after you've won it'). The teddy bear display was very impressive, and symbolic of the affective links between home and school, private and public life, pupil and teacher.

The 'caring spirit' did not cease at 4 o'clock. When Shakeel's house burnt down, Mrs Brown took Shakeel (one of seven children) into her own house until the family could be found new accommodation. She felt that he knew her, and she could provide some emotional as well as material support for her pupil. 'Rotten, isn't it, just before Christmas?' This indicates teachers' readiness to 'take the role of the other' to put themselves in the children's position and see things from their perspective.

Teachers occasionally acted the role of pupil. For example, eleven or twelve plus transfer is known to be a traumatic event (Measor and Woods, 1984). One morning a group of senior girls did a play they had made up about their first day at their new school. To the delight of all, they triumphed over all the standard alarums — being late, getting lost, losing friends, having new teachers etc. After the play, the teacher in charge, after asking them a few questions, incorporated his own experience into the event:

> You may be a little bit anxious going to a new school, new things always are. But once you get started it's all right. I remember my first day at new school — it was the John Lee, do you know it? Can you imagine that picture, that long drive up to the gate? I can still remember my first morning walking up that drive — it seemed to go on for ever and e-e-ver. But once I was there, with my friends, in the lessons, I realized my worries were very silly.

Again, in an assembly where a class had tape-recorded accounts of a number of accidents, the teacher's voice appeared among them, describing how he was cycling along a road near the Red Lion Inn. He 'turned right without looking, was hit by something, did six somersaults through the air and landed on his feet. All because he wasn't looking where he was going'. 'Who was that?' the teacher asked. 'It was you-ou-ou!' 'Yes it was me. I was lucky, very lucky'.

When the second king fluffed his lines in 'We three Kings', Mr Butcher excused him quickly, got the other soloists to do it, and then told a story against himself: 'When I was that big, no that big (his hand goes up and down — the audience laughs), 'I had to do that. I opened my mouth and said the words but nothing came out. I was all trembling. So it's not easy . . . '.

Introducing some announcements after an assembly, Mr Butcher asks,

Who's a good cook? (a few hands go up)

Who's a pretty good cook? (more hands go up)

Who's a fair cook? (majority of hands go up, including his own)

Why am I asking you this you may wonder, well it's because it's coffee morning with the PTA on Friday and we'll all bake gingerbread men and buy from each other for school funds ...

He made a few more announcements, then 'When I say "now!".' This was a secret formula, and they prepared themselves in readiness. 'Now!' They folded arms and sat bolt upright, stiffly silent. For some seconds there was absolute stillness. Suddenly, however, behind the teacher, the boy at the xylophone, was overcome by an involuntary twitch and clipped a note — Ping! This immediately punctured the thrall greatly to everyone's amusement. Mr Butcher added to the humour by pretending to be much startled at the sound.

This illustration, among other things, contains a device for securing order some might associate more with purely authoritarian modes. If this were the case, there would have been a different outcome from its rupture. Here, the device *and* its rupture are incorporated into the teacher–pupil interaction.

Teachers at times slipped naturally into representing the world from the pupils' viewpoint:

Right! Come on! Mrs Brown's back now! (after her enforced absence during the morning, and whatever latitude they had been allowed, it was now back to normal).

Teachers took part in activities with children. In a taped 'Music and Movement' lesson, Mrs Brown became a 'showery raindrop' 'fluttering her fingers' ('Ready Raindrops?'), quickly jumping up and running on tiptoe, pausing only to banish Hemang and again illustrating the limits ('It didn't say race round doing what you like!'). Later, she skipped with them round the Mulberry bush. She gave her 'news' when they gave theirs (telling how she won two raffles, one a big rag doll!) On the sponsored walk in the park, teachers walked round with pupils, and Mrs Brown had a race with some of hers at one point. In playground games, Mrs Brown changed into her '10-year-old pumps and husband's blue socks and laughed her head off' with the children as they had team games with footballs, balancing balls on bats, beanbags on heads and skipping. All had great fun together. Teachers joined with pupils in singing and responses in television programmes. They joined in the conker and teddy bear competitions. Mrs Brown's 'family tree' was on the wall with the pupils'.

On occasions, pupils were encouraged to take the role of the teacher. They sometimes conducted assemblies.

'Good morning everyone.'

'Good morning, everyone.'

Even the youngest at times led the prayers:

> *Pradeep:* Let us say a prayer together. Let us think of the good things
> we share with our families.

This interchangeability of roles was again part of the general ethos of the school. Drama and role-play were common activities in classroom and halls, and much appreciated by all concerned. Sometimes I found it difficult to grasp what was happening in a pupil 'made-up' play, but the pupil audience did not, invariably craning forward to see with much interest and responding to all the cues. Few opportunities were lost by teachers to try to put them in the position of the 'other'. Thus, in an assembly on St Paul, they were asked to consider what it was like to be blind. A volunteer was blindfolded and asked to 'go and find Mr Thompson'. She set off, unsteadily groping her way, bumping into Mrs Brown and then Mrs Durrant. 'Have you found him?' She nodded, much to everyone's amusement. Three prominent messages came out of this little scenario — (i) an element of appreciation of what it was like to be blind; (ii) reinforcement of the friendly relationships with teachers (the activity was uncommonly like the game of 'blind man's buff'); and (iii) the moral of the exercise that one can undergo profound change, in this case from 'nasty' to 'nice'.

Teaching

A teacher may be a friend and a parent to a pupil, but she must also teach them something as well. Without this, friendships would not develop — it legitimates the teacher's whole position (Musgrove and Taylor, 1974). Ironically, however, much of its requirements run against the affective grain. For, while the ideology of pupil-centredness has a measure of control vested in pupils and instruction taking place on demand, the fact is that most teachers are forced through lack of resources to operate a part pupil- part teacher-centred approach. In this, instruction and teacher control figure as prominently as pupil discovery and creativity and pupil self-control. These are, however, blended into a coherent and consistent pattern through a quality of omniscience, or what some have identified as 'awareness' or 'withitness' (Kounin, 1970; Lacey, 1977) and through a process of what I will term 'orchestration'. I will consider each in turn.

Teacher Skills and Strategies

Omniscience

Yeah, Mrs Brown knows everything (one of Mrs Brown's pupils).

The skilful teacher's knowledge of, and influence in, her classroom seemed boundless. In a class of some twenty-five children, some working individually, most in small groups on different topics or subjects and at different stages, she knew what each one of them was doing and when they were not doing what they should be. Even though there was a constant noise as pupils discussed, read or reflected, her finely tuned ear soon detected any variant to a legitimate 'working noise', when a brief signal cutting through the swathe of sound quickly restored the situation. It might be a name, a certain tone of voice in what she was already saying, a noise or utterance, or, if necessary, a reminder of different categories: 'I don't mind you talking but I won't have silliness'.

The skilful teacher can see round corners. The classroom with its cupboard and shelves, nooks and crannies, playhouse and reading corners with carpet provide opportunities for quiet work — or concealment and idleness. Where people are is imprinted on her memory and the linkages are maintained by brief signals without the teacher having always to patrol the room. 'How are you getting on ... ?' 'Are you doing that properly ...?' 'How far have you got ... ?' 'How many have read so far ... ?' 'Is everything all right on the floor?' (Ye-e-e-es!) On one occasion, Tony was banished from the corner reading group 'I've been watching you ... that's the second complaint I've had ... now get on with some writing'. Later Mrs Brown laid emphasis on the privilege of being in the 'advanced reading group', where they could get on on their own in a comparatively private and select area of the classroom. But 'some children had been silly and lost the opportunity'. Here the teacher is attempting to construct a social structure within the classroom which all will accept and which then will run itself without her constant vigilance and being sustained, perhaps, only with some of those briefest of signals. The teacher, herself, is part of that structure. In a sense, she remains its guardian. The better it runs itself without intervention from her, the fewer and lesser the signals, the more successful she has been in constructing it. But it still depends on her, or at least some other with similar abilities and powers, as was demonstrated, when the structure collapsed sometimes when some other occasionally took over.

However, the skilful teacher's influence lives on in the classroom, for a time at any rate, in her absence. One morning Mrs Brown had to leave to teach another group, leaving the class with a pre-service student. After getting them in good order ('Are you listening?' 'Kaushik, get your bottom down!'), she gave them a firm reminder of the rules before she went, to lay the platform. The entry in my field notes reads:

66

Her influence lingers on, the 'spell' of her warning impressed on memory.

Once established, the structure can be reaffirmed with signals. The signalling can take many forms. It can become progressively more imperceptible to an outsider, and take the form, almost, of a game:

(After one assembly): Mr Butcher quietens them down with hand signals (rather like the comedian who cuts off the piped applause — and he has a similar effect). The palm held out, depressed means quiet but at ease; when the palm was turned up, they all sit up briskly like soldiers coming to attention.

The gamelike qualities of this tactic were demonstrated when, having got them all quiet and orderly prior to leaving the hall while the closing music played, the Maori music (which was the tape of the day) suddenly began with a loud grunt. Mr Butcher jumped and retreated in some trepidation, to everybody's amusement. My notes record a 'good, relaxed, consociable, orderly start to the day'.

Mr Butcher later told me of the other signals in his repertoire. For example, one finger-snapping click means 'attention', and two means 'relax'. He sometimes moves his lips soundlessly — 'you can hear a pin drop as they try to make out what he is saying'. These signals are blended smoothly into the pattern of events:

Mr Butcher picks out a choir (all hands go up), orders the verses, snaps his fingers and a boy goes out to the front without a pause in the teacher's approach.

The teacher's omniscience, omni-awareness and fine-tuning may seem to indicate superhuman powers. It is easy to see how a lay observer might develop that impression. However, if this were the case for pupils it would run against the grain of the kinds of relationships we have been talking about. The teacher's mystical expertise needs balancing therefore with more identifiably human properties. A certain fallibility was therefore evident — not too much, just enough to show that the teacher was human. A certain humility in the teacher's approach helps to substantiate this.

In some maths blackboard work, Mrs Brown has to draw dogs, birds, rabbits, and cats. The pupils laugh at her pictures, and she joins in with them. 'My rabbits are not very good!' On another occasion commenting on her blackboard artwork she admitted 'I can't draw fingers. I always draw sausages'.

Sometimes the fallibility is genuine, sometimes contrived:

In a maths lesson, Mrs Brown sometimes makes deliberate mistakes on the board:

$$\begin{array}{r} 19 \\ \underline{04} \\ \hline \end{array}$$

'I add nothing . . . ' 'No-o-o! The other side!' '9 add 4 equals 13'. She puts 3 under the line. 'No-o-o!' 'There's no catching you lot is there?'

Teachers must know many things. She must have an idea of standards and each pupil's capabilities and personalities, how to develop them, when to intervene, when not to intervene, when to be cross, when to be nice, to punish, or reward etc. This is illustrated, as so often, by comparison with some of my own efforts. I had ticked Sheela's work as having reached what I thought was a reasonable standard. But at a later stage Mrs Brown, who, of course, knew the pupil's capabilities much better censured her:

Sheela, you're making silly, silly mistakes, you're not concentrating. Your maths yesterday was not good, not careful enough work. You know why, don't you? You're always talking that's why.

Orchestration

Hey! Not rude! I don't mind fun, but not rude!

Omniscience in itself is not enough, for the teacher must know how to put it all together in practice in a harmonious whole. This applies not only to her knowledge of subjects, of pupils, of the classroom and so on, but of her potentially discordant roles. Orchestration is an appropriate term for this for she must not only plan and organize her work accordingly (with the score), but rehearse and conduct a not always attentive and cooperative orchestra.

Much is a question of striking a balance — in the week, a day, or lesson. Teachers ring the changes to get the best out of their pupils. On a typical occasion a spelling test was scheduled to follow a viewing of 'Music Time' and to be followed by playtime and a story. 'Music Time' involved teacher and pupils enjoying a game of 'question marks'. It worked on the same principle as 'Simon says'. If the person at the front asked a question, they all drew a big question mark in the air with their fingers accompanied by a 'Neaoiow — Ping!'. If the person simply made a statement, they remained silent. This, then, was an instructive game in which we all participated.

This was followed by a spelling test which required some control. This was a rare event, following on this occasion a number of carefully planned lessons on short vowel sounds. The admonitions, motivators, teaching encouragement and control were subtly interwoven into the main text on the basis of agreed rules:

No talking now. Clean pages please. Right — yes, I'll have the date . . .

John, come on.

This is the first word. PUT, when you *put* something somewhere. Look up and look at me when you're finished. Have you finished Samson? Then look at me so I know . . . GOT. GOT. It's easy if you listen hard you can hear all the letters. GOT. HEMANG!

If anybody cheats I shall be *so* cross. It's not that important. You don't get into trouble if you get them wrong. So there's no point in cheating, you're only cheating yourselves because you've not been bothered to learn them.

JOB. Go do a JOB today. It's only got three letters and you can hear all of them. JOB. JJJOBB. Make sure that nobody's written JO*D*. All written JO*B* have you?

Right! Next one — there's something special to remember about this one. I shan't tell you next time when there's something special to remember. TOM. The name TOM.

Finished Pradeep? Look this way if you have. Right. DOG. Woof, woof. DOG. (some whispering) Shh!

Right! An even easier word this time — ON. Robert! If I hear your voice again (angrily) woe betide!

Another easy one — TOP, either a spinning top, or the top of something, etc. etc. . . .

Without a sound, swop with the person next to you. Don't use crayon. No talking. Put away your pencils. Tell me first of all which is the odd one out, and why (Sheela says it is 'Put' because it had a 'U' instead of an 'O'). Good girl! You can have a house point for that.

I will write them for you and you can mark them. Can you not talk! (angrily) . . .

(She invites a pupil to spell each one, and write them on the blackboard.)

> . . . JOB. Not G–O–B! But *J O B*. Usually with a J it's a softer sound.
>
> TOM. If you haven't got a capital T, it's wrong. I've given you five weeks to learn that.
>
> (Angrily) I'm not going to do any more and I'm going to start taking time off your dinner hour. Nobody, but nobody should be talking except Richard. If anybody else talks I'll put a line through your work and write 'cheated'! Now listen! (There is silence as the next few words are spelt out.)

In this formal activity which contrasts strongly with some of their independent work, these 7-year-olds are learning as well as spellings the difficult lesson of self-control. There are rewards and punishments, lighter and harsher tones, softer and louder pitch, gradations and inflexions of the voice as the circumstance warrants. Reasons are given. And in spite of the changes it is all part of an integrated and continuous presentation.

John had his spelling test crossed out and awarded nought for disobeying and being consistently naughty. Those who got them all right received a star. Afterwards a general reward in a sense ('put your head on your arms and rest if you want to, and listen') was to have read to them the story of *The Little Match Girl*, a sad story with a Christmas message of love and charity. This reflected the general school 'caring' ethos, and made a neat foil to the earlier disciplined activity.

Another, even more relaxed, foil was to follow, for at the end of the day came the distribution of Christmas cards sent through the school post. John received a card with no name on it, and the teacher made a point of going over to him and sharing his pleasure and thus neutralizing her earlier anger and restoring their friendship (another aspect of orchestration). 'It's either a secret admirer or a very forgetful person.' The teacher herself received a card, ('To Mrs Brown, you are very good, kiss, kiss and no name'). 'They're too ashamed to tell you — it might be a boy' opined John. This was a familiar event — expulsion, followed by enfolding. On another occasion a boy who had been very naughty was roundly scolded and told to stand near the door facing the wall (symbolically outside the culture of the room). When he was told to go back, the teacher joined him to explain what to do, her physical proximity, help and kindly voice reaffirming the basic relationship.

Later in the year, with the rules of interaction more firmly established, the emphasis was more consistently on rewards:

> The class are writing up the story of Peter and the Wolf. Winston is congratulated. 'That's the best work you've done since you've been here. You've remembered all your full stops and capitals — they go hand in glove I always say'.

'Daniel, whereabouts are you in the story, love, because you're going to find this ever so hard to copy up.' He says 'where the duck comes out of the wolf'. 'Oh, that's all right then, love.' 'Ann, are you writing in neat, yet?' 'Yes Mrs Brown.' 'Come on, then.'

Gentle cajolery usually had its effect, but not all the time. After persuasion had failed, bright but lazy Tony's unsatisfactory work was torn up and he had to begin again. 'I'm not having it! Go and do as you are told!' Ann also had been tardy though being given plenty of opportunity to finish, preferring talking to writing: 'I think you'll have to finish your work in playtime this afternoon, outside the headmaster's office — or inside. This work should have taken you half an hour'.

With some individuals and on some occasions it is possible to combine a nudge and a joke:

'Hemang, I'm going to wind you up, Eeerk, eerk, eeerk.' (winds him up)

'You children in the corner are making more noise than the monkeys in the zoo!' (a combined admonition and joke which had both effects)

'Those that are in the line stand like soldiers, not like old flowers that are drooping.' (laughter)

There are many ways of bridging divides. In the following a teaching technique is carried over into the informal area and this demonstrates their command of the role. The pupils' amusement at it derives from the incongruence:

A music lesson from Miss Steele practising rhythm. They clap hands and slap knees after her. Mrs Brown and the student join in. Miss Steele asks them to sing their favourite colour in 'so-me'. 'Pi-ink' 'Re-ed'. When the lesson is finished Mrs Brown sings in 'so-me', like a vicar, 'When you are ready will you stand u-up'. 'Richard's ta-ble' (i.e. being given permission to leave). Mrs Durrant comes in and chants 'Can I have a word with you, Mrs Brow-own?' And they have a 'so-me' conversation.

In a sense, this helps to put the music lesson in its place — within the realm of ordinary experience — as well as consolidating the pitch of the notes.

A difficult part of the school day to orchestrate is the gaps around the edges of planned activity. At Albert Road, there was inevitably some time-filling of a purely occupational nature (given the inequality between pressures and resources). Time needed to be filled in case holes appeared into which disorder might flow. Here again the perceptive teacher had a keen eye for the distinction between 'constructive disorder' (which worked in part on the principle that pupils needed some space during the day to interrelate, to explore freely some aspect of their work, to release their minds in the interests of creativity and their own control over their learning) and destructive anarchy. Otherwise, time-fillers were devised that fitted in generally with a learner-centred approach. While a teacher might build up a repertoire of time-fillers, there is a need for freshness and relevance which taxes inventiveness:

> 'While we're waiting (for assembly), how many saw some fireworks last night?'

Tony did not go into assemblies, and when the school celebrated Diwali, faced a very long wait on his own. So he was asked to write an account of a competition he had been in.

At the end of one day when there was a gap, teacher and class struck up (with actions):

> One finger one thumb one nod of the head
> One stamp of the foot
> One flap of the wings
> One tap of the nose
> Stand up sit down (shouted)
> . . . Keep moving, we'll all be merry and bright.

On another occasion (with actions, and missing out a line with each repeat though preserving the actions):

> In a cottage in the wood
> A little old man at the window stood
> Saw a rabbit running by
> Knocking at the door
> Shouting Help me! Help Me! Help Me! he said
> Before the huntsman shoots me dead
> Come little rabbit come to me
> And forever we shall be.

After missing out a line each time, the last reprise was the whole song 'as loud as you like this time', which finished just on 'going home time'. Sir Thomas Beecham could not have arranged or timed it more perfectly.

The achievement in orchestrating is highlighted by considering some failures. The first is a probationary teacher quoted by Pollard (1985):

> If you're easy going, you're easy going, you can't suddenly become very forthright can you . . .? I had a very easy home background, very easy relationships at home . . . no particular struggles through life . . . I've never been a leader, even all through school with friends

. . . I'd rather follow anybody than lead anybody, and to stand up in front of the children and suddenly become this horrible person who had to be nasty to get control . . . it wasn't me in the first place which is why I found it difficult to do. (p. 33)

This might have been Mandy, a student teacher in another school of the research, of whom her supervising teacher said 'She was so wet, she couldn't control five kids, let alone a class. You have to get cross with them sometimes!' I sympathize with Mandy having myself struggled at times with groups of five pupils, and knowing exactly why she found it so difficult to shout at them — you don't usually shout at your friends. Another student teacher reported by Hollies (1988, p. 31) liked working in junior school, but felt teaching was not for her because she was not able to be strict enough: 'I liked the teaching, but I don't think I was the sort of person that could be strict enough. I am strict, but I love them too much. I think you've got to be this high-powered woman who stays up here and never comes down. That's what I've seen of infant teachers anyway.' While this student identifies correctly the components of the problem, she fails to see that the solution lies in bringing them together. One can be over-teacherly as well as over-friendly, and thus miss crucial links with the pupils that actually promote learning or some other positive function. One class of children complained of an occasional teacher who 'shouted at them, wouldn't let them out for wees, was horrible, wouldn't help them'. A supply teacher who came in occasionally was also cast in a more traditional mould. She looked for explicit rules, formal timetables, taught transmissionally, used strange language ('Don't be so forthcoming!'), asked strange questions ('Why must small girls and boys always talk?'), separated boys from girls, used a strange tone of voice (authoritarian — though their usual teachers might be stern with them on occasions, it was contextualized within a more democratic pattern, not, as here, providing the context). The children treated her with respect, but were kept at a distance, and worked half-heartedly, only by rote on those occasions. Some of them told one of the staff 'It's murder when she comes'. In some ways this may seem a little uncharitable, given the problems of very occasional supply teaching. But in this case an element of fixation in the teacher role as dictated by her basic conception of teaching did appear to obstruct progress with these children. Connell (1985) similarly describes a teacher who, in response to early disciplinary problems 'came down hard on the kids' with the support of the school hierarchy, and established silence and order. 'But she soon came to see this as the wrong solution. She had control, all right; but the kids were not learning anything'.

These examples concentrate on one side of the role or the other. Equally unsatisfactory, some might argue, is the teacher who alternates between one and the other, now a firm disciplinarian, now a bosom friend. Much will depend upon how it is done, but a stilted presentation with sharp divides typical of inexperienced teachers might bring accusations of two-facedness or of multiple personalities. For the pupils will associate self with role, and will never know for sure which one is coming on stage. Such a teacher is not to be trusted, not one to converse with intimately, not one to count amongst one's friends.

These roles, therefore, can be combined in ways that are mutually damaging. One of the secrets of successful teaching in the primary school, it seems, is combining them in ways that are mutually enhancing. This takes considerable skill that seems to derive from experience in ways that are difficult, in the press of day-to-day events, to characterize and to record. Hence the belief in intuition, and the explanation for a certain action that 'It just felt right to do it that way' (Jackson, 1977). Hence, too, the view of teaching as an art, the need to be innovative to cope with the unforeseen, to be creative in process, to orchestrate activities into an aesthetic experience (Eisner, 1979).

Some twenty years ago, Morrison and McIntyre (1969) were writing on the skills of orchestration on a more limited front. Here, all is in perfect time:

> Management and instruction are so closely interwoven that it is hard to tease out the components either chronologically or conceptually. In skilful teaching, the distinction can be difficult to make because shared understandings by teacher and pupils, often built up over a long period, make overt management actions largely unnecessary or such that they become absorbed in the smoothness of the total activity. This is not so, however, in classrooms where the teacher is inexperienced or where there are 'disciplinary' difficulties.

Morrison and McIntyre are describing here a transmissional mode of teaching of which the major components were control and instruction. The first sets up the conditions for the second. The skilful teacher combined them so the seam did not show (see also Hargreaves, 1981; King, 1978; Nias, 1988b). The skilful teacher of today does this and more, for she incorporates a strong affective element within the blend to a greater degree than formerly. She/he is a teacher (involving instruction and control), parent and friend all in one, blended imperceptibly together. It is the same kind of balance noted by Hartley (1985) in a teacher described by a colleague as 'brilliant', though 'it's difficult to explain. Mrs Carter doesn't shout a lot, doesn't punish a lot, but she gets the most amazing work out of these kids. She's fantastic. She treated children exactly the way they ought to be treated — not harshly, not soft; just right' (p. 113). It is the same kind of subtle intermixture observed by Nias (1987) in the interactions between a head and a deputy in which 'task and personal concerns, instrumentality and affectivity, rationality and feeling were inextricably blended . . .' (p. 26). How teachers handle these conjunctions is arguably the essence of the primary school teachers' art or craft, the secret of their professionalism, the basis of their 'educational connoisseurship' (Eisner, 1979). It is the attainment of a kind of 'ecstasy' which brings 'intellectual, volitional, and emotional functions into play together' and yields 'the intensity of consciousness that occurs in the creative act' (May, 1976).

Conclusion

The analysis presented here suggests that part of the skill of the primary school teacher derives not from proficiency at any one particular style, but from their successful combination. Primary school teachers are possibly more distinctive for what they have in common than for their differences. This in turn suggests that further consideration of more teachers on the lines of how they manage role conflict and resolve dilemmas (Berlak and Berlak, 1981) might be a fruitful line of enquiry.

I have argued that the primary school teacher role is intrinsically conflictual. The need for strong affective relationships between pupil and teacher (whether progressive, traditional or whatever) is demanded by the teachers' parental role, by their own interests among which enjoyment figures large (and much of which is derived from their relationships with pupils), by pupil needs. And so teacher-pupil friendships are formed. This is the other side of the coin to that identified by Davies (1982) wherein she argued for the separateness of children's culture and the particular meaning of friendships among children themselves. That argument, I believe, still holds. It does not preclude the possibility of the relationships I have discussed here.

However, it is difficult for teachers to escape altogether some old-fashioned instruction and control, whatever their ideals and beliefs. There are pressures operating on them from central and local government, from school and parents, from pupils, from themselves, to meet objectives and achieve results. With adequate resources, these might be achieved through purer pupil-directedness. Where they are inadequate, the 'purity' will go down on a proportionate scale. At one extreme, we may find the 'survival' syndrome where teacher strategies are focused on survival rather than pedagogy (see Chapter 4). More often, and especially in primary schools for reasons stated earlier, one might expect to find a productive blend.

The skills that go into its manufacture are fashioned, I would argue, from three main resource areas:

(i) personal abilities, beliefs, attitudes, commitment — Teachers will not strike a happy combination if, for example, they do not like children, or if they are too 'wet' to shout at them occasionally, or if they do not like teaching; conversely, those that have a certain flair or charisma have a head start.

(ii) training and education — This undoubtedly adds something to a teacher's 'omniscience' — subject-knowledge and the craft of pedagogy.

(iii) teaching experience — The day-by-day experimentation over the years, that reveals what works and what does not, the progressive compilation and refinement of techniques and strategies, smoothing off unnecessarily abrasive edges, tightening up on indulgent or slack approaches and activities, knowing one's abilities as diplomat, negotiator, socializer, increasing knowledge of pupils and themselves and their interrelationships in the classroom . . . and so on.

Success in all these areas as manifested in a 'good teacher teaching well' almost defies analysis and comes back to a conception of teaching as an art. It involves combining roles, solving dilemmas, and inventing patterns of events and relationships, that, seen in their entirety, have a certain beauty. Herein lie the greater rewards of teaching — for both teachers and pupils.

Chapter 3

Cultivating the Middle Ground: Teachers and School Ethos⋆

Rutter *et al.* (1979) suggested that the most important factor in both academic and behavioural achievement among pupils is school 'ethos', which they saw as the distinctive culture or pattern that any fairly self-contained organization develops. Though they did not pursue the idea very far, we suspect from our experience and from other studies (for example, Power, 1972; Reynolds, 1976; Mortimore *et al.*, 1988) that the Rutter team have touched on something of great importance in the way schools are run and in their effects. But if we are to make it a viable area for study, we must add some substance to the rather vague notion of 'ethos' as it stands, and for this, we would argue, we need qualitative techniques. For 'ethos' involves elements not susceptible to statistical analysis. But that was the cast of the Rutter research, and they did not study items they could not measure. The same point can be made of the host of psychological studies that have been made of classroom 'climate' or 'atmosphere'. Valuable as some of these are in characterizing elements of the phenomenon, they are unable to convey any sense of the dynamic process which, to us, constitutes the essence of any ethos (For useful reviews of work in the area see Anderson, 1982 and Fraser, 1989).

Whatever it is, 'ethos' is not a thing, nor a settled state of affairs with constant parameters to which all subscribe in equal measure. Our view of it rather suggests a moving set of relationships within which different groups and individuals are constantly in negotiation. It is expressed largely in symbolic form, notably in language, appearance and behaviour. Over time, these symbols may become cryptically abbreviated, intelligible only to insiders. Accordingly the most appropriate method, we feel, for the study of these processes is ethnography, for it is the task of the ethnographer to 'describe a culture', focusing on process, symbolic meanings and construction of realities. Because an extended period (in our case, a year and a half in

⋆This chapter was written with Lynda Measor

one school) is spent in concentrated study of a single institution, the ethnographer observes and experiences the full gamut of day-to-day life within the school. Over time, the ethnographer may come to recognize some general patterns from the many and various interactions witnessed and taken part in. In other words, any ethos is identified from within, in its natural setting and in terms meaningful to the inmates.

In a recent study of a 12–18 mixed (comprehensive) upper school (which we shall call 'Old Town') we discovered a distinctive ethos. Teachers spoke of the 'Old Town way'. They had a clear sense of the values that distinguished the 'Old Town way', and contrasted their good reputation in the town, and favourable academic and behavioural results, with the two other upper schools in the area. We cannot, however, at this stage evaluate the ethos in terms of results — that would involve a comparative study which afforded other schools equal examination. Nor can we, in one chapter, illustrate its full pervasiveness. What we aim to do is to demonstrate the viability of a particular method for discovering the character of a particular ethos, and how it is engendered and sustained in the day-to-day life of the school. A number of further such studies of other schools would enable us to analyze general features of the phenomenon.

Our observations led us to a conceptualization of the ethos of this particular school as one of the 'middle ground'. Basically, teachers sought to make links with pupil cultures, by appropriating elements of them that promised to further their aims. They thus constructed an identifiable 'middle ground' between teacher and pupil cultures upon which the official business of the school was conducted. Conceptualizing this as 'middle ground' has the advantage of recognizing the existence of powerful and prior cultures and sub-cultures within the school based on, for example, ethnic, social class and gender differences; and of 'front' and 'back stage' regions, where contrasting value systems are frequently displayed (Goffman, 1971); and indeed of individuals, who differ in personalities, abilities and resources.

This complexity of differences within the school has led some to deny even the possibility of a school ethos (Acton, 1980). However, teachers and pupils, whatever their origins and allegiances, share the problem of how to live together within the school. On occasions there may be 'culture clash' as value systems collide and promote conflict (Willis, 1979). On others, more open negotiation (Woods, 1978) produces, at the very least, a compromise; at the best, possibly, understandings that transcend the conflicts and contradictions between opposing cultures that would otherwise prevail. There can, of course, be no absolute blending of cultures. This is why we term this a 'middle ground', for it represents the meeting point of two or more basically different and opposing cultures. The common ground between them, however, on which their interrelationships will be based, is not readily apparent. It has to be continually worked at and strived for. And if there is any transgression of the rules, sanctions may ensue, such as punishment from a teacher, uncooperative behaviour from pupils. It can have, therefore, a brittle, unstable quality.

Again, a set of values and modes of implementation may be agreed at a level of policy, often with as many implicit as explicit features, but then has to be mediated and remediated through many different situations involving, for example, individual teacher and groups of pupils, curriculum area, setting and time. These factors may scramble the intended ethos and promote the divisions. In our school, however, this did not appear to be the case. Its chief characteristic was an attempt sometimes to penetrate, sometimes to indulge, the value systems of the pupils and to incorporate them into their own teacher styles and in curriculum material. This strategy was promoted and practised within a strong disciplinary framework, which appeared to reflect the pupils' home backgrounds. Also, there were no concessions to power-sharing. Though many of the tactics and strategies employed by the teachers disguised divisions and power imbalances, the divisions remained, and power was used when the middle ground collapsed.

The ethos promoted by the staff of the school, therefore, has to be seen within this framework, and with these provisos. In the rest of the article we shall delineate its main features. Teachers appeared to work along four main lines: (i) adopting and tolerating modified appearances; (ii) utilizing a common language; (iii) employing humour; and (iv) role-distancing. We shall examine each in turn, and try to illustrate how they worked in practice. There is, of course, much overlap between these themes in practice, but we feel that each is of sufficient prominence to merit separate attention.

Appearance

Appearances are generally recognized as a matter of great symbolic importance (Stone, 1962). The fact that school uniform was mandatory, and certain basic requirements had to be met, illustrated the school's basic traditional mould. Girls wearing black skirts instead of the regulation blue were sent home to change. However, there were many areas of flexibility, as a result of teacher–pupil negotiations in the past. There was no demand for hats or caps, nor regulations about outside coats or jackets — though their removal in school was rigidly enforced. Latitude was also allowed over shoes, many of the boys wearing fashionable 'drapes' and 'winklepickers', and girls wearing high-heeled shoes. Thus the expression of pupil culture was allowed within the general framework of school uniform. Ties were knotted in various ways (though roll-neck pullovers were permissible for those who objected to ties), jewellery was worn, and the favourite bag for carrying school books and equipment was plastic, bearing the name of a favourite football team.

A set of flamboyant male hair styles was allowed to proliferate. Some had their hair cut as short of baldness as possible (the shorter the hair — unlike as with Samson — the greater the strength and toughness symbolized), some had hair shaved in stripes, others in squares, dyed alternately orange and green. Institutional opposition to this was limited to teasing insults — 'Yes, I trust you, you're lovely, at least you were before you had your hair cut'. The remonstration is put in jocular form.

As pupils were allowed to modify their appearances to an amalgam of formal and informal, so some teachers modified theirs according to what might appear to be values teachers and pupils held in common. One needle-work teacher, for example, sported a fashionable and varied wardrobe, with many frills and flounces. The girls always found her appearance a major interest, though they disapproved of the amount of eye shadow she wore. A male teacher, whose youth had been in the 1960s, also dressed casually, in, for example, big striped sweaters, casual black jeans and suede desert boots. He had long hair and a full beard. Another also dressed informally, never wore a tie, and cultivated almost a nonconformist attitude. A typical posture, for example, was standing at the front of the class with one foot on the floor and the other on the desk. These attitudes were not strategic ones, designed intentionally to appeal to pupils. But appeal to pupils they did, by simply staying true to their own sense of individuality against the pressures to conform to a more formal image.

Language

We have noted the supreme symbolic importance of language. Stubbs (1976) speaks of a 'metalanguage' teachers typically employ to secure their control, and Barnes *et al.* (1969) demonstrated the difficulties for pupils in much ordinary teacher language. But language can also speak to a 'middle ground' between teachers and pupils (Woods, 1979). There were many illustrations of this in the school. Most teachers were themselves conscious of its importance. One experienced teacher, a member of the counselling staff, warned a probationer, 'Even the way you talk, OK, it seems natural to you, but they can feel you're trying to put one over on them, they can feel got at, just by the sort of words you use and the accent you have. You have to be aware of that.'

In general the teachers used a classroom language shared between themselves, the local community and the ad-mass world, and not one derived from their own academic professional culture. This indicated a communal bond which could be appealed to on the formal occasions of keeping control and trying to teach. Thus one male teacher reproved a girl jauntily with 'Ey, we'll 'ave less of your cheek, D.C.' The sting of the discipline message was thus modified by the use of the girl's familial nickname. Another teacher frequently referred to older girls as 'Sweetheart' when asking them to do things for him. He addressed one sixth-former as 'Ey, Erotica,' and then asked, 'What you on about?' He rarely pronounced his 'h's.

Apart from appeal to the personal bond symbolized by use of pet names, teachers had recourse to other elements of pupil culture, for example colloquial language. One addressed his classes semi-jokingly as 'Rubbish', 'Garbage', or 'a Shower' when disciplining them. When the noise level rose too high, he ordered them to 'button it', again not in aggressive and abusive tones, but with a tinge of face-saving humour. Similarly, another teacher, when separating two deviant boys, instead of issuing a straight injunction, said, 'Mark, I've just had an idea. There's a lovely table over there that's all lonely on its own, and I want you to go and sit at it and keep it company.' When Mark hesitated, he was urged, 'Come on, shift your carcase!' On another, similar occasion he said, 'Come on, remove your loathesome, horrible form to that table at the front'. The pupil remarked as he prepared to go, 'It's a long way to walk'. Thus the teacher achieved his objective, but not at the expense of pupil dignity. By subtle use of humour the formal is made to meld with the informal. Again, when a boy attempted to avoid work because his 'brain hurt', this teacher offered to 'treat him for it at four o'clock', adding, after a pause, 'if you insist on not working' in traditional teacher language. Sometimes teachers used the pupils' own vernacular, actually entering informal territory to effect: 'I'm not having you dossing about and doing nothing.'

As in matters of control, so in teaching. Subtle use of language was made to achieve teacher aims and to bridge the gap between 'highbrow and popular culture' (Williams, 1968). Teachers traditionally identify with the former, but at this school they stood at the interface, trying to convey the essence of one in terms of the other. In a poetry lesson, for example, when a pupil, after repeated teacher attempts, failed to grasp the point of short lines breaking up sentences for effect, the teacher finally said to the amusement of the class, 'That's how the chap wrote the damned thing!' The remark may sound dismissive, but the colloquial use of language and the accompanying facial gesture of helplessness and puzzlement helped the class address themselves to the point, and go on with their attempts to write poems of a similar type. The same teacher asked his class to 'OK, stick up your pinkies if I've said you deserved a house point'. When inspecting some old and decrepit textbooks, he referred to his own copy as 'cranky', and he sought the help of the class in mending them in these terms: 'Because you're such a nice set of people I'll ask you to do something about this tatty collection of objects'. Such language helped promote a relaxed atmosphere in his lessons, in which English literature could be approached in a simple way and not as part of an unattainable other world.

Sometimes colloquialisms were mixed with a subject of pupil interest in vivid metaphor, as when one teacher announced, 'Today I want to put my foot down on the accelerator and go like the proverbial clappers. I want you to get it written up and given in.' The English teacher cleverly used metaphor against himself in one poetry lesson. When they were discussing why the image of 'petals on a black bow' was a good description of people in a subway, one idea was that petals suggested the softness of skin on their faces. Though accurate, the interaction was becoming stilted and formal, but the teacher broke the mood by observing that his own face was more like a 'dried leaf than a petal'. This led to a range of comparisons in a relaxed, informal atmosphere.

Humour

It should already be clear that humour is an essential ingredient of this particular ethos. Its coping properties and abilities to bridge differences are well known (Woods, 1983b). It was an important element in both teacher and pupil cultures, and both were drawn on in the humour of the middle ground.

Part of teachers' humour came from spontaneous manipulation of material which arose in the day-to-day activity of the class. The German teacher, for example, used German sound combinations that were unfamiliar and amusing to the English children. He was demonstrating that in German the letter 'w' is sounded as 'v', and made up a silly sentence, 'Germans can't say "w", they say "v". Villy was a vicked rotten vaster.' An art teacher was encouraging a class to paint with care and precision, and to look after their brushes. 'There are lots of ways of using a brush, and, depending on what sort of person you are, by the end of the lesson it will still look like a brush, rather than a wet budgie or something.' Some teachers were good at puns. In one lesson, the word 'ruff' appeared in a story about children in Elizabethan times. He said, 'You know what that is'. The pupils made appropriate gestures around their necks. 'You know, it's what a dog says when you ask him how he is — "ruff, ruff".'

The bridging qualities of humour are perfectly illustrated when teachers and pupils join in making it. Sharing jokes was one form of this, often involving a form of 'ribbing', a common activity within the teenage peer group. In a way, teachers almost became honorary members of the pupils' own informal culture on these occasions. One example was when a girl instructed a teacher to repeat after her a number of 'iced' items, which ended with 'iced ink' ('I stink'). The teacher repeated it all faithfully, amid great laughter from the class, and entered into the spirit of it by extending it. 'Anyway,' he said, 'I don't, I've got the protection of Brut 33, me and Henry Cooper.' For some, however, this confirmed the teacher's noxiousness, for that was 'terrible stuff, it smells awful!' This kind of banter was common. In one poetry composition class the pupils were asked to think of couplets beginning 'Did you ever see . . .', with the second line a metaphoric comparison. This brought a number of humorous efforts. One began, 'Did you ever see the dentist?', to which the teacher quickly responded, 'Oh, that's a good one, you can really get your teeth into that!' In another humorous exchange a girl explained to a teacher why two pupils were so late — they had taken home a cat which had followed them to school. The teacher said, 'Oh, they must have been kidnapped', and the girl said, 'Yes, by the cat!' The class laughed, and the teacher continued, 'Can't you see the ransom note? The cat will demand seven thousand tins of Whiskas in flavours of its own choosing!' Such incidents, which drew freely on the ad-mass world, helped to create a bond between teacher and pupil.

Sometimes the humour in incidents or jokes had become ritualized (Walker and Adelman, 1976). For example, one teacher and his classes played on his known fondness for Polo mints. When he announced, 'I'm afraid I'm going to have to give you homework over the weekend,' they reacted, 'Oh, please, no! We'll save up and buy you sixty packets of Polos . . .' In another lesson a girl of considerable artistic ability was helping other pupils illustrate their poems, and this teacher suggested she charge a Polo per drawing, and give them to him. The Polos were an ongoing joke shared between the teacher and his pupils — a resource they could appeal to to soften division and dispute and to cement their relationship. One girl reported, typically, 'These lessons are fun. I can hardly keep a straight face in them'. As a matter of fact, eating in class was not allowed — yet the teacher ate Polos all lesson and colluded with pupils in doing so. It illustrates a curious feature of the ethos — communality was sometimes earned at the expense of a general rule. Rules were there not to be obeyed but to be negotiated against together. On occasions, infraction of a rule could be the best way of achieving a purpose enshrined in the ethos. This particular teacher had excellent relationships with all his pupils, because, we feel, he had incorporated deviance and 'having a laugh', which pupils usually initiate for themselves, within the formal structure of the lesson.

At other times, teachers acted almost as comedians, holding pupils' attention and moral support through their ability to entertain. One woman teacher remarked, 'I think you need to be a bit of an idiot or a goon in this job'. A male teacher opined, 'I've always seen teaching as flirting on the fringes of show business anyway. We are all clowns, really.' This manifested itself in several ways, but notably in pantomime and silly voices. One teacher, for example, grasped his head in mock horror at pupil answers to his questions. He grabbed pupils by the throat in a teasing way and exaggeratedly 'strangled' them for getting answers wrong. When a pupil pointed out that this teacher had made a spelling mistake on the blackboard, he fell against it in dismay and begged the forgiveness of the class, pleading exhaustion, it being very near half-term. The German teacher embroidered his play-acting with a thick German accent. 'Aaarghh! Strangle him!' (in a pronounced guttural tone) was his response to a wrong answer. To yet another one, he clutched his head in theatrical manner and exclaimed, 'Dummkopf!' Some of his teaching techniques were reminiscent of children's theatre, as when he held a competition between boys and girls as to which could recite the days of the week in German the faster and the louder. Again, a wrong answer brought 'Mein Gott!' and an ostentatious collapse into a chair. Teachers mimicked the funny voices of certain television comedians. And the German teacher rarely missed an opportunity to illustrate new words and idioms by noises and actions, as when he barked, panted and wagged his tail like a dog. Pupils could hardly fail to give such teachers their attention — they were the best act in class!

Humour allowed teachers to defuse some potentially explosive incidents and fraught feelings. Many of the latter attend the difficult matter of adolescent sexuality, but teachers coped with this frequently taboo subject also. Thus a teacher struck an imitation stripper's pose as he took off his jacket. When they read about a boy whose voice was breaking in the novel they were studying, he took the opportunity to normalize the development: 'You know — that horrible time when your voice does this' (appropriate imitation) 'and you don't know whether you're a boy or a girl' (laughter), '— no, I mean a boy or a man, Oh! What do I mean?' We all go through such experiences, even teachers. When a girl remarked to an art teacher that at their previous school they painted on newspaper and all the boys would get 'page 3' and study it, he shook his head in mock anguish and said, 'Yes, well, I suppose I used to do that, even a fine upstanding man like me.'

Humour aided discipline. It allowed control to be exercised in a way that emphasized the bonds between them at the same time as informing pupils they were behaving inappropriately. Thus a boy leaning a long way back on his chair was told, 'A chair has four legs, you know. Those are the things that are on the floor, that's the thing that stops you falling through into the room below. Use all four legs, will you?' On another occasion some pupils were hanging out of the window, which brought the teacher's comment, 'Glass is a wonderful invention, it gets rid of the necessity to hang out of windows, endangering life and limb. Come inside! Another teacher, having a 'tidiness' purge, made remarks like 'I think it would be better if I got two of you to look after that drawer with your work in it. At the moment it looks like the feed tray at the farmyard'. Such a discipline technique allows the pupil — and others in the class — to laugh. There is something on offer other than censure, abuse or negative feelings. Even if an individual pupil chooses to be hurt, the bond between the teacher and the rest of the class has been endorsed once more.

Humour can afford the pupil status at the same time as exercising control. A difficult boy in a woman teacher's class was dubbed 'Menace' and continually referred to as that. Five minutes before the end of the lesson she said, 'Menace, come over here and talk to me,' and then spoke to him quietly about the need for good behaviour. Publicly, she had afforded him a status which allowed him to retain dignity while setting him up for the major message conveyed privately. The following week there was a 'Menace No. 2'. The teacher called the attention of the class to the problem with 'We will have to see whether they are going to be good kids or wombles next week'. Here again elements from the pupil's world are incorporated into the discipline message.

In a similar way, a male teacher appropriated a group of boys' discussion of Kamikaze pilots, with its noisy side effects. 'Do you know about Kamikaze pilots?' There was a confused buzz of response. 'Yes, yer, he commits suicide.' 'Yes, well, that's what you're heading for — big trouble — if you keep that kind of behaviour up!' His first question had produced amusement, the second an amused acknowledgement of defeat, which left them quiet, but not resentful. In another lesson a boy preoccupied with the Derby being run that day and doing little work drew the comment from his teacher, 'I hope your Derby horse runs faster than your work, sunshine,' which raised a smile all round and caused him, for a while at least, to go on working.

On occasions, teachers employed stronger sanctions. The cane and detentions were both used at times in the school, and teachers also expressed anger. But they were unusual occurrences, for emergencies when the normal order broke down. Humour was used to help preserve the normal order, and after an incident of 'trouble' it rapidly reappeared. Thus after a teacher had berated a class one week for unsatisfactory homework, and subsequently received much better work, his return to the use of humour was a signal that relations could again relax. For example, he explained the next homework very clearly, 'so those of you who very nearly got murdered last week have no excuse this time'. The class relaxed, and began to share the joke. 'You wouldn't really murder us, sir?' 'My excuse would be,' replied the teacher, 'are they really human?' His final comment, and the reference to 'murder', were peculiarly apt, for the incident had threatened to savage their carefully established relationship.

Sometimes teachers made mistakes in their use of humour, which usually they were quick to repair. One such incident was when two girls were chatting and failed to respond to the teacher's stare, whereupon he waved at them and said, 'Cooeee!' to attract their attention. They blushed, returned to their work, and the rest of the class laughed. The teacher, however, immediately went up to the two girls to offer them personal assistance with their work, thus countering his error of appearing to laugh *at* pupils instead of *with* them. Had he not done so, the girls might have been deeply resentful at having been embarrassed.

Teachers' humour strategies did not always work. When the music teacher asked the class to sing *The Streets of London* one boy appeared very unwilling to do it. 'You weren't doing it,' the teacher remarked, 'Your lips weren't moving. You must be a ventriloquist. You could make a lot of money doing that, but not in my lesson.' The reproof was successful in that all laughed, and the boy did join in, though it would appear only for form's sake, for he remained hostile to the subject, saying to his friend afterwards, 'That was boring.' A better result was secured in another lesson, where a boy was not paying attention but idly conducting some music being played. The teacher exclaimed, 'Geoffrey, I don't know what you're doing, but if you think you're waving to that castor oil plant there, it won't wave back!' The class were hugely amused, Geoffrey included, the humour being sufficient on this occasion to tip the balance.

Role-distancing (Goffman, 1961)

Teachers distanced themselves from the traditional teacher role in two distinct ways: firstly by identifying strongly with certain elements in pupil culture, many of which might have been thought to be opposed to teachers' basic values; and secondly by emphasizing their human qualities against the bureaucratic pressures of the teacher role, which some had found distinctly dehumanizing (see Chapters 2 and 7).

Teachers frequently put themselves in the position of the pupil. The music teacher 'managed' talking about a classical musical concert with comments like 'All those men in penguin suits, parading up and down'. When teaching science the headmaster recognized some basic difficulties with nomenclature. 'This German bloke did it, he called himself Fahrenheit, I don't know why it couldn't be Schmidt or something.' Similarly, another teacher, seeking a definition of a 'scimitar', having established that in addition to being a car it was a curved sword, said, 'Yes . . . from the East, you know —

Clacton and Norwich way. No, in Asia, over there.' Once when the headmaster spoke of 'having a bit of a hiatus' in a lesson the previous day, he corrected it, as puzzlement began to spread on pupils' faces, to 'I have brown sauce on mine'. These examples illustrate attempts to incorporate the pupils' social world into the curriculum. The headmaster tried to explain the relevance of science, 'It's real life, it's everyday, but it's science and maths. Don't be put off because it's called science, it's just problems you're solving every day.' He felt obliged to teach about Fahrenheit, for example, because 'In the factories around here they are still using Fahrenheit'.

At times, teachers reversed roles completely as pupils introduced certain terms. One girl used the term 'siren' in a poem to describe a certain woman. The teacher congratulated her, but from the common standpoint, 'You've used a flash word there'. A maths teacher, having said, 'You've got to simplify the fraction,' immediately added, 'There's another of those posh words — "simplify",' and went on to explain. Teachers also put themselves in the position of parents. Thus when one of the counselling staff met some parents new to the area, he adopted a particular style in his conversation with them — 'Don't you, er, 'esitate, you just come up 'ere when you want'. He did not normally drop his 'h's. He had adapted his style to theirs for the purpose of his aim — putting them at their ease.

One aspect of how certain elements of a middle ground can develop out of the confluence where its component cultures meet was nicely articulated by the headmaster one day in a science lesson: 'I have been used to measuring in feet and inches, you have been taught to measure in centimetres. We could make up our own measuring system and call it "groggles" or "sturmers". It doesn't matter, but if we all use the same, then it means a Chinaman can come to England and buy a Marks & Spencer's shirt.' A male teacher appreciated some of the more noxious elements of pupil culture, and used it to effect. When warning the class about using too much thick paste glue he said, 'It will squash out of the sides of the paper and look like you've sneezed all over it.' When pupils committed a minor offence teachers appropriated children's own terms of abuse, such as 'burk' or 'silly idiot'. They showed that they understood pupils' views about homework: 'Now Mr Jones is going to say a rude word – yes, that's it, "homework", and about time.' 'If you cast your mind back a hundred years to last week,' and 'Back in my youth, about 1764', or, in explaining the meaning of 'octogenarian', 'That's someone even older than I am. He's eighty — no, Mark, I'm not telling you how old I am.' This appreciation included pupil sensitivities. For example, when school photographs had been taken, one teacher refused to let her pupils see photographs other than their own, and handed them out face down. Another made teasing capital out of it. 'If anyone messes about this afternoon, I'll show everyone his photograph.'

Teaching and teenage culture were made to appear relevant to each other. When the art teacher asked pupils to bring in a picture to copy, they were allowed to choose from the full range of modern graphic design. Many brought in pictures of rock musicians. The teacher spent part of the lesson discussing their respective merits with the pupils. When one boy brought his drawing of Debbie Harry to him he exclaimed, 'How could you do that to Blondie, the woman I love?' He thus announced his knowledge of and attachment to the youth culture.

Further curricular links were noted in music and poetry. In music, the similarities and connections between classical and pop music were brought out — how Handel was the 'pop' artist of his day, and how many classical tunes lay behind pop music and TV jingles. In poetry, the teacher drew on rock music to help pupils understand the imagery of love poetry, which was all of warmth and heat: 'When people talk about love and stuff like that in poetry — and pop music is a sort of poetry — they talk about it together with warmth, like "Come on, Baby, light my fire". Mm, well, maybe that's a bit old for you. Well, "You are the sunshine of my life," then.' The point thus was established firmly within the context that had most meaning for them.

A keen interest in transport and 'wheels' was also recognized. One teacher ran a vehicle maintenance course for 16-year-olds in the school. One lunchtime he was rather late, and explained he had been trying out a bet with some fifth-formers as to whether his car would do 80 m.p.h. He had packed several of them in, and driven it along a local road to prove his point, describing his skids round roundabouts with delight. Not only was there a shared interest and pleasure here, but also an illegal act, which, however, reprehensible, clearly did something to deflate the traditional righteous image of teachers which mark them as people apart — the pleasure-spoiling standard-bearers of morality.

The pupils at the school were largely working class, and elements of what teachers perceived as working-class culture were freely incorporated into their teaching. Both French and German teachers used bingo games to teach numbers. When one found all present one day, she called, 'Full house!' to which the class shouted a response. Teachers had lengthy discussions with pupils on football, and organized regular fishing competitions.

Further to this, however, several of the male staff actually *became* working class during the holidays, in the sense that they took on heavy manual labouring jobs to supplement their income. One sheared sheep during the summer as a source of tax-free income. Another welcomed half-term. 'It means I can get another job and make some money. I'm broke.' He actually worked for the father of one of his pupils in a cement-works making reinforced concrete moulds. 'You come 'ome knackered, and all colours —

one day it's red, the next it's blue; depends what they're working with.' Both teachers freely expressed to pupils their admiration for the physical strength of the men who did such jobs. The man who ran the concrete firm, for example, "as muscles out 'ere. Charles Atlas has nothing on him. 'E lifts up bloody big blocks of concrete easy, by himself — and it's wet concrete. I've seen 'im load a five-ton truck by 'imself.' Teachers were thus seen to be interested in working 'instrumentally' (Goldthorpe *et al.*, 1971), and to value strength and toughness — matters of considerable concern to working-class pupils.

Television was also shared in common by teachers and pupils, and teachers readily capitalized on it. 'Haloes', for example, were explained by reference to the 'Saint' and not by more formal representations. The relevance of the decimal point was conveyed through reference to the winter sports currently filling the screen and the fine gradings of competitors' times. All the pupils in the class seemed to have seen the programme.

Again, however, it must be noted that there are legitimate and illegitimate entries into the pupils' world. If a teacher goes too far, it can be seen as intrusive and ingratiating. In discussion with some pupils one day, Lynda said she was going to a Stranglers' concert. She was, in fact, going not out of personal enthusiasm for this punk group but to observe a group she knew appealed to the pupils. The pupils seemed to detect this, and were guarded and negative in their response. On another occasion when Lynda told them she was going to see The Who there was no such reaction. The Who, therefore, as an 'older' group, were permissible; the Stranglers' was 'their music' and Lynda was made to feel she had invaded their territory. In fact any slightly laboured attempt to incorporate the pupils' world was very quickly detected and punished by pupil scorn. The middle ground has to convey sincerity. If teachers are seen to be merely play-acting to secure a hidden purpose, pupils will not join.

It has to be said, too, that not all teachers could carry the ethos off. Some on occasions tried too hard, especially with humour that fell flat. Some pupils preferred to keep their distance from some teachers. Thus, though several pupils were known by their peer-group, nicknames, they were for use only by 'approved' teachers. Matthew Plumm, for example, took strong exception to his form mistress, a teacher he did not respect, calling him 'Plummy' when taking the register one day, though earlier he had grinned delightedly when another teacher did it. This suggests that teacher personalities have to be aligned to the ethos, or to be seen by pupils to be so aligned, for them to succeed in it. Sometimes, too, teachers themselves were laughed at by pupils without intending it. One young female teacher's references to the 'Viking's stop-motion screw' in a sewing machine, and her advice to 'Touch up your stencil points' reduced the class to laughter — but laughter *against* the teacher when that had not been her intention. Such sexual innuendoes are excluded from the middle ground, and they sneak in here, through a young teacher's inexperience or lack of knowledge, in opposition to its principles.

On a wider dimension the middle ground by no means prevailed over divisions that lie deep within society. For example, the attempt to import youth culture into cross-gender areas of the curriculum to try to increase their relevance to pupils did not work. Boys were never going to take to needlework, even if it was called 'Fabrics' and they were allowed to make football shorts and posters advertising their favourite clubs (Measor, 1983).

In the second kind of role-distancing, teachers were keen to emphasize human mastery of the role, and the human properties of the school, where teachers and pupils were basically people of equal status. Many teachers, and not only counselling staff, spent time in the pastoral care room, where they relaxed in armchairs and chatted informally to pupils on a range of subjects. They would smoke, drink coffee, read newspapers. One would have the *Sun*, which older pupils borrowed, accusing him of 'excessive page 3 interest'. Sometimes a pupil would sit in the head of house's chair while he perched on his desk. One teacher regularly offered pupils a lift home in his car. Another deliberately reversed aspects of the role. For example, we are accustomed to teachers banning eating in class, but this one ate to amusing excess himself. A second-year class entered his room one day and caught him eating a large piece of sticky chocolate. He was unable to speak to them 'as he oughta' for fully three minutes, except in grunts and mumbles as he tried to free his jaws. The class found the situation very funny, and advised the teacher to stick to Polo mints in future, for it was indeed he.

Teachers were also willing to open up their private world to pupils in some degree. One was wont to discuss his childhood family background, and some pupils pressed him for further details of his relatives. Another made frequent reference to his main leisure interest: beer and pubs. 'As I was on my way to a very important meeting — with the local brewery' was a typical gambit of his. On school trips teachers brought their spouses and children, some in push chairs, much to the delight of pupils, and a holiday atmosphere attended these occasions. Another teacher brought his two-year-old child to the playgroup run by the Domestic Science department one afternoon. He would sit in lessons with his father until the group began, to the amusement of the class. The teacher capitalized on it further, asking in mock stern tones, for example, when the child began to gurgle, 'Who's making all that noise, then?'

On occasions a teacher acted in a way completely opposite to that expected. One day, for example, after a particularly difficult test, a teacher walked round the room giggling delightedly if anyone had got an answer wrong. One clever boy asked whether he had got one wrong, but 'No, no, you got it right! That's awful! How dare you get it right!' These are all examples of 'playing at the role', now circling round it, now directly opposing it, now meeting some of the requirements — but always in command of it, and never its servant.

A range of extra-curricular activities also helped the formal blend into the informal. There were chess clubs, cooking clubs, and a weekly disco. There were also community-based activities like sailing and badminton. There were trips to places of educational interest, a skiing holiday, and a summer camping trip in the South of France. These events were always attended before, during and after with much enthusiasm. One teacher sent all his classes postcards when he was away, with detailed notes on his activities. The activity, however, that perhaps best epitomized this particular school's ethos was a fishing competition, which aroused tremendous excitement among the boys, and which was actually won by one of the first year's ace delinquents. There was something within the general offering for almost everyone.

Conclusion

We have attempted to convey the flavour of one school ethos which we have characterized as 'middle ground'. We have presented an ideal type of this, drawing the prominent features from the full range of staff, though individual teachers relate to it in varying degrees. Its dominant feature is the attempt by teachers to interlock key communicative elements in pupils' background culture into their own concerns. This 'pupil-centredness' is apparent in appearances, language, humour and attitude towards the institution and roles within it. The middle ground is distinguished by openness and flexibility, by equality of treatment, by sincerity, and by friendliness. But it is also notable for its boundedness and for its limitations. The sincerity involves an appreciation of the limits — relating, for example, to appearance, language, music, basic rules, leisure interests, family life — beyond which teachers and pupils would not go. 'Pupil-centredness' is by no means 'pupil dominance' and is, in fact, more apparent than real — it is a means to teacher ends. The 'friendliness' worked as long as pupils responded in the expected way. The sense of 'togetherness' collapsed if unwritten rules were transgressed. Beyond a certain point in entering, or flirting with, pupil cultures, teachers might begin to offend their own values. Then they would not only negate their teaching aims but be suspected of ingratiating postures, and thus offend the basic communal value of sincerity. And, quite clearly, there were private areas on both sides that were jealously guarded.

The middle ground therefore, in this case at least, is not a blending of cultures, nor the creation of a new, situational one transcending all others. It is, rather, an overlapping of 'penumbras', with teachers exhibiting wares and appropriating those expressive elements of the satellite pupil cultures that will increase their chances of capture into the teachers' field of gravity.

From whence is it derived? There would appear to be a strong generational element. The teachers contributing most to middle-ground culture (others were more socially distant and culturally isolationist) were nearly all in their late twenties or early thirties, possibly nearer the values of pupils as a generational cohort (Mannheim, 1952), than those of older teachers. Some of their attitudes and actions were probably reaction against teachers of their youth. One teacher, in fact, often told pupils about the 'snob' school he went to as a child and how he 'hated it'. It was a public school, with strict uniform regulations, Latin and Greek on the curriculum, and boys having to take girls' parts in Shakespeare's plays. Grammar schools, of course, were modelled on these, and that indeed was the origin of most of the school's teachers. They could well have been contributing to a reaction against the closed, divisive academic culture of the old grammar schools, particularly if they themselves were of working-class roots.

However, the middle-ground approach of this school was part of a positive policy, spearheaded by the headmaster, inspired by his example and direction, and largely controlled by the appointments to staff that he made. Several of these had been strongly influenced by counselling courses they had attended, (see, for example, Hamblin, 1978). It is tempting to speculate that the policy has something to do with comprehensivization. Does it not reflect the spirit of comprehensive ideology, with its emphasis on sharing, togetherness and equality? Is not the welfarist overtones with the reserved 'academic' and 'dominant' position what we might expect of an amalgamation of grammar and secondary modern cultures? It could take other forms, but we strongly suspect that the middle-ground ethos we have depicted is in line with the ones described by Rutter *et al.*, that produces highest academic and behavioural achievement. This was certainly true of the school's own immediate area, and it is supported by the work by others. However, we must not jump to conclusions. We have attempted to show what some of the elements of such an ethos look like. We have also tried to indicate how a particular method can illuminate its main features. We have not considered how the pupils react, the exact nature and degree of any cultural bond, pupils' own input from their own cultures and possible appropriations or distortions of the teachers'. Such consideration in similar qualitative terms is now urgently required to facilitate evaluation of the efficacy of the school ethos, and to advance its conceptual refinement.

Chapter 4

Teaching for Survival

Institutions, once established, generate a certain momentum and interdependence. The establishment, development and gradual expansion of compulsory education and the drive since the last war for equality of educational opportunity created an ethos of beneficence about the education system, which has only been seriously disputed within the last two decades. This disputation was the product of developments in society which were to bring into question the structures on which the education system of industrialized societies rested — the changes accompanying advanced technology, the nature of work, upheavals of class and community cultures, the extension of the media, 'affluence', shifting definitions of morality, changes in child-rearing patterns and the growth of the social sciences. However, at the same time that the system was coming under attack, it was still, of course, receiving substantial support from within. Changes in structure, such as comprehensive education, and new developments in educational theory, notably child-centredness, were adaptations to the changing social scene, which carried an air of healthy reformism to those within, though it was rhetoric and reification to those without.

Now, one way to explain the resistance of the system to radical change is to see it as the agent of the capitalist state. It is then dependent on economic forces and structures in society, and only changes in those structures can bring about any real changes in the education system. Another way to explain it is to view it as the product of institutional momentum. We can secure a more interactional viewpoint which would allow the actors more autonomy and furthermore enable us to make distinctions among the actors, by introducing the notion of commitment. I refer to the term as used by Kanter (1974):

> Commitment is a consideration which arises at the intersection of organizational requisites and personal experience. On the one hand, social systems organize to meet systemic 'needs'; and on the other

hand, people orient themselves positively and negatively, emotionally and intellectually, to situations. Since social orders are supported by people, one problem of collectivities is to meet organizational requisites in such a way that participants at the same time become positively involved with the system — loyal, loving, dedicated, and obedient. This requires solutions to organizational or systemic problems that are simultaneously mechanisms for ensuring commitment through their effects on individuals — their experience and orientations. Commitment, then, refers to the willingness of social actors to give their energy and loyalty to social systems, the attachment of personality systems to social relations which are seen as self-expressive.

As Kanter has observed, this analysis links maintenance of the self with maintenance of the system. We might regard institutional momentum as the collective sum of commitment of all the actors within the institution.

One of the major social system problems involving the commitment of actors is its continuance as an action system. This involves cognitive orientations bearing on profits and costs, and generally implies a commitment to a social system role. 'The individual who makes a cognitive-continuance commitment finds that what is profitable to him is bound up with his position in the organization, is contingent on his participating in the system' (*ibid*, p. 132). There is a profit in remaining there and a deficit associated with leaving. Continuance is accompanied by 'sacrifice' and 'investment' processes. As a price of membership, members give up something, make sacrifices, which in turn *increases* commitment. So does investment, which promises future gain in the organization. Members take out shares in the proceeds of the organization and thus have a stake in its future. They channel their expectations along the organization's path, and the more they do so, the more they increase the distance between this and other possibilities. They grow more remote as commitment grows larger. In this way the process is self-validating, self-reinforcing and frequently irreversible. Members go on further to lay down what Becker (1960) calls 'side-bets' as other, unanticipated, sources of reward appear, once the line of action has been chosen.

Another process accompanying commitment is what I will term *accommodation*. This refers to the solving or riding of problems thrown up by the organization so as effectively to neutralize the threat to the actor's continuance in it. One of the most common techniques of accommodation is rationalization, which frequently follows decision-making. What previously might have been perceived as problems are explained away once a course of action has been chosen, and often reappear as benefits.

Continuance commitment among teachers is strong. It's their job —

they are not trained for any other. Investment takes the form of career-bound choices — doing certain jobs, such as the timetable, accepting certain roles, taking courses. Also, the sorts of trials teachers go through in their first one or two years of teaching are a kind of initiation rite, a matter of pride to those who have successfully negotiated them. Sacrifice is considerable — alternative careers and the pleasures and profits associated with them. Once embarked on teaching, few turn back or alter course. Perhaps the large demands in commitment that teaching makes help to explain why so many opt out at training stage (Lister, 1974).

Contributing towards institutional momentum is institutional development, reformist educational theory and much teaching tradition. A great deal of the latter already involves much 'accommodation' to perennial constraints and difficulties thrown up by such matters as the teacher-pupil ratio, the length of the teaching day, week and year, resources such as book provision, buildings, compulsory education and examinations. While we cannot deny that generally conditions in schools have improved over the last hundred years, it is equally true that in some respects, in terms of demand on teachers' accommodation capacity, they have worsened in recent years (see the Introduction).

Concerning reformist educational theory and institutional development, the teacher operates within a climate of dynamic change. The growth of departments, institutes and colleges of education, of the social sciences and their application to education, of in-service training, of general interest in and recognition of the importance of education have contributed to this. While theories about comprehensive education, mixed-ability teaching, the integrated day, Newsom courses, child-centred education, progressivism, vocationalism, multiculturalism, anti-racism and so on also pressurize teachers to adapt further. Support of, and attachment to, these theories is itself, of course, a product of societal developments but all, or nearly all, are framed within the same institutional context and assume its continuance.

With regard to the trend of societal developments mentioned earlier, the social consequences of technological growth are manifested for teachers most prominently in the nature of their clientele. Musgrove (1974) has likened the school system to a 'network of bear pits' (p. 46). Webb (1962) found the teachers of Black School distinguished by fatigue, and hence motivated by the avoidance of circumstances that might add to it, and *fear* — fear that 'playground chaos' would spill over into the classroom. That picure has become much more common today and the problems deeper and more diverse. Every week there is talk in the educational press of growing rates of violence and truancy in the schools. And there is much teacher disillusionment. One rank-and-file member told Musgrove, for example, 'because of the pressures teachers work under, because of the system, they find they have no real control over how they teach and how they carry out the job. And this is a very degrading experience' (Musgrove, 1974, p. 165). Since this comment was made the situation has grown even worse (see Introduction, and Chapters 7 and 8).

I conclude, therefore, that the pressures on teachers' accommodation capacities have increased, are increasing, and are likely to go on increasing. But, of course the pressures differ according to (i) type of school — there are enormous differences among secondary schools as well as between secondary and primary; and (ii) teacher commitment — the less the commitment, the less the accommodation problem. If we envisage for a moment teachers in the most besieged situation — strongly committed, but having to cope with a number of difficult classes — their problem might be construed as a crisis wherein the whole basis of their commitment may be called into question. The investments and sacrifices made, the side-bets laid down, are all at risk. They face career bankruptcy. It is, in short, a survival problem. What is at risk is not only physical, mental and nervous safety and well-being, but also continuance in professional life, future prospects, professional identity, way of life, status, self-esteem, all of which are the product of an accumulating investment process. Because of the concomitant sacrifices, for most people there is no second chance, no closing down and investing in another career. Teachers are stuck, and must do as best they can. They cannot leave their positions, they cannot change the social order, they therefore must adapt. They must accommodate these problems. Where the problems are numerous and intense, accommodation will prevail over teaching. In easier circumstances, teachers can concentrate more on educational interests. However, it is not quite as clear cut as that. The problems are of such a nature, teachers' commitment so complete, their position so circumscribed, that accommodation requires considerable ingenuity. It can, as I shall demonstrate, 'double' or masquerade as 'education'. I should make clear that I am talking of 'education' here as 'the transmission of knowledge', the model overwhelmingly subscribed to by all teachers at the school that first alerted me to the phenomenon, a secondary modern in the late 1970s that I called 'Lowfield' (see Woods, 1979a, for a full account).

Survival Strategies

Teachers accommodate by developing and using survival strategies. Normative means of control enshrined in the punishment structure are quite inadequate. They are after all devised for normative children. It is the kind of control one needs in order to teach. And survival, of course, involves more than simply control, though that is an important part of it. I define control in this instance as successfully dealing with incidents which fractures the teacher's peace, or establishing one's power in a situation which pre-empts such an occurrence. We can illustrate this by the techniques Waller (1932, p. 198) observed teachers using to secure control: (i) command; (ii) punishment; (iii) management or manipulation of personal and group relationships; (iv) temper; (v) appeal. These can be subsumed under more general strategies, for example, command, punishment and temper are all features of the general survival strategy which I term 'domination'; the others, of the general survival strategy of 'negotiation'. But these are only two out of eight survival strategies that I have observed in our secondary schools. The other six are socialization, fraternization, absence or removal, ritual and routine, occupational therapy, and morale-boosting. If control is conceived of as the handling of incident, survival includes that, but also involves the avoidance of incident, the masking or disguising of incident, the weathering of incident and the neutralizing of incident.

A feature of successful survival strategies is their permanence and ongoing refinement. They contain the seeds of their own continuance and growth, often outliving their usefulness, and festering, causing another problem for which survival strategy must be devised. They do not take a problem out of the arena, as it were, leaving more room for teaching. Rather, they expand into teaching and around it, like some parasitic plant, and eventually in some cases the host might be completely killed off. However, like parasites, if they kill off the host, they are a failure and they must die too, for they stand starkly revealed for what they are. The best strategies are those that allow a modicum of education to seep through. Alternatively, they will appear as teaching, their survival value having a higher premium than their educational value. Theoretically, it is not difficult to point up the difference:

> the intention of all teaching activities is that of bringing about learning . . . If therefore a teacher spends the whole afternoon in activities the concern of which is not that the pupils should learn . . . he cannot have been teaching at all. In these terms, it could be the case that quite a large number of professional teachers are in fact frauds most of their lives because their intentions are never clear . . . [they] may be lost in a welter of secondary intentions. (Hirst, 1971, pp. 9–10).

The term 'frauds', though technically correct, carries unfortunate moral connotations. My analysis shifts responsibility largely from teachers to the situation in which they find themselves. The factors of which I have spoken have led to teachers suffering from 'a crippling sense of uncertainty about what they are for' (Judge, 1976, p. 21). Only their commitment with its capacity for accommodation keeps them going. And the immediacy of the survival problem, as Jackson (1968) has noted, determines the action. I want to emphasize this situationist point. Deutscher (1969) has stated the extreme case:

> The social situation is a notion which is different in kind from the constructs culture, social structure and personality. These gross abstract forces not only provide little understanding of why people behave as they do in everyday life, but, unlike the social situation they are fictions constructed by the social scientist; none of them, in fact, exists . . . These concepts are all inventions, myths, fantasies, which often blind the analyst to the very real constraints imposed by the immediate situation in which the actor finds himself. (pp. 28–9)

Becker (1964, p. 59) also stresses the importance of the situation with regard to personal change in his notion of 'situational adjustment', whereby individuals turn themselves into the kind of persons the situation demands:

> If we view situational adjustment as a major process of personal development, we must look to the character of the situation for the explanation of why people change as they do. We ask what there is in the situation that requires the person to act in a certain way or to hold certain beliefs. We do not ask what there is in him that requires the action or belief. All we need to know of the person is that for some reason or another he desires to continue his participation in the situation, or to do well in it.

Clearly I would not want to write off 'structure' as completely as Deutscher seems to do, since I am concerned to account for the situation in wider forces. But if we are to understand behaviour we must examine thoroughly the circumstances people find themselves in, and their own perspectives on it.

One work which illustrates how teachers' perceptions of pupils contribute to this is that by Jenks (1971). The teachers in the primary school that he studied characterized most of their pupils as 'difficult'. Consequently they distinguished among them according to their 'controllability'. 'Thus the strategy of coping with the present situation involves a central notion of control, usually exercised as silence: this is what is sought often, and against this success in the classroom is measured.' Control became an important part of the curriculum. Instead of a curriculum of writing, spelling and maths, it became writing and control; spelling and control; maths and control. 'Child-centred' methods were considered inappropriate by the older teachers for *that* type of child (see also Sharp and Green, 1975; Denscombe, 1985; and the Introduction).

It is these contingencies that threaten to predominate in many schools. Westbury (1973) has observed:

> The interaction between the demands on the classroom and the constraints within it cause it to be a social setting that has only limited potentiality for manipulation by teachers. The recitation is a teaching strategy that permits teachers to deal, in at least a minimally satisfactory way, with the tensions that this interaction between demands and constraints creates; it has persisted through the fifty years that Hoetker and Ahlbrand have explored because the fundamental characteristics of the classroom that have made the recitation adaptive to the needs of teachers have persisted through these fifty years. (p. 100)

Westbury, however, concludes that 'the classroom does not alter the essential character of these teaching tasks, but it makes their execution more complex'. This provides us with a more humane view of traditional pedagogical processes such as formal teaching, question and answer and so on, whose inadequacies as educational vehicles are more usually simply exposed. It is what Westbury calls a *coping strategy*. However, survival entails more than coping, and I would contend that it does quite often alter the essential character of teaching tasks. Significantly, Westbury only takes into account rather mechanical or demographic constraints, such as rooms, desks, resources, *numbers* of pupils, within a general context of these other constraints. What we have to inject into this model is a more dynamic factor, namely the nature of the pupils, within the general context of these other constraints, which materially represents the pull of societal forces; together with an element of teacher creativity.

I want now to give some illustrations of survival strategies that I noted during my year at 'Lowfield', the Midlands Secondary School of my research (for a full description see Woods, 1979a). I try to show in these illustrations how pervasive the survival aim is, as opposed to other aims that have been imputed, such as educating for 'social control' or 'educating for democracy' in some cases; lack of interest of anomie, for example, in others.

Socialization

'Teach them right'

Some regard conflict in schools as inevitable. Only the degree of it varies. Where there is little, it might be that fewer constraints are operating on the teachers, and/or they have perfected their survival techniques. Some, mainly private schools, enjoy the benefit of matching prior socialization. This is the ideal state for pedagogy, where both sides have common standards, values and beliefs. Most schools spend an enormous amount of time and effort in trying to inculcate them. While some of this might be in accordance with a general 'citizenship' aim, the volume and intensity of many programmes has to be understood in existential survival terms. As noted previously, many children take to schools a culture which is not conducive to good order in the institution. The culture might value, for example, initiative, single-mindedness, activity and individualism; the school, on the other hand, invariably favours receptivity, malleability, docility and conformity. Most schools have some blanketing techniques which achieve a veneer of these qualities and hence a working relationship. For example, many schools adopt 'mortifying techniques'. They aim to strip pupils of certain parts of their 'selves'. Certain roles are prescribed, and the role of 'good pupil' highlighted. This will involve deference patterns (how to address members of staff, how to respond, etc.), loss of identity (as one of a group — a class, a House, a school, entities which submerge the individual), will-breaking contests, and rewards, of course, for 'proper' behaviour. Great emphasis is put on the management of the pupils' appearance. Clothing, hairstyles, cosmetics and jewellery are closely controlled, so that individual expression is limited. Most school uniforms in turn are drab and coarse, unless there is a well-presocialized intake. Pupils are given drill in how to move about the school, sit in desks, raise hands, speak to teachers, eat their dinners, treat their fellows; and the puritan ethic of hard work, sober living and good manners is continuously urged upon them. Some would interpret this as 'education for domestication', that is, concerned with the successful induction of the young into the industrial-political system (Freire, 1972). It is perhaps better viewed as accommodation. This is hardly a survival strategy in itself. It is an anticipatory manoeuvre. It tries to fashion pupils so that they will not cause other contingencies to arise. Thus other strategies depend upon its success or failure. Generally speaking, unless pupils are already well disposed toward the official culture, socialization programmes are just as likely to alienate as to win over, and most of them have a hollow ring to them. Most teachers, therefore, have to have recourse to other methods.

Domination

'Keep them down' (headmaster's advice to new teacher)

Generally speaking, teachers are bigger, stronger and wiser than school-children. If survival is basic, nothing is more basic than these facts and recourse is frequently had to them. Corporal punishment abounds in school. If formal use of the cane has been abolished, there was still at the time of the research a great deal of punching, knuckling, tweaking, clouting, slapping, slippering, hair-pulling, twisting, rulering and kicking. One teacher told Becker (1976) in his Chicago study:

> Technically you're not supposed to lay a hand on a kid. Well, they don't, technically. But there are a lot of ways of handling a kid so that it doesn't show — and then it's the teacher's word against the kid's, so the kid hasn't got a chance. Like dear Mrs --, she gets mad at a kid, she takes him out in the hall, she gets him stood up against the wall. Then she's got a way of chucking the kid under the chin, only hard, so that it knocks his head back against the wall. It doesn't leave a mark on him. But when he comes back in that room he can hardly see straight, he's so knocked out. It's really rough. There's a lot of little tricks like that you learn about. (p. 150)

I witnessed several such incidents. One teacher I asked about the legality of this kind of treatment said: 'The secret is to hit them where they don't bruise.'

Verbal aggression is even more widespread. Humiliation is common (Woods, 1979), as is the threat of physical aggression imbued with a special tone of nastiness for extra effects:

> If I catch you chewing gum in my lesson again I'll ram it down your throat; you'll have indigestion and you won't go for a week!

The threat is often accompanied by 'transfixation' whereby the victim is held in a vice-like grip and subjected to a wide and wild-eyed nose-to-nose confrontation. Often, of course, anger is simulated — it is part of the teacher's 'presentation of front' (Goffman, 1971).

With regard to commands, Waller noted some factors which might weaken their efficacy. One should not explain a command, for that immediately introduces doubt and weakens it. Nor should one express a grievance, whine or moan, threaten or exhort. Waller, of course, is talking about the establishing of authority, and in the 1930s when he was writing that, traditional forms of teaching were much more universal and teacher-pupil relationships much more stable. There are still many teachers who would agree with him, but given the nature of the pupils today, it is extremely doubtful if the formalization and mechanization of commands that he recommends as being most efficacious in his time would still be so. This provides us with a good example of a survival technique which has outlived its usefulness and in fact turned into a problem itself, thus requiring some other technique to accommodate it.

It is an accumulatory process, and there is something awfully inexorable about it. Webb (1962) speculates about a new idealistic teacher going to Black School:

> Secretly he despises his colleagues. He will never be a drill-sergeant as they are. In class he tries to be relaxed, treats the lads as equals. This does not work, because they play him up. He is a chink in the armour of the system which oppresses them. At first he looks upon fighting for control as a game. So do the boys. Then he begins to get tired. There is ridicule from colleagues. The head seems to be saying 'good morning' rather coldly. A game's a game, the new teacher thinks. But the 'blighters' don't seem to know when to stop. And he has not enough energy left at the end of the day to do anything worthwhile. After spending the first week of the holidays in bed, he resolves to do as a kindly colleague advises — to 'really get on top of the blighters next term from the word go.' In a year or so, if he is not qualified to move, he is another drill-sergeant. Thus Black School perpetuates itself. (p. 269)

Physical superiority (and preparedness to use it in some way) and nastiness are useful attributes in maintaining order, for few pupils, like any other group of people, would push any interaction to the extremes where they are employed.

Sometimes this is an integral part of one's teaching. It is perhaps best illustrated in the gymnasium. It is no coincidence that many PE teachers progress to senior positions with special responsibility for discipline. For many of these, 'survival' and 'teaching' are synonymous. The survival techniques of games teachers are built into the structure of their teaching, and are based on relentless efficiency, continuous structured physical activity (which pre-empts any countering), strong strident voices (backed up by whistles, hooters, megaphones, etc.) used to prevent the activity from flagging, and a display of potential physical aggression (in short, singlets, track-suits, muscles, and the smell of sweat and embrocation, etc.). This is fused into the normative order, so that barked commands like 'Stand up straight!', 'Don't move!', 'Pull, boy, pull!' appear as part of the manifest curriculum. It is the accepted, legitimate technique for the aim in view.

A certain momentum is created:

> Well done! . . . This is where it begins to hurt! . . . Keep going!
> . . . This is where it counts! . . . Come on! . . . Another twenty
> seconds! . . . You can get three more in! . . . Pressure, now, pressure!

The strict control of activities, the stentorian voice and the aggression are used to socialize:

> Somebody's changed places, who is it? Come down, whoever it was!
> (*Boy comes down from wall bars.*) Why did you change! I don't know
> why! (*Boy mumbles.*) Now why did you do it? (*Boy mumbles, inaudibly.*

Teacher, very loudly) Don't be so dishonest, lad! Let's have some guts and courage here! If you don't like the people you're playing with because they're weak, do something about it make them stronger! That's no way to show you're a superior sportsman, is it? You're here to learn to lose!

Mortification techniques are freely at the disposal of the games staff. PE and games are often compulsory, there are the showers, and various stages of undress. Stripping people of their clothes strips them of part of their 'selves'.

I made them all do PE in their pants the first week I was here, just to show them who's boss. (Woman PE teacher)

Games and PE thus perform an important function in the life of the school. Not least, of course, they release a great deal of bottled-up drive and energy that otherwise might be released in more sedentary lessons. These techniques are employed variously by others teachers.

The same form of verbal aggression is employed during assemblies and other such rituals. Some moral message is usually offered, and enshrined in prayers and a hymn. These are often enunciated with frightening force, as if validated by holy authority. The function is both to alarm and to rally, but the aim is singlefold — conformity. Even if nobody joins in, the first function is hopefully achieved — the headmaster and music master at Lowfield, for example, by the sheer power of their voices and terror of countenance, established themselves as forces to be reckoned with, backed by mystical power.

Negotiation

'You play ball with me, and I'll play ball with you'

The principle of this strategy is exchange. Commonly used are appeals, apologies, cajolery, flattery, promises, bribes, exchanges and threats:

I'm sorry I'm talking a lot this morning but bear with me, please. I do want to get this finished.

We'll call it a day after this one, you've worked hard this morning well done!

I thought in the second period we'd have a film, then I thought next week we'd do the nature trail in Aspley Forest, but first I want us to make up those notes.

You can go when you've finished, and not until.

Often the commodity the teacher offers in exchange for good order and a representation of 'work' is escape from or relaxation of institutional constraint — films, records, visits, outings, breaks, an 'easy time'. In the pupils' reckoning, these are not 'work'. Nor are they always such in the teachers'. Thus on one occasion when a teacher found he had the wrong film, not even remotely to do with the subject in question, he felt he had to honour the bargain and offer the class the film regardless. Otherwise he might have had a survival problem. They accepted, for otherwise they might have had to do 'work'. 'Community Service' also comes under this rubric. Most pupils I spoke to 'had a good time' while doing it. Many did all that was required of them — gardening, shopping, making tea, etc. — but it was not that obnoxious commodity, 'work'. Neither were 'projects, whether connected to examinations or not. One can hide somewhere, have a smoke, and fill in the worksheet later from somebody else's. Certification that allows for this kind of coursework is, in fact, a considerable aid to teacher survival. It draws many more pupils into the mainstream culture of the school, and still allows pupils their secondary adjustments. Thus, as some pupils told me, if you fall behind on your essays in English, you can always copy somebody else's, merely changing a few words; or you can submit your brother's or a friend's specimen in woodwork — and so on. These examples all support Bernstein's theory that

> when (the pedagogical) frame is relaxed . . . to include everyday realities, it is often, and sometimes validly, not simply for the transmission of educational knowledge, but for purposes of social control of forms of deviancy. The weakening of this frame occurs usually with the less 'able' children whom we have given up educating. (1977a, p. 99)

All this adds to the teacher's resources. There are various types of admonitions teachers use. These include appeals to civilization and society in general, and the individual's fitting into it. 'Right' conduct and attitudes thus will provide access to the promised land. Waller (1932, p. 209) mentions appeals to the parents' ideals, fair play, honesty, chivalry or self-esteem. There are appeals against the fracturing of peer-group norms ('spoiling it for others', group punishments for individual offences), and appeals against the fracturing of a common bond between teacher and class. Of course, the particular strategies a teacher employs will depend on other factors — conception of children, view of teaching, ideological make-up. Great contrasts can be found within one school. One teacher might be essentially dominative and to keep an edge on her technique cultivate 'social distance' from her pupils; another might be predominantly negotiative, and aim for social nearness. Of particular interest here is the development of a sense of 'we-ness' between a teacher and a retrograde class of school 'failures'. These constitute the biggest potential menace to the school, and hence require a special security arrangement. This frequently involves assigning one teacher to the class full time, so that a notion of separateness develops between the backward class *and* their own teacher from the rest of the school. Strong identification is made within the unit, with feelings of loyalty, comradeship and regard, so that it acts as its own survival agent. Appeals, if made by their own teacher, rarely fail. Other teachers, however, are invariably driven to other techniques with these forms.

There is a more general negotiation strategy that teachers use based on compromises over rules. Many teachers work out, through interaction, with each set of pupils, norms and standards common to the group as a whole. Everybody feels bound by such democratic procedure. Thus teachers might choose to ignore certain forms of behaviour as long as they are not perceived as institution-threatening or publicly flaunted. 'Smoking behind the cycle shed' is an obvious example. The same can apply to 'work'. Teachers often feel obliged to abandon their absolute standards and settle down for what they can get from a class, or from an individual.

Fraternization

'If you can't beat them, join them'

> One of the ways to resolve extreme conflict between teachers and children is for the teachers to become less adult and in some sense enter into the world of children. This requires isolating oneself from adult interactions and assuming some of the language and style of children. (Waller, 1932, p. 207)

Some staff were

> not altogether sympathetic with the social aims of the school, but fulfilled an informal role which was functional for the school organization in defusing conflict within the pupil identity of working class children which might otherwise have made it difficult for them to continue in the upper years at the school. As such, these staff acted . . . as a 'safety valve institution', channelling discontent and hostility, while keeping intact the relationship within which the antagonism arises. (Welton, 1973, p. 9)

> The concern with interest and motivation as exhibited through practical problems in the schools owed as much to the aim of preventing disruption, as to the aim of promoting the inculcation of knowledge. (Denscombe, 1977, p. 253)

A prominent survival strategy is to work for good relations with the pupils, thus mellowing the inherent conflict, increasing the pupils' sense of obligation, and reducing their desire to cause trouble. It might be thought that this is fairly central to certain forms of teaching. Indeed, it is the main element in the school ethos described in Chapter 3, and its contribution to teaching is also evident in Chapters 2 and 5. But the teachers at Lowfield strongly opposed this kind of teaching. It is taking place therefore within more authoritarian styles. Thus, while some of the activity described below is very similar to that in Chapter 3, I argue that it carries, in this context, largely different intentionality (see Woods, 1987). The same behaviour can be symptomatic of teaching or survival or both. One needs to trace through how far the behaviour is linked to learning or creating the conditions for learning and how far to simply 'surviving'. There seemed sufficient of the latter in the examples below to warrant their inclusion here.

Fraternization takes many forms. Young teachers, especially, by their appearance, style of dress, manner, speech and interests frequently identify strongly with the pupils. They are often very popular. Implicit alliances can form against the main structure of the school, but, as with teachers of 'backward classes', it can ultimately work in the school's interests, since much bad feeling is defused through this bond with members of staff. On the other hand, of course, pupils with their own survival problem might try to increase their benefits by playing off one teacher against another ('so and so lets us chew in *his* lesson'), so it can promote instability. Older teachers can assume parts of this role. For example, they can display signs of alienation from the official culture, especially where it seeks to dominate. Explicit or implicit disapproval before pupils of a rule or action, especially if perpetrated by the upper hierarchy, is common. In fact it has been suggested that a major function of the head and his deputies is to soak up a lot of the bad feeling in the school, leaving a pleasanter field for front-line teachers and pupils to work in. Some identify with the pupils against outside aspects of the establishment:

> I loathe the vicar, who goes up, takes his watch off — and you know you're going to get your twenty minutes' worth — and he says 'I've got four points to make' — and he's only done two of them after fifteen minutes . . .

(Interestingly, this teacher betrays himself before these pupils by identifying with the establishment at all!)

Many teachers share in cultural influences which cross generations. Thus some have recourse to an earthy humour which marks them not as 'a teacher, a man apart', but as 'a man of the people'. Dirty jokes are not excluded, and seem to be particularly appreciated by rebellious male elements in the school.

Another shared cultural influence is television. Some lessons I observed abounded in references to popular television programmes, advertisements included. While this might have a pedagogical value, it also has important survival repercussions for the pupils' perceptions of the teacher's identity. Sport also can form a bridge. For example, gangs of adolescent boys follow a football cult. Their discourse consists of jocular abuse directed at others' chosen teams and vigorous championing of one's own at all costs. This aggressive banter is typical of their lifestyle and is indulged in as a form of play. On these terms it is open to teachers and sometimes they take advantage of it.

Much survival teaching takes the form of entertainment. It is quite often reflected in styles of speech and associated with culture-identification. Thus one teacher I observed employed a colloquial style of speech in his teaching, which he indulged to good effect from the control point of view. Another had a cosmopolitan, youthful, 'with-it' style which reinforced his identification with the pupils. Another related almost everything he said to television programmes, making liberal use of standard phrases, and copying situation and character comedy. Less 'identification' associated are forms of teacher wit and humour. A stage manner helps, and the fun is often directed good-naturedly and matily toward the inmates. The displacement of reality in humour neutralizes any potential conflict.

> Oh, my God, that smell. Is that that 'Brut' again? Open a window, stand back. (*Hangs out of window, gasping. Returns to desk.*)
>
> Oh, my God, those socks (*Covers eyes with hands, puts on sunglasses.*)
>
> Now who saw *Maxim Gorky* last night? That's the programme you tune into between Mickey Mouse and Long John Silver.

By this form of humour the teacher retains control and reinforces status. It is a kind of humorous, rather than aggressive, domination technique, but the aggression lurks in the background.

Sometimes, however, teachers direct laughter upon themselves, frequently belittling their formal role. These divergences from the mainstream expected behaviour place them in a wider context and invalidate the narrowness of the immediate scene. Impersonation is a favourite vehicle:

Example 1

The teacher is talking about raising hands when the pupils wish to reply:

> In Germany — and don't do this here, please, other teachers might not like it — the pupils go (*here he snaps his fingers together*) . . . and

at the back they even do this (*does it with both hands, jumps up and down and shouts* 'Sir! Sir!')

Example 2

A pupil comes into the room and requests the 'German helmet and gas mask'. Teacher goes into cupboard and comes out wearing them: 'Mein Gott in Himmel: Ve haf ways of making you talk!', and gives a five-minute impersonation of Hitler.

Many aspects of modern teaching embrace the entertainment principle. The use of film, television, radio and records, and devising the projects, fieldwork and so on, have control as a major aim. Interestingly, many general courses depend almost entirely on film and television. Teachers also devise their own little tactics. Many of these, for example, took the form of quizzes of one sort or another. One teacher punctuated a formal question-and-answer technique with 'hangman' games when no one knew an answer. Class involvement and hence control was always greater during the games.

Another form of fraternization is indulgence. This is consciously to allow the pupils a far greater measure of liberty than is customary for teachers. In negotiating, the teacher goes to the extreme of bargaining counters. The norm of behaviour is displaced entirely towards the pupil culture. Here is an extract from my note of the beginning of one such session:

(I sat in a corner at the back, as usual, next to Mark Godfrey. He was peashooting away.)
Mark: Great teacher this is!

PW: I don't know, is he?

Mark: Yeah, he fixes things up.

Steve: It's a muck about.

Mark: No, it's not that, 'e's great. (*He aims off another pea, scores a hit on Peter Matthews, who prepares to retaliate.*)

Paul (loudly): Cor, Steve! You done a fart in English, you done one now! (*Paul gets up and moves over to teacher; suddenly there are more shouts from this corner, and a mass exodus.*)

Mark: Bloody 'ell, Dunsley, you've dropped one again! (*He holds his coat collar up. Paul comes back, groans and goes away again.*)

On the other side of the room a group of girls are very noisy. Michelle is whooping and squealing — they have a letter. Janet appeals to teacher loudly, but humorously: 'Tell her off, sir, she's getting on my nerves!' Teacher (*attending to an individual*) ignores her.

The lesson continued in this vein for the whole period. Yet is was not the anarchy it appeared to be. The teacher did much individual and small group tuition. None of the disorder was directed against him, nor did it involve less yield of work than was normal for his form, whom I accompanied to all their lessons. Another indulgent technique is the indiscriminate backing of 'winners'. Sometimes pupils do become interested. Teachers capitalize on this interest. No doubt this frequently has pedagogical value, but equally it is often done unrelated to the lesson as planned, and justified only *post hoc*.

In co-educational schools flirting is a widely used technique, especially by male teachers with female pupils. Since sex is one of the most prominent interests of the more rebellious girl pupils, it can be a great aid in securing their goodwill and co-operation. Many of these pupils see school in purely 'social' terms, as compared with instrumental or vocational, and their idea of 'social' differs a great deal from the school's 'social training' or 'education for citizenship'. It is much concerned with the basic elements of interaction, and is rooted in their own culture. Some teachers spend their careers fighting this, others capitalize on it, while perhaps denying it:

Teacher: Don't flash your eyes at me, Susan. It might work with your dad, but it won't work with me! (*However, his expression and tone indicate that it is working.*)

Susan (faking embarrassment): Oh! Oh!

Teacher (mimicking): Oh! Oh! (*He carries on up the row, flashing his eyes at the girls, who smile and giggle in mock confusion.*)

The sex element is strong in games. I noticed during a mixed game of volleyball that occasionally, when serving or receiving, an individual would be the centre of attraction, but that one's failings in this arena are laughed at and experienced in a different way from lessons, when they might have felt embarrassment. In the role of 'female' as opposed to pupil, all seemed to recognize that it was quite acceptable, even perhaps desirable, to be incompetent at games. The girls responded with complementary ruses like ogling, putting out the tongue, pretending to hide confusion and so on. Thus their participation in the game was sublimated, and they found salvation in the sexual front. This technique was more used by 'incidental' games teachers. Full-time games staff were much more dominative and aroused far more resentment, especially among teenage girls. This was because they were permitted only the role of 'sportswoman', and their failure at games was of prime importance.

Here is an extract from my observation notes of an incidental games male teacher and a group of teenage girls round the trampoline:

Teacher: Who wants a double bounce! (*Pet puts her hand up.*) Right oh, give us a push up. (*Two girls help push teacher up by the backside.*) Hey, watch it! (*good humouredly*) (Teacher and Pet have a double bounce, teacher working Pet to state of collapse and confusion. As he gets off, he pulls another girl on, and she collapses, bouncing and laughing, in the middle of the trampoline.)

Absence or Removal

'Teaching would be all right if it wasn't for the pupils'. (Teacher folklore)

One certain way of ensuring survival is to absent oneself from the scene of potential conflict. Some teachers achieve this by upward mobility or early retirement at one end, or by never starting at the other (in 1986, for example, 40 per cent of newly-qualified teachers chose not to take up posts).

However, most do not achieve such absolute absence. They have to make do with partial absence, some official, some unofficial. Because it is the most efficacious and the most relative (i.e. one usually gains only at the expense of others) of survival techniques, it is the cause of intense and sometimes bitter struggles. This is why the timetable is of such critical importance. 'Survival' features prominently in its construction. 'Weak' teachers have to be protected, 'good' ones rewarded. 'Weak' ones can be given fewer lessons, none of the hard classes and the most favourable rooms (a good example of how incompetence might be rewarded in our educational system). Whence then come the rewards? Fortunately for the hierarchy there are some 'in-between' teachers consisting of a faceless group of those who have not yet 'arrived' at the school, a 'disloyal' group consisting of those who are leaving or applying for other jobs, and a 'rebellious' group who for some reason have got in bad favour with the hierarchy. These take up the slack of 'bad' forms, poor rooms and overloaded timetables.

Manipulation of the timetable protects the weak, rewards the good and penalizes the unknown and unworthy. The same applies to timetable adjustments that have to be made in the day-to-day running of the school. One of the 'rewards' is free periods. The importance of survival as an organizing principle in the teacher's day is evidenced by the neuroticism attending this topic. Losing free periods can be quite traumatic, for survival becomes that bit harder; it can be very much harder if, in exchange for an idyllic 'free', one is confronted by somebody else's extreme survival problem — a 'bad' form in 'bad' circumstances.

Failing the legitimate acquisition of 'free periods', one can absent oneself in other ways. Unloading the worst troublemakers onto others is a common device, and is legitimated in schools where certain teachers have been given financial and status compensation in return for a 'counselling' function. One can take days off school, though the folklore regards this as defeatist. It also saddles equally hard-pressed colleagues with extra responsibilities. Thus it is more customary to steal extra minutes at the beginning and end of 'breaks', use delaying or deferring tactics during lessons or work absences into one's teaching. Many new courses and styles of teaching that have come into vogue are characterized by a large amount of absence. Link courses, work-based courses, Community Service, fieldwork, individual and group projects, all aid teacher survival by virtue of separating the combatants for much of the time. Techniques such as pupils taking assemblies, running parts of lessons or initiating and controlling work on their own cleverly turns the opposition back on itself and neatly fits into fashionable educational philosophy, while the teacher sits on the sidelines.

If teachers choose to maximize their survival programme, they will follow a policy of non-volunteering, 'keeping out of the way', and 'keeping one's nose clean'. Some teachers have their 'secret places'. Some feel the need to go out — often to a local pub — during the mid-day break. Some are strictly 'nine-to-four' teachers, often for survival reasons rather than lack of interest or sense of vocation. Teachers can be absent in spirit. They can 'be away' and have their 'removal activities' as well as the pupils (Goffman, 1968, p. 67). Teachers occasionally daydream, fall asleep, look out of windows, fail to pay attention, defer or ignore problems, pass or waste time, pretend something is happening which is not and otherwise evade the head-on conflict with reality.

Ritual and Routine

'You'll be all right once you get into the hang of things'

Bernstein (1977) has described the symbolic function of ritual as

> to relate the individual through ritualistic acts to a social order, to heighten respect for that order, to revivify that order within the individual and, in particular, to deepen acceptance of the procedures which are used to maintain continuity, order and boundary and which control ambivalence towards the social order. (p. 54)

In British state schools, rituals

> facilitate the transmission and internalization of the expressive order

of the school, create consensus ... deepen respect for and impersonalize authority relations. They also serve to prevent questioning of the values the expressive order transmits. (*ibid*, p. 65)

Much ritual is to be located in the expressive order of the school. But there are ritualistic qualities about certain forms of teaching. Bernstein again has noted the social control element that lies behind much systematization of our teaching:

> Where knowledge is regulated by collection codes, social order arises out of the hierarchical nature of the authority relationships, out of the systematic ordering of the differentiated knowledge in time and space, out of an explicit, usually predictable, examining procedure. (*ibid*, p. 106)

He has observed:

> It would also not be entirely wrong to suggest that the incentive to change curricula arose out of the difficulties secondary schools were experiencing in the education of the non-élite children. (*ibid*, p. 164)

In turn, this suggests the possibility that survival strategies based on ritual and domination were becoming counter-productive, and needed to give way to more negotiative strategies.

In pluralistic, industrialized societies the value systems are various or ambiguous, and because of other societal developments which I spoke of earlier,

> the social basis for the ritualization of the expressive order of the school will be considerably weakened and the rituals may come to have the character of social routines. (*ibid*, p. 60)

Perhaps the best example of this is morning assembly. Morning after morning the school where I did my research went through the formula of mustering, saying a prayer, singing a hymn, and listening to a peroration and exhortation from the headmaster. However, teachers would find it difficult to do without routine. Musgrove (1974) explains the problem:

> The computer will take much of the routine out of teaching in schools, and will make possible far more learning which is not school-based. Although most people complain about the routine in their jobs, they would probably go mad without it. Without routine we are constantly dealing with unique, unprecedented, non-recurrent and non-standard events. This may be exhilarating; it is also

exhausting. We can expect teachers to be in a state of constant exhaustion. (p. 45)

That prophecy for the future is for all too many teachers ancient history: routine, systematization, drill, have provided a safeguard. Black School provides a vivid example. Because of the boys' 'irrepressibility, rule-breaking and spontaneity' and the teachers' fatigue and fear of playground chaos spreading into the classroom, they insist rigidly on good behaviour and adopt a rigid style of teaching. Consequently, only rather mechanical skills can be taught:

> Only certain rigid work and conduct standards can be conveyed by drilling. And these make or maintain dislike and therefore the need for drilling. (Webb, 1962, p. 265)

Teachers can become addicted to routine and ritual. Once instituted, they are extremely difficult to get rid of. Rituals become associated with 'tradition' and to change them means discontinuity and disjuncture. An ethos can become ritualized in the interest of a dead hand of control. Routine is a narcotic, taken to soothe the nerves and mellow the situation. Once established, to do without it would involve the teacher in severe withdrawal symptoms.

Routine imposes a structure on school life which pupils and teachers almost automatically come to accept, and serves as a basis for establishing control. Registration, form periods, assemblies, timetables, lesson structures and so forth are the bones of the school day. Within this overall structure, individual teachers establish their own routines. We are all familar with the archetypical teacher of fiction, middle-aged, soberly dressed, extremely mannered and eminently predictable in all movements.

As Webb noted, this carries implications for what and how one teaches. Gump (1971) has shown that self-paced activities involve more difficult pupil management problems than in externally paced activities. Westbury (1973) has portrayed recitations and textbook teaching as coping mechanisms. Furlong (1977) has noticed, from the pupils' point of view, that 'work' and 'learning' is a desiccated, skeletal, structured and measurable form of knowledge. To them, learning is 'measured accomplishment'. Britton (1975) found that a large percentage of the writing done in school is done for the 'teacher-as-examiner', and not for the purposes which might do more to foster pupils' learning and development. 'Teacher-as-examiner', it must be realized, is masking 'teacher-as-survivor'.

Many a teacher who has tried an experiment, and felt it has not been working and disorder threatening, has reverted in mid-stream to more formal techniques. The best example is the dictating of notes. This is an extremely useful device from the survival point of view for it gives pupils to believe they are being spared doing their own 'work', and thus secures their co-operation, involving quiet application, for considerable periods at a time. This is not to say that much activity associated with 'new' teaching techniques does not have a strong 'routine' component. Work cards, structured exercises, group activities, programmed learning, audio-visual techniques all provide for it, and perhaps their persistence is to be explained by it.

Occupational Therapy

'It passes the time'

The principle of pupil therapy is bodily involvement accompanied frequently by dulling of the senses. The aim is to take the edge off boredom or fractiousness, and thus prevent incident arising. Pupils sometimes try to provide their own therapy such as playing cards, carving on desks, doodling on paper, reading comics. But though therapeutic, these activities are counter-official. Education must be seen to be going on. This is the purport of the 'busyness' that Sharp and Green talk of. The injunction to 'be busy' is legitimated by the philosophy of child-centred education (see the Introduction).

Within the secondary schools of my knowledge I have encountered many therapeutic techniques. Drawing maps, pictures, patterns is good therapy. This is one of the reasons why art is a popular subject, particularly among bored and rebellious pupils. History, geography and science teachers make good use of the knowledge. 'Play' is also useful. The simple experimental kits provided for pupils' tinkering in science lessons allow for this, and for this reason the practical subjects — woodwork, metalwork, cooking, needlework, etc. — have strong therapeutic value. De-inhibiting activities such as free, unstructured swimming are wonderful therapy, and can spread their beneficial effect over several classroom periods before and after.

Pupils often fill in time with 'jobs'. 'Have you any jobs, sir?' is a common refrain from bored, inactive pupils. So teachers request blackboards cleaned, drawers tidied, corners cleaned up, pencils sharpened, files ordered and so on. It can be the major 'official' activity of older pupils outside the mainstream of the school, especially in their final year when there is common acceptance of the failure of the special 'official' programme designed for them. The girls can make tea and wash up for the staff, the boys can repair gates or glasshouses, paint sheds and so on. They are usually glad to do these jobs, for therapy is a more lasting and satisfying antidote to boredom than 'mucking about'.

A teacher can engage in therapy unilaterally. Busying oneself can help, when all around is chaos and threatening. Marking books, setting up equipment, giving individual guidance can occupy one's mind and cut out the general scene. Sometimes a teacher's whole programme is little more than therapy, like a series of science lessons I observed. Here the teacher carefully constructed the equipment for his experiment, and went dutifully through the procedure from beginning to end, explaining as he went, and elaborating on the application to the modern world of what he was doing. It was a model lesson in many respects, but none of the pupils in these classes listened. Moreover, they obviously were not listening, but clearly divided into their own groups and devised their own entertainment, often quite noisily. The two elements, teacher and pupil, though in the same room, seemed totally oblivious of each other. The only time when they came together was in the last ten minutes of the two-hour period when they were dictated the results of the experiment, and they recorded them in their exercise books. This teacher neutralized the control problem by concentrating exclusively on the 'stimulus' aspect of teaching and totally ignoring 'response'.

Another form of therapy takes the form of 'spinning-out' exercises. One example that came my way involved non-examination, non-scientific subjects allocated half-day slots because of their parallel grouping with science subjects which were reckoned to need that kind of block provision. I observed some of these sessions, and always enormous time-wasting and time-passing was resorted to as a survival technique. It was taken up with arriving late, finishing early, chatting with the pupils before and after, preparation of lesson and materials for it (during it), interruptions (which seemed to be welcomed and capitalized upon), peripheral story-telling and general nonchalant pace.

Morale-boosting

'We have to believe' (deputy headmaster)

Just as socialization is an anticipatory strategy, morale-boosting is a retrospective one. For teachers need a survival strategy to 'account for' their other survival strategies. They mentally neutralize the survival problem, and they do it in two ways — by rhetoric and by laughter. I am speaking of rhetoric here as Green (1977) has done, i.e. 'it explains and constructs the necessity of the conjuncture within the disjuncture. It constructs the paradox in the teacher's actions and perspectives as itself a conjucture.'

Aiding this is another aspect of commitment, group cohesiveness. Kanter (1974, p. 128) defines this not in terms of sociability and mutual attraction but rather in terms of the ability to withstand disruptive forces and threats from outside the group ('sticking together'). This sort of commitment involves primarily 'forming positive cathectic orientations; affective ties bind members to the community, and gratifications stem from involvement with all the members of the group. Solidarity is high, and infighting and jealousy low. Group cohesiveness among teachers is high, though it frequently pertains to sub-groups within a staff. Friction between these is only another feature of the internal cohesiveness of the groups.

The deeper the commitment, both in terms of continuance and group cohesiveness, the more extensive the rhetoric, and attachment to it. Sharp and Green (1975, p. 121) give a good example in their discussion of 'busyness' as already noted. To the teacher 'there is a logical relationship between her notion of busyness, her educational philosophy and her actions'. If the children are 'busy' and 'getting on with it on their own' or 'finding something to do', this is well within the spirit of child-centredness.

Well-established rhetorics attend many of the techniques discussed here in relation to secondary schools. I have touched on the legitimation of certain forms of absence and removal. Pupils running lessons, taking assemblies, going on projects are in line with 'progressive' philosophy, as are certain aspects of therapy ('more involvement') and fraternization ('treating the pupils like people'). There is now a vast thesaurus of 'progressive' vocabulary and idioms, from which teachers might draw to construct their own vocabulary of motives (free expression, integrated learning, activity-based learning, project work, free choice . . .).

All of the specific instances I have mentioned have a rhetoric closely attending them. Young teachers, for example, are best 'thrown in at the deep end', it is 'good experience', and better known sooner than later whether they are going to last. School uniform is championed in the interests of 'equality', preventing the poor being exposed by the sartorial elegance of the rich, of school 'ethos' and the qualities of pride and loyalty, and of 'utility', for identification purposes. Mortification procedures and dominating techniques are represented as socializing devices in the interest of the individual, whose naturally savage and uncouth character must be tamed and channelled along the 'right' paths to a civilized society. The latent survival function of the separated form of potential trouble-makers with their teacher is occluded by a rhetoric which asserts the peculiar characteristics of these pupils — personal, environmental, mental — which 'entitle' them to special preferential treatment; and the relationship they develop with the teacher concerned, which ensures the success of the survival manoeuvre, is presented as evidence of the justification of the rhetoric. Thus the problem is collapsed back into the situation and contained within a solution that masquerades, very powerfully and convincingly, as education. Even the 'jobs' that they do as therapy are justified as 'education'. In one case, for example, the boys in fifth year had to decide 'how much paint was needed', 'who was going to do the job', 'how they were going to order the materials', 'how much they were going to cost', 'how long it was going to take' and so on. This was the view of the teacher in charge of the educational value of one particular job the boys did. In essence though this is not far removed from Mr Squeers's technique:

> We go upon the practical mode of teaching Nickleby — the regular education system. C-l-e-a-n, clean, verb active, to make bright, to scour. W-i-n, win, d-e-r. winder, a casement. When the boy knows this out of book, he goes and does it. (Dickens, 1839)

The growth of the counselling function in schools has legitimated the 'removal' technique, as mentioned above. Moral crusades and deviance amplification in the service of Parkinson's Law have provided a vast amount of rhetoric to support the counsellor's position, function and raw material.

In the struggle for survival, detection and celebration of the enemy's weakness is an enormous morale-booster. Hence the teacher's insistent representations of pupils in psychological terms as 'thick', 'idle', and the prevailing 'norm of cynicism' to be found in many staffrooms (Hargreaves, 1972). One of the two beliefs on which the ideology of Black School staff was based was that the boys were rather hateful (Webb, 1962). From this, the individual teacher might draw renewed strength, after flagging perhaps, towards the end of a double period and allowing the pupils to gain the upper hand. The greatest danger is that teachers should doubt what they are doing. Usually the supportive voice of colleagues available at key points of the day provides sufficient reassurance of beliefs and reinforcement of status. Thus pupils invariably come to be held fully accountable for failings. They are responsible and free agents. Thus, with regard to the segregation that occurred in the school as the result of the subject-choice process, I was told by some that 'they had the choice' (Woods, 1979). There was no acknowledgement by these teachers of factors such as pre-conditioning, group perspectives and channelling procedures which constrain and direct these choices (though *some* were well aware of them). More of such factors are so completely beyond the control of the school that knowledge of them could possibly undermine commitment and hence powers of accommodation. As I have elaborated it, commitment provides for its own defence. Teachers, therefore, would resist such knowledge.

For teachers to 'get on' in their careers, they must 'believe' in these ways; and the more they get on, the more they must believe. The firmer the commitment, the greater the accommodation. This applies particularly to belief. There are several other reasons for this. Sharp and Green (1975) point out that the deputy head in their school had to 'contend more directly with the general crisis in school–parent relations than the other staff. The ideology of domestic pathology has become more sharply articulated for her as a device for understanding and handling her situation' (p. 121).

Webb (1962) imputed *guilt* to the upper hierarchy in Black School, though not to the rank-and-file teachers, whose drill-sergeant role was too narrow for them to have enough freedom to be held accountable. The headmaster eases his guilt by busying himself in administration, or exaggerating the school's achievements. Perhaps also, guilt helps the upper hierarchy to invent and sustain a higher level of rhetoric.

However, it need not necessarily be a product of guilt. It is the responsibility of the head and deputies to facilitate the teaching task for the staff. The provision or reinforcement of a rationale to support their survival strategies is a service to them, while, of course, the head's own responsibility for the school in general, as opposed to the teachers' classroom problems, causes survival problems of a different order. Headteachers are supposed to lead and guide. Where the scope for educational policy is limited they should be experts in accommodation policy.

Less committed teachers who have less of an accommodation problem often see through this rhetoric and boost their own morale by absence. This is one of the main subjects of staffroom humour, a supremely important factor in teacher survival (see Woods, 1979).

Conclusion

Such an analysis of teacher behaviour links the self with the system. At a systems level I have spoken of institutional momentum and societal developments, which may or may not run counter to that momentum. At the individual level I have spoken of commitment, which is bound up with institutional momentum, and the nature of the clientele, the pupils, which is bound up with societal developments. I have introduced the notion of accommodation, which is a product of the confrontation of these two factors. Where the confrontation is intense teachers will meet with a survival problem which they relieve by use of survival strategies. These do not necessarily facilitate teaching. They often take the place of it, and even assume its guise. Success ensures the establishment of a strategy, but many outlive their usefulness and turn into problems themselves. New teachers are quickly initiated, and so the system perpetuates itself. If there is a 'hidden curriculum', there is also a 'hidden pedagogy' (Denscombe, 1985).

What are the implications for teaching? Westbury (1973) concluded that

proposals for change in classroom behaviours that do not address the issue of tasks and resources do not show how change in teaching real groups of students can be effected, [and that] the ideology of open education articulates goals which the conventional school cannot address. (p. 18)

This is no surprise to such as Illich (1973) and Holly (1973), who see schools as places where modern society puts children because it has nothing else to offer them, and that teachers and schools are trapped in the logic of custodial institutions. Teachers, rather, are trapped in the logic of survival. Consider the raising of the school leaving age recommended in the 1944 Education Act. By the time it was implemented in 1972 there were more powerful reasons for bringing it down. But teachers have had to accommodate, and that very process will ensure its continuance, especially when the most committed and most powerful — the headteachers — are so strong on morale-boosting. This has nothing to do with custodialism.

So much of what counts as 'teaching', therefore, can be a fake commodity. This is certainly alienation of a sort, but not in the sense that Holly (1973) talks about, whereby

education is defined for the pupils by the dominant forces in society, (and) education is removed from the essential being of the learner and objectified as an alien commodity which can be consumed or rejected (or whereby) schools make alienation preparatory to life. (p. 59)

This alienation is a result of pressure on the teacher, not a conspiracy on the part of capitalist society. This appears to be Musgrove's (1974, p. 179) meaning when he says 'What is alarming is not that we have a high degree of alienation (we don't), but that so many people invest meaningless activity with meaning, trivial work with high significance.' This pressure is the reason why there has been so little real change in our educational system and why despite the Education Reform Act of 1988, there is likely to be little in the future (see Chapter 8). For example, at the time of the research at Lowfield, there was much latent objection among teachers to team teaching, open-plan schools, integrated teaching. This was because they threatened the privacy of teachers in their classrooms; in other words, they threatened to destroy the whole basis on which their survival strategies had been constructed and on which they depended for continuance. In exchange they offered doubtful benefits, but certainly a whole new range of survival problems of unknown order. While teachers are shackled and threatened by continuing situational constraints, notably the teacher–pupil ratio, the required working week, compulsory education until 16, they will be unable to break out of the protective cocoon they have spun themselves. For they will be forced to continue to think of survival first, and education second. The 1988 Education Reform Act and other developments surrounding it are unlikely to affect this situation while leaving these constraints untouched. I develop this view in Chapters 7 and 8.

Chapter 5

Strategies, Commitment and Identity: Making and Breaking the Teacher Role

There has been much interest, of late, among sociologists in teacher strategies (Lacey, 1977; Hargreaves, A. 1977, 1978 and 1979; Pollard, 1982; Woods, 1979 and 1980; Denscombe, 1985). This is partly because the concept offers a way of getting to the heart of school action, until recently an under-researched area; and partly because it allows for the consideration of the influence of both structurally generated constraints and of individual biography.

Thus Hargreaves (1977) came to see strategies as the meeting point of societal determination and individual construction in the concept of 'coping strategies'. While this draws attention to what has to be coped with, to the problems and constraints that are externally determined, it also recognizes the act of creativity on the part of the teacher. Hargreaves (1978) argued that teachers are wrestling with educational goals in current capitalist society that are fundamentally contradictory, (for example, 'egalitarianism' but 'socialization for the occupational order'), operating under material conditions which are a product of planning and politics, and assailed by a number of differing educational ideologies. Strategies are given a further twist by institutional mediation of these constraints.

However, to the extent that Hargreaves has developed the model (1977, 1978 and 1979), he has so far tended to emphasize the constraints, at the expense of teacher creativity. We have adaptations, given in the examples of strategies of 'policing' and 'confrontation avoidance' (Hargreaves, 1979). But he does not discuss negotiations, which arise from a dialectical interplay of teachers' own intentions and resources and the structurally determined conditions that confront them.

In attempting to correct this imbalance, Pollard (1982) makes two significant inputs, one at the middle level of the institution, in the form of the influence of children in interaction with teachers, teacher culture, and what he calls 'institutional bias'; the other in the area of teacher biography. He points out that while constraints are important, there are other, equally important issues of 'what it is that "coping" means, how coping is defined by the participants, what criteria are used to judge degrees of coping, what goals do the participants bring to the interaction?' (1982, p. 13; see also Hammersley, 1980). In offering one kind of answer to these questions, Pollard has recourse to symbolic interactionist theories of the self. A key idea is that the self is not a constant, homogeneous whole, and different facets of it are realized depending on coping requirements. Pollard introduces Schutz' (1970) concept of 'interests-at-hand' to analyze these facets of self. In these, motivational relevance is governed by situational demands and interests, which are 'juggled' depending on how priorities are perceived as classroom processes evolve (see also Pollard, 1980 and 1985).

These are important developments, but they need to be taken further, and considered in relation to more teachers. For example, what governs interests and priorities? Again, while the self might not be a consistent whole, is there not some aspect of it that has more permanence, that has repercussions for our actions? One possible kind of answer to such questions, which offers to elaborate the biography end of the model, was suggested to me while reconsidering some data on two teachers, gathered during a year-and-a-half's observation in their school in the mid-1970s. The method here is akin to that of analytic induction. It is assumed

> that the exceptional instance is the growing point of science and that cumulative growth and progressive development of theory is obtained by formulating generalizations in such a way that negative cases force us to either reject the generalization or to revise it. (Lindesmith, 1947, p. 37)

Such a strategy 'makes necessary the intensive analysis of individual cases and the comparison of certain crucial cases' (Denzin, 1970, p. 197). All cases should fit the theory or model, but if one deviant case be found, it should not be discarded, but rather the theory or model should be adjusted to accommodate it. By examining and comparing the two teachers in some detail, therefore, we can test some areas of the Hargreaves/Pollard model, and possibly suggest some refinements and additions. The comparison is not as thoroughgoing as I would wish it, for the analysis is being applied long after leaving the field, and the opportunity for theoretical sampling through 'pinpointing' (Glaser and Strauss, 1967) has passed. My analysis, therefore, has the status of a first enquiry, suggesting areas for future focused attention.

The two teachers were ideal for a critical case analysis for they were two remarkable men in a rather remarkable situation. The situation was a traditional secondary modern school (Lowfield'), with an authoritarian-paternalistic head of very fixed views one year short of retirement. The school also was about to undergo a profound change in status, to comprehensive. It was not, in short, the most propitious moment to try to introduce radical change.

This was rather irksome for our two heroes, who held radical views. Tom was head of art, in his early fifties; Dick in his twenties, at the other end of the teaching career, taught social studies. The difference in age and career stage might appear to invalidate any one-to-one comparison, but in this particular instance, the data suggests that their different achievements may be a product of other differences between them. I shall suggest that one possible reason why Tom had survived for so long, despite his radical views, in what seemed a hostile environment, and that Dick lasted for so short a spell (one year at the school, though he had spent each of the two preceding years at two other schools) was to be found in their types of commitment and their conceptions of identity. I want, first, to establish their similarity in views of teaching, and to illustrate their different strategical orientations.

Views of Teaching

Tom and Dick were very similar in respect of their values and beliefs about teaching. They were contributors to that style of teaching that Hammersley (1976) has called, following Schur, 'radical non-interventionism', or that Dale (1978) has characterized as the 'hippy' strand of the progressive movement.

The most explicit example of this for both teachers was in their views of and approach to pupils as equals, their rejection of the traditional teacher role, and their dislike of institutional and bureaucratic aspects of the job. Tom compared himself with the headmaster. They had heated discussions on how and what to teach pupils. The head's line was 'when you go in there you should say "you *will* do this!"' But Tom preferred the gardening metaphor. He saw himself as a gardener — the seeds arrive and he will help them grow, now and then applying a little fertilizer (*cf* Parlett and Hamilton, 1972). He was a strong believer in community education. He was the only member of staff to live in the village, fraternizing with the pupils and the parents, many of whom he had taught of course, out of school. For him, school had to be seen in this context — as part of the community life. There was frequent reference in his talk to kids as 'human beings' and as 'adults'. Thus, much of the organization of school and of the curriculum militated against treating pupils as human beings (for example, there were inadequate resources to make the 'block system' work), and he was for sixth form colleges, for they allow them to be more adult. He 'loved people'. But the more his love, the greater the frustration at the hundred and one petty administrative things like collecting money, answering letters, the caretaker (a 'union' man and a big problem), and 'poor teachers'.

Dick had the very same heroes — A.S. Neill in particular. He also articulated the philosophy — education from within, liberation, anti-bureaucracy, and anti-hierarchy. He had had some experience in a Village College, but in his view its progressivism was only skin deep. He had heard some dockers talking about the Liverpool Free School. He gave them A.S. Neill to read. 'If we can get through to parents like this' he said, 'it's a beginning'. He contrasted himself with his predecessor, whom he gathered was rather 'authoritarian'. His approach was rather different, more 'free and easy, trying to make *them* forthcome'. His whole efforts were devoted to trying to get pupils to think for themselves, as opposed to trying to force them to do things. The answer was inside oneself, rather than seeking it outside. There was so much talking down to pupils in the school — he tried to operate on the same level with them. One example of the elitism he so loathes was when he proposed taking a party to the House of Commons. The headmaster thought that a good idea, but of course 'he would have to take the more able ones, — the "other lot" the intellectual stuff of the House of Commons would go over their heads!'

Dick reiterated the Neill philosophy. The main point about it was *trust* of children. He was for 'living' as opposed to 'lessons', 'emotions' as opposed to 'headwork'. He had faith that Summerhill type schools would become more common. Though he did not doubt initial difficulties. Neill's success in getting children ultimately to respond to their new found freedom by doing creative things and to change for the better, made him optimistic. They had free choice of lessons, no science (though there was a laboratory for 'discovery purposes'), and a far healthier attitude to sex. Above all, they had a large measure of self-government, which was the basis for social control in the school.

Despite the thirty years or so then that separated Tom and Dick in age, they were broadly of a mind as regards views of teaching and learning. How did they try to realize their aims and what did they achieve?

Strategies

This takes us to a consideration of strategies, and here they were remarkably different.

Dick's strategies took three forms:

(a) constructive progress,
(b) ambitious experimentation, and
(c) radical departures

Perhaps the most generally recognized constructive contribution Dick made was a brand new social studies CSE programme, carried through despite 'all the headmaster's suspicions and growlings' (for example, he would not hear of Community Service carrying 30 per cent of the marks). 'But he had worked on it with the head of department, Mrs Lane and, indeed, with Tom, and eventually the head had agreed. It contained not only new subject matter, for example on consumer education and the running of schools, but also new methods, with much project work, a good deal conducted outside the school with the pupil as roving researcher. Interestingly, it was not acknowledged as Dick's invention. Once he had approved of it, the headmaster spoke of 'our brand new social studies syllabus, which Mrs Lane and the humanities' department have devised'.

Dick's year at the school, however, was characterized more by frenetic and ambitious experimentation. For example, he was very keen on films, and not just ordinary films. Films in lessons, between lessons and in the evenings with the school's film club, which he founded and ran. Swedish sex education films, Dr Martin Coles' sex education film, and the BBC film of Summerhill were all shown. But to what effect? The A.S. Neill film was shown to fourth and fifth years. The film shows pupil self-government, Neill himself being out–argued and outvoted, and nude bathing in the swimming pool. It also contains two clear messages for aspiring imitators. One was the time it took for the children to become socialized into the A.S. Neill frame of thinking. The other was a comment by Neill that we do not live in a free civilization. 'If I allowed my pupils double beds', he said 'the DES would close my school'. Even Summerhill has limits.

But those of Lowfield were much narrower, and Dick was in a much less powerful position. He was working within a completely different world of meanings and values, where the general culture and other agencies of socialization were much stronger than him, and simply absorbed him within their framework. Thus the reactions of the class to the films were to titter at the bathing sequence, and to demand to see that particular bit again. More seriously, one opined 'It don't seem natural'. Another said 'what happens when they leave and come out into yer actual world? They'll be in a gap'. The tone of the whole discussion afterwards was critical. Asked by Dick if they would have liked to have gone to such a school, there was a massive 'no'. A spokesman declared 'you wouldn't learn anything. They don't have no lessons. You've got to have some order'. Some would argue that these pupils, whatever their lack of academic prowess, had learnt their lesson.

The pupils did not know how to respond to Dick's innovations. When he sent them out on projects some found it difficult to handle their new gained liberty. There were reports of shoplifting and irate telephone calls to the school from law-abiding citizens which caused the headmaster to hold an enquiry. When Dick gave them a comic strip sketch on consumer rights, and asked them to fill in the blurbs, they vied with each other in inventing obscenities. When they got bored during a part of one lesson when he was addressing the whole class, and began to talk, gradually louder and louder, *he* was the one who shut up, standing and facing them in silence for a full ten minutes while the storm raged around him. It was that master symbol of the institution, the bell, that brought the disorder to an end, not Dick's new technique.

It is possible to argue that he did achieve something through his approach. Some thought he was a 'great teacher' because he 'fixed things up' 'did interesting things' 'treated them like human beings'. Others however found him 'rather "queer", not like a proper teacher — he never tells you off'.

The same is true of the staff, a few of whom were, for a time at least, captivated by his ideas and enthusiasm while the rest looked on askance. What could have been a forum for change became more of a caucus of malcontents, who steadily became more divisive and rebellious as the year progressed.

So Dick was eventually emboldened to try something more radical. He attempted to reform the government structure of the school by establishing a School Council. Its initiation was prepared by way of a press campaign through the school's new newspaper, whose editor was, of course, Dick.

The newspaper raised questions about corporal punishment, under the heading 'retribution by physical violence', urged pupils to help change the direction of power within the school structure, to join the School Council and the NUSS, advertised films like 'Strike' and pamphlets like 'Peace News', and advised, 'Don't let them get at you kiddo — come and see us at School Council'. The draft constitution when it appeared declared amongst other things that 'The School Council shall be responsible for making representations to the appropriate bodies on behalf of the students of the school on all matters affecting the day to day running of the school, and shall also act as a consultative body when new rules and regulations are deemed necessary'.

These were all, clearly, radical departures from the school's usual customs and structure. While it was going on, according to Tom the headmaster was girding his loins, going along with it in form if not in content. Thus, when he was asked to expound on his constitutional position to one of Dick's classes, he did so to the letter, reading out the articles of government for all but ten minutes of the period', and in a tone of voice and with a fixity of stare that dared anyone to challenge him. Tom reckoned the head was quietly but definitely preparing a dossier, including all the minutes of School Council meetings. Soon, he had more material available. Dick refused to attend a Speech Day evening. The head told him it was a required duty, but Dick insisted it was against his principles. Another member of the 'anarchists' trust' capitulated, because he was on a short-term contract and wanted the head's reference for a new job, but Dick refused to yield.

When the head tried to breathe life into the wilting house system, Dick entered into the spirit of it with his usual enthusiasm, spending over £7 of his own money to requisition badges for his house, bearing the name of the house and the motif of a black clenched fist on a red background. With this simple trick, it seemed to the head that Dick was threatening to subvert the most hallowed of institutions. After a day or two of furore and debate, during which another master proposed for his house the motif of a Churchillian cigar with a V sign on a blue background, badges were banned, apparently because of their 'communist implications'. Nobody could accuse Dick of being a retreatist or for lacking resource. He sat down immediately and began a long letter to the Chairman of the Governors.

Generally, Dick and the head began to clash more frequently, as when one of Dick's pupils allegedly set off the fire alarm, and had the whole school turned out on the field in a snowstorm. The head was heard by the multitude thundering at Dick to send the miscreant at once to his room, where he proposed to 'put him over his desk and thrash him'. Dick was heard by those near him to reply that he would do so only when the headmaster had 'calmed down a little'.

Eventually, however, Dick's resolution snapped and he resigned after a series of incidents, when the head had exerted himself and reinforced the *status quo*. An interruption of one of Dick's lessons to instil a different structure of expectations, an exertion of authority over the whole school in which the head caused everybody to suffer because he had been worsted in an incident with two errant fourth formers, and other such happenings, and Dick gave up with a suddenness that stood in stark contrast to the total vigour and resolution of his former application.

Tom seemed to have started out like Dick, but had modified his approach later. He told me about several incidents in his early career similar in spirit to those of Dick. For example, he had got the kids to produce a newspaper. They had a referendum on sport, and 99.9 per cent of them had disapproved of rugby. This went up on the wall, with the other information, and the games' man of the day 'had apoplexy. He was soon round having a right do — "you're undermining my authority" — and only one person in the staffroom would speak to him'. Another edition had a Tarzan-like picture, 'not particularly well endowed, a few hairs on the chest'. The senior mistress saw it and was horrified, fetched the head and down it came. On another occasion he initiated a 'great debate' about school uniform but he was the only one to speak out against it. They accused him of trying to sabotage the system, but 'no' he said 'I'm a democrat, I accept the majority vote.' Tom's libertarianism was contained. For instance, the examples above were one-off attacks on parts of the system on an opportunistic basis, in contrast to Dick's calculated, total assault. Also it could be argued that Tom by virtue of his subject was more peripheral to the main life stream of the school. A somewhat bohemian style could be functional for the school, offering pupils a form of therapy (see Chapter 4).

These days Tom takes it more quietly. But he has not lost sight of his vision and his ideals. Basically he says it's depressing. You just can't 'do it' in the state system. But he does what he can, speaking up now and again in heads of departments' meetings on the lines of more freedom, occasionally winning a small victory. Most of his colleagues think he's mad, so he shuts up, he knows he'll never get anywhere.

Just inside the art room door is a little sign — 'Conform or Else!' — mocking the system. It applies to staff as well as to pupils. He has learnt the art of compromise. When editing the school magazine, everything had to be submitted to the higher judgment and occasional censorship of the headmaster. He complained, the head insisted, he went through with it. There are, however, limits to Tom's tolerance, for example certain people, who in his opinion were inadequate, being made head of the forthcoming Faculty of Design. He did not necessarily wish it for himself, in fact he thought he had talked away his chances, but he did want somebody with vigour and vision.

Yet, though far from satisfied, Tom does enjoy a measure of achievement. He does teach his own kind of art. He likes the summer season best, when he can take the pupils out. They get on a bus and go out to villages, have a snack out, go in a Wimpy and so on, escape the boundaries of school. Or he sends them in small groups to places, to colleagues of his, whom he has contacted beforehand. In school he creates his own kind of environment — informal groupings, pop music, coffee and so on. The art room is a place where pupils like to go. He is always pleasant with them, laughing, joking, teasing, enquiring about family, extra curricular activities, softening the institutional boundaries, showing the human side of teaching.

Another feature of Tom's strategies that differ from Dick's is their range of application, for he teaches in evening classes, and fraternizes in the local pub, or elsewhere in the local community. To Tom, school is part of life, to be encompassed within the larger design. Dick also had a grand design, but in his spare time applied it to a different community. The close integration of the various compartments of life is an important factor for Tom. He can achieve things in his evening school and at large that he cannot in day school, but which he can nonetheless lay the basis for and form connections with.

Dick tried to revolutionize the power structure. Tom worked to gain power within the system, and to influence those in the upper hierarchy. Tom had gained a position. He was the senior art master and Head of Creative Design. He was a personal friend of the Chairman of the Governors, a local leader of the religion Tom shared with him. The Chairman also shared with Tom his views of teaching. It was this very chairman who received Dick's letter of protest about the house badges and who could do no more than try to quieten the matter down. For Dick, therefore, he was the end of the road. But for Tom, he was an avenue to some accomplishment, over and above the power structure of the school, that could nonetheless be fed back into it.

Tom had not only an administrative influence, but also an academic one. For one of his old colleagues at the school, of similar views to his own, had been appointed a county adviser, and visited the school quite frequently when long discussions between them, often over a pint at the local, took place. The deputy head, heir apparent to the headship, was also a kindred spirit, up to a point, often calling in the art room for a coffee and a smoke. Tom, in fact, felt that he had helped secure his position as deputy head, by frequently alerting the head to the fact that he was doing all the duties required of such a position. He had also secured this man's appointment as staff representative on the steering committee to oversee the school's transition to comprehensive status, against the Head's initial wishes. In these ways, Tom made his influence felt, and got his views represented. This influence was within the legitimated power structure, and at some important and influential points. One should also note Tom's influence in the community in general, where he was well-known and respected. Parents, seeking a consultation about their children, often bypassed the formalities and went straight to him.

In summary, Tom's approach to teaching carries a veneer of compliance, but he provided therapy for the pupils, a sociation centre in the school, attempted and accomplished the occasional innovation, had an impact on some influential opinions, and linked these efforts with his wider concerns. It was through this partial accomplishment, I suspect, that Tom had managed to preserve his philosophy intact.

How can we categorize these differences between Tom and Dick? Lacey (1977) spoke of three modes of strategic orientation among teachers: (i) strategic compliance, wherein the individual accepts the prevailing system though entertains private reservations; (ii) internalized adjustment, where the individual believes the prevailing system is the best; and (iii) strategic redefinition, where individuals actually achieve change by 'causing or enabling those with formal power to change their interpretation of what is happening in the situation' (p. 73). Tom's prevailing mode might be seen as an example of the third variety though with a large injection of the first at crucial points. Dick's might be seen as a 'failed' attempt at strategic redefinition.

Lacey gives an example of one such case among his sample of student teachers. 'Peter' had become vulnerable because of his espousal of the classic 'risk' syndrome of strategic redefinition, collectivizing strategies (i.e. where 'the problem is shared by the group whose collective opinions legitimize the displacement of blame, p. 86), and 'radical direction of displacement of blame'. In these situations, Lacey argues, success depends on the individual's ability to redefine the situation, and, if necessary, to employ compliance strategies at crucial points (*ibid*, p. 89). Lacey describes this ability as 'sensitivity to the environment and to significant others within it' (p. 90) and quoted extensively from Miller and Parlett (1974) on 'cue-consciousness'.

Kounin (1970) noticed a similar quality among teachers, which he termed 'with-it-ness'. There was, I feel, a marked difference between Tom and Dick in this apprehension, and specifically, to my perception, in sociological awareness. Dick's failure to draw the lessons of Summerhill, to appreciate the difficulties arising from the environmental and temporal circumstances of the school he was in, the limitations as well as possibilities of pupil and teacher cultures, the power vested in the ongoing organizational structure of the school — all this seems to suggest shortcomings of an awareness which was necessary in a situation where radical political change was being attempted. Tom, by contrast, appeared to have a sound theoretical knowledge of the situation geared to practical action which rose above the recipe knowledge one often finds in beleaguered schools. Time and again, in his discussions with me, he showed intuitive understanding of such refined sociological areas as labelling theory, the amplification of deviance and teacher typifications (see Chapters 1 and 6, and Woods, 1987). Also, the general strategical drift discussed above suggests a considerable sociological awareness.

However, to leave the analysis there would be a mistake. It would be to suggest that Dick was defective in either native ability or knowledge, and I believe neither to be the case. Other factors lay behind this apparent difference in awareness and, to identify them, it is helpful to characterize Tom's strategical orientation as pragmatic, and Dick's as paradigmatic. I borrow the distinction from Hammersley's analysis of teacher styles (1977).

> By paradigm I mean views about how teaching ought to be, how it would be in ideal circumstances . . . The pragmatic component of teacher perspective is concerned with what is or is not possible in giving circumstances and with strategies and techniques for achieving goals. (p. 38)

Hammersley draws attention to the difficulty of unravelling paradigmatically and pragmatically motivated elements of teacher perspectives. However, I would argue that in this case Dick was drawn towards an orientation that allowed no compromise on his view of how teaching should be, while Tom equally clearly shows a concern for 'what is or is not possible in given circumstances'. We can go further, and on the basis of the evidence that Tom and Dick afford us, claim that, in the paradigmatic orientation, as well as ideals and principles being uppermost, there will be little or no situation adjustment (Becker, 1977). Any 'collectivizing' (i.e. sharing problems with colleagues and seeking a collective view) will be undertaken in the service of those ideals and principles rather than in the more pragmatic teacher culture or sub-culture (Lacey, 1977). Inasmuch as the norms, rules and values prevailing in the institution are at variance with those of the ideals and principles, they will be subverted, not accommodated. Inasmuch as the power structure is tilted against the ideals, attempts will be made to swing the balance.

In Tom's kind of pragmatic orientation, there is situational adjustment but also some partial redefinition. Tom has come to prefer 'privatization' of his problems, near-conformity of career structure, and acquisition of power within the prevailing framework. All this takes place without the loss of the vision of ideals, though inevitably there is compromise of principles in practice. The mode is characterized by opportunism, testing out chances on a limited front, and seizing whatever possibilities present themselves to further one's aims. They are not necessarily limited to the school.

The comparison of Tom and Dick is suggestive in the area of strategical orientations. Clearly, there is something interposing between ideology and strategy that causes Tom and Dick to go their separate ways. Differences in age and subject specialism may obviously be important. But, since Dick's teaching career came to such a sudden end, there would appear to be other factors. There, was, I believe, a marked difference in 'awareness' between them in some respects. But the characterization of their strategical orientations as paradigmatic and pragmatic leads us to other areas on which this difference in awareness may be dependent. My analysis suggested the related concepts of commitment and identity.

Commitment

In Chapter 4 I described a form of commitment known as 'career-continuance'. In a study of 100 primary teachers (thirty men, seventy women), Nias (1981 and 1989) has identified other forms of commitment. These are first, commitment as vocation — this involves a 'calling' to teach, and the examples include a missionary sense deriving from religion, or the promotion of other ideals, or 'caring' for children. Secondly there was commitment as profession — a dedication to one's skill as a teacher, involving a continuous search to improve one's knowledge and abilities, and to do the job really well. Thirdly, there was commitment as identity — here, teaching offered people the opportunities to be the sort of people they wanted to be. Fourthly, Nias did recognize the 'career- continuance' kind of commitment identified in my previous research (see also Kanter, 1974). Of course there was overlap in practice among these four analytical forms.

Lacey also, from his questionnaire study (of students on PGCE courses) noticed differences in forms of commitment. One common form was to education in its broadest sense. Teachers with this kind of commitment 'acquire jobs in the schools which they feel will give them the freedom to teach in the ways they wish (comprehensive schools), and already see their careers taking them outside the classroom and outside the school' (Lacey, 1977, p. 126). They are committed to a set of ideals about education and society, not to teaching as such and, if blocked from achieving their ideals through teaching, will explore other means of bringing them about. This roughly corresponds to Nias' commitment as vocation.

The other form Lacey noted, corresponding to Nias' second category (commitment as profession) was a professional commitment to teach, to a career in the school, and to subject-based teaching. They rated their teaching abilities very highly, and were dedicated to their advancement.

Nias points out that one of the differences between these two forms of commitment (vocation, profession) and the other two (identity, career), is the willingness of the individual to give scarce personal resources — time, energy, money — to one's work (see also Lortie, 1975). Tom and Dick would clearly both be included among the former categories on that basis. But there were, nonetheless, important differences between them.

It is not surprising that Nias, among primary teachers, and Lacey, among student teachers should find a preponderance of vocational and professional commitment, while in the beleaguered secondary modern school of my research, the prevailing mode was career-continuance. What is surprising, perhaps, is that we should find in the latter two teachers whose forms of commitment were more in line with those in the former categories. However, the type of school forced a crucial difference between Tom and Dick to be revealed. Both Tom and Dick showed 'vocational' commitment. But that does not get us very far, and it misses entirely the real point of contrast between them. For while Tom, by my estimation, was just as committed to ideals as Dick, he was also more committed to the principles and practice of teaching, and over a wider range of application. This enabled him to 'juggle' his interests. Pollard has demonstrated how teachers do this in the immediacy of the classroom situation (1980). Tom illustrates how one 'juggles' or 'negotiates' on a wider front. I gained the strong impression from him that his own position in the school was always precarious, that is to say his sense of fulfilment, and confidence in what he was doing was perennially a matter of doubt for him. This was perhaps inevitable given the wide gulf between his views and those prevailing within the school at large, which yielded a reality far removed from that desired by Tom.

This position would have been intolerable were it not for those other two broad areas of commitment. The first was to the principles and practice of teaching. Tom was a professional, who, while seeing many faults in the system, nevertheless recognized the need for administration and bureaucracy, for control and examinations and the like. This is illustrated in Tom's approach to the subject choice process, which forces teachers and pupils alike to face the realities imposed on them by structural considerations. Though not a front-line subject, art, by virtue of entering for examinations faces the same pressures:

A lot choose art, yes, and you know why, don't you? I'm not fooled. I say to them, 'Why do you want to do art'? I say, 'I know, but come on, you tell me', and they say, 'Huh, I don't want to do old biology or whatever, all that homework and so on'. It's an easy option, and they go for it on both lines. My results this year were pretty poor which rather proves my point. But what I do is this. I pick those with most artistic ability and I like it to be seen to be fair. I don't spring this on them either. I tell them all this at the beginning of the third year. I tell them they'll be judged on the quality of work that goes into their folders, and then, towards the end of the year, I get them to lay it all out, so they can all see, and, of course, some are very good and some are pathetic. There's no other way, not if they want to take the exam. If they just want a skive, they can do it somewhere else.

Here, one might have expected a wholesale commitment to Tom's ideals to have operated against examination results leading the decision-making. The whole tenor of this statement, also, would have been different. As it is, it contains the vocabulary, idiom and implications of traditional teaching — pupils trying to outwit teachers for an easier time, the experienced teacher easily recognizing the attempted subterfuge, poor results, skiving, and the strategy that appear to bridge the gap between ideals and practice — the demonstration of ability by fair procedures.

Despite his own periodic fulminations against bureaucracy, Tom recognized the need for organization. He was himself Head of Art and first year tutor, the first carrying responsibilities for the subject specialism, the second involving important counselling functions. This latter post was another bridging device between ideals and practice, for it enabled Tom to indulge some of his most cherished ideas centred on interest in the person, including their whole background. But it also brought about frustrations when the channels of communication between Tom and parents were obstructed by the hierarchy.

Dedication to subject specialism was also prominent. Lacey (1977) identified strong student subject sub-cultures, and argued that these operated as latent cultures within schools. There were signs that Tom was influenced by and contributed to such a sub-culture, sustained by his relationships with other art teachers in other schools and colleges. Its guiding feature is 'creativity'. Art is regarded as a creative subject — it comes from within. Techniques can be learned, but their deployment in the act of composition is fundamentally a creative process. There are certain implications for teaching style — a relaxed atmosphere, gentle encouragement, a removal of restriction, constraint and conflict, indeed the creation of an environment where pupils can find expression. Art has therapeutic qualities, therefore, both for pupils and for teacher, for whom it is another bridge between aspiration and accomplishment.

The point is neatly made again by the stark contrast between the view of Tom and those of the headmaster. According to Tom, the head was concerned 'only with the production of nice pictures'. He had 'no conception of what teaching art involves'. Having given this trenchant opinion, he would say 'I never bloody well could understand art!'. He was interested usually only when visitors were coming. The art room was one of the front line show places and he therefore wanted the best pictures up. Tom strongly disagrees with that. He wants the *pupils'* best pictures up. But art teaching involves so much more than just the production of pictures, you have to do so much groundwork on basic dispositions, getting them in the right frame of mind. This is why he plays pop music in the art room. The pupils like it, it's a place they want to come to, they can feel more at home there, less threatened, less constrained. But the head objects, 'not so much to the principles of the method, as to the music. It's "infra dig". Now you can go along to the music room and there'll be strains of Bach. That's OK, it's socially acceptable, it doesn't matter that nobody's listening'.

Despite his frustrations then, Tom is able to derive some satisfaction from his teaching, both from a subject-based and personal point of view, without sacrifice of principles. This delicate balance between gains and losses extends to his view on changes and forthcoming changes in school organization. They enable him to keep the principles in sight, while their full realization is likely to be obstructed. Thus the 'block' system of time tabling was devised on principles embodied in the Newsom Report (CACE, 1963) and not just administrative convenience. 'That would be OK' Tom argued 'if we had the resources to make use of it'. For example, he could hire scaffolding at £1 a day to decorate the walls, make new gates at the front and rear of the school — they needed his vocational orientation. Then he had mates at the Art School and the Technical College who would have the pupils for a day, and that would be one less day at school, they needn't wear uniforms, they'd be with adults, they'd be human beings, and if some of them did well it could be extended to 1½–2 days.'

Tom was for comprehensive education, though against 11–18 all through schools. He favoured sixth form colleges where students could be more adult, and he also preferred smaller 11–16 schools which allowed for teachers 'knowing the kids and where you all grow up together'. He did not approve of sacrificing humanity for a dubious equality. At the time, the school did not exceed Tom's size requirements, allowing him to know a large number of pupils in the way he thought desirable.

This leads me to the other main aspect of Tom's commitment facilitating the achievement of his aims, namely that to the community in which he lived. He was the only member of staff who lived in the village, fraternizing with the pupils and their parents out of school. If he met any pupils in one of the local pubs, he would nod and turn his back, he wouldn't 'welsh' on them, which could have a deleterious effect on his relationship with them in school. These relationships were everything. He believed in community life — and school is part, only part of that life. Others thought him odd as he was the only one living in the village, but he thought it was 'the only way'. The pupils knew he fraternized with their parents, many of whom he taught himself. At every first year parents' evening he would meet a whole horde of his previous pupils who were now parents of pupils he was teaching, so it was all reinforced. And by the fifth year, these pupils knew him just as well.

Generally mixing then, with the people of the village, in pub, street and church, probably in that order, was one aspect of this wider commitment. Another was his association with the adult education evening classes held at the school, of which he was the principal. Again, the main plank of his policy was the fostering of social relationships, because he believed that was why people came — for therapy. Therefore he liked to be in the foyer at the centre of operations, welcoming all and available to all. The head tolerated it, but regarded it as still *his* school, with much greater priority. Evening school was frequently more satisfying than day school, because he preferred dealing with adults, the relationships were more mature and complete. The environment was much better, clear of all the constraints of compulsion. But you could still have frustrations. For example, the caretaker wanted to lock up at 9 p.m. sharp and this was quite a huge problem.

Tom aspired once to go on a 60 per cent evening and 40 per cent day school basis. He would have loved that because he could have got out of assemblies, staff meetings and so forth — all the things unconnected with teaching. But for that he needed a roll of 500 in his evening classes, whereas he only had 360. He could work to build it up, but it would take two years and they wouldn't guarantee him the headship.

But he oscillated. At the time he was disposed to give up evening schools because of 'a hundred and one petty administrative things like collecting money, answering letters, the caretaker and poor teachers, who often were unprepared and boring'. At other times, he felt he should abandon his day work. But this oscillation is my point. The swings and roundabouts of Tom's existence kept him going. The rewards and penalties varied from time to time in each sphere, but while there were rewards somewhere, they were banked against career-continuance.

The main feature, therefore, of Tom's commitment was not its vocational or professional orientation but its range, both in respect of his teaching within the school, where his application to the practice of teaching, the teaching of art as a subject, and school and curriculum organization balanced the strong commitment to ideals; and in respect of his whole life which was dedicated first and foremost to the community, of which the school was only a part. His range of commitments allowed Tom to ring the changes on his options and keep them all open, as now one area gratified and another disappointed, and at another time, *vice versa*.

Dick, on the other hand, did not have the same range of commitments. He had outside interests, notably in the Society of Friends, and this association, I would argue, helped to sustain his 'ideas' commitment. He corresponded with people with similar views to his own, and he told me of their aspirations to create a new Summerhill in the south of England. This no doubt helped sustain his vision aginst the continuously disappointing reality of the school he was in. He certainly gave a great deal of his time and energies to the school — in sporting activities, in running, swimming and football teams, in organizing the film club, in preparing lessons and projects. The simple truth is that the more one puts into an organization or activity, the greater, or the more single-minded one's commitment, the greater will be the frustration and desperation when aims and aspirations are dashed. This must be even more so when the commitment is primarily one of 'ideas'.

This greater commitment to ideas, was often at the expense of practice. I have argued that Tom, in his professional commitment, showed a capacity for situational adjustment which left his ideas intact. I observed no such capacity in Dick. My feeling is that he had the 'vocational' or 'ideas' commitment of Lacey and Nias in excess in this particular situation, to which he was unwilling or unable to adjust. It seems unkind to label somebody with Dick's tremendous energies and dedication as non- or unprofessional, but in the strictest sense he was. There were those on the staff who said 'he was his own worst enemy', and those among the pupils who said 'he was not a proper teacher'. Grace (1978) has noted some teachers in his study of inner-city schools who resisted 'immersion' into the school since it involved 'a threat to their intellectual and social vitality' (p. 187). Dick however did 'immerse' himself, for there were few who equalled his input into the school while I was there, only to extricate himself by resigning when he felt the 'threat to his intellectual and social vitality' realized. This may have been Dick's central problem — an inability to do anything other than immerse himself wholeheartedly in any enterprise he chose to engage in, coupled with a very strong commitment to principle.

This would help to explain some curious anomalies. For example, while Dick certainly had had three schools in three years, it was not his search for a more accommodating billet that was responsible, as I shall show shortly. Curiously, too, in spite of failure at each, by his own admission, his career was from more progressive institutions to less — from Cambridgeshire Village College to West Country Comprehensive to East Midlands Secondary Modern. Moreover, jobs were still fairly plentiful at the time. He talked at length and with great enthusiasm about Summerhill, junior schools and so on, and of a plan he and some friends had of founding a real community school in the south of England. The further his own experience got from his ideals, the more adventurous those ideals seemed to become.

For a more adequate explanation, however, we must move into identity theory.

Identity

Identity theory 'begins with the notion that each of us has an interest in being or becoming somebody special, sufficiently different from his (sic) fellows to save him from anonymity, and different in ways that enable him to command some admiration, respect or affection. Our cultures provide us with a repertoire of possible selves . . . from this . . . each of us chooses or assembles a package and he gives people to understand that this is the sort of person he is . . . (These choices) constitute in effect, a set of claims we make about ourselves. Having made these claims, our public reputations and our private satisfaction with ourselves depend on our success in fulfilling these claims' (Cohen, 1976, p. 49).

This has been demonstrated many time, especially in the field of deviance, for example in the abortion clinic (Ball, 1972), and with various types in Rubington and Weinberg (1978) — 'shoplifters, nudists, check-forgers, queers and peers'. All illustrate the managing of identity. 'Identity establishes *what* and *where* the person is in social terms . . . One's identity is established when others *place* him as a social object by assigning him the same words of identity that he appropriates for himself or *announces*' (Stone, 1962, p. 93). The distinction is often made between personal and social identities. Personal identity is the image one has of oneself — social identity is the image others have. These are sometimes distinguished as *self*, ego as known to ego, and *identity*, ego and his self as he appears to alter (Stone, 1962). There is continuous interplay between the two performed through symbols — language, appearance, acts — and mediated through interpretive frameworks. For interaction with others to be able to occur, there must be at least some correspondence between presented self and assigned identity, between personal and social identities (Ball, 1972).

Identities have a temporal dimension. Ball has distinguished between situated and substantial identities. The latter have a more stable and enduring quality. Situated identities are more transient, more dependent on time, place and situation, though they interact with substantial identities and may affect them. If there is a wide divergence between the two, a great deal of negotiative work may be required by both actor and audience to salvage the substantial identity.

We shall find these distinctions useful in our consideration of our two heroes. My main argument is that Dick was concerned to claim a particularly radical personal and substantial identity, and that this was one of the main factors, ultimately, behind his eventual surrender. This would help to explain the consistency of his behaviour, in fact *escalation* of attempted innovation, despite the evident lack of success. Albert Cohen (1976) argues that 'for some of us, a key portion of our identity is our claim to be among the vanguard of some movement' (p. 51). Once certain areas have been achieved, or even perhaps simply broadcast, we need to move on to still more thoroughgoing aims:

> Disillusionment with the ineffectiveness of a less radical posture may play an important part and so may, paradoxically, the experience of success. Success, by altering one's conception of what is possible, may encourage a revision upward of aspirations and therefore of greater extremism. (*ibid*)

I would argue that both factors, failure and success, albeit a 'phoney' success, paradoxically played a part in the maintenance of Dick's radical identity. He had moved to three different schools in as many years. I believe that Dick wanted to be a reformer, and that his brief excursions into these three schools *each* gave him a glimpse of that characterization before threatening to undermine it. For all institutions have a certain elasticity. The norms and rules of the prevailing cultures may be strong, but ill-defined, if only because they are so rarely challenged. When they are challenged it takes time for the upholders of the culture to marshal their defences. In that space, that area of 'give', Dick enjoyed momentary but largely phoney success with his film club, his clique of malcontents, his newspaper, house badges and school council. Once the strength of the prevailing forces began to outweigh his apparent successes, it was time for him to test the pliability of some other institution. That this overall movement showed a trend towards situations that were less and less likely to favour his aims, supports my argument that Dick was acting in the service of his own preferred identity, rather than seeking out ways of creating the conditions that might help some of his ideas become practice. Of course one could argue that trying to set up a school council etc. was his attempt to create those conditions, and that his failure was simply a product of superior forces or his own misjudgment or inexperience. But Dick was neither a novice nor unintelligent. And there could be fewer less propitious moments and situations for such a reform.

In the terms of the model of identity with which we began, it enabled Dick to pass off the situational identity as part of his substantial one, whereas Tom played off one situational identity against another in an always precarious juggling feat. Moving fairly rapidly from place to place was Dick's way of managing his identity as a radical reformer, dedicated to certain ideals and principles, which admitted of no compromise, and which called for vigorous and persistent prosecution of method. Further, what others might have interpreted as warning signs and gathering powerful opposition, was an essential component of Dick's identity. For in the shaping and honing of these identities we need not only supportive feedback from others, but also contrastive. Thus opposition would be converted to gain in Dick's (and Tom's) perception of others. Thus when Dick and Tom criticized the hierarchy, 'craftsmen' handiworkers, time-serving nine to four teachers, as they frequently did, it was not simply a question of attacking policies and ideologies, but an 'attempt to render worthless the currency in terms of which the identities of those who dwell comfortably within those institutions are currently valued' (Cohen, 1976, p. 52). The counter-criticism was a useful mirror for Dick, or as Cooley described it, 'the looking-glass self' (Cooley, 1902).

Dick's identity was projected with his usual vigour and clarity, from his long hair with hair band and other unusual symbols of clothing to the laying bare of his spiritual self in his confessions of his innermost thoughts and feelings in his assemblies. Gregory Stone has argued for the importance of appearance, as well as discourse in the establishment, maintenance and alteration of the self (1962). The headmaster and most of his staff realized this in their preoccupation with school uniform. Of course the kind of identities the head was trying to promote among the pupils was greatly at variance with that of Dick.

This clash of identities, in which appearances were paramount, is illustrated by an incident which sparked off a series of events which led to Dick's eventual resignation. It is important to realize that Dick, even though periodically he spearheaded a clique, was an individualist, even more so than Tom. He was a marginal man, who championed other marginals in his teaching — tramps, gypsies, alcoholics — with passionate ideas but lacking the roots that Tom had sunk over the years.

He was not one of the staff as a collective body, and in some respects he was anti-professional. He would not have subscribed to the 'collective ideology' of the staffroom (Hammersley, 1977). Nor would Tom in many respects, but he admitted to accepting the majority view. If decisions were made that he did not like, he would not seek ways of overturning them, but of adapting them. Dick, however, could not bear to be associated however remotely with certain decisions. The occasion in question was when the head took his revenge on the whole school, for having been worsted by two fouth form boys, laid his conformist philosophy on the line, 'denigrated them as human beings', and ordered a harsh uniform and general appearance inspection the following day, as if to signal the birth of a new order. Dick marched into the staffroom afterwards and immediately declared 'That's it! I'm leaving! I'm off! Can't stay in this school any longer'. It was not only the philosophy, but the fact that the head had declared that 'he was going to see to it that *his* teachers carried out his new totalitarian oppression policy'. Dick resented this association. He 'wasn't going to bloody do it'. Some boys said that at times it was like the SS with the head as Hitler. Between the verbal fury of the onslaught, however, and the deed itself — in this case, the uniform inspection of the following day — there was a world of difference in which both teachers and pupils could manoeuvre, as most of them did, including Tom. They knew that the head's outburst, not any new policy or regime, *was* his revenge. Thus, you could go up the line of pupils under his charge, pretending to inspect them but making amusing comments, neutralizing to a large extent the previous day's damage. This mutual 'face work' (Goffman, 1967) enabled Tom and the pupils he inspected to preserve their substantial identities while going through situational motions. By making a pretence of the inspection, Tom was projecting an image of self detached from that particular framework. And by their smiles and knowing looks, the pupils confirmed the image.

Dick could not bring himself to do this any more than he could attend speech day. It is possible that he saw his particular attack as just as much an attack on him as on the pupils, since much stress was laid on the importance of *appearance*, and what certain deviant forms of it (for example, long hair) indicated. His reaction may, then, not have arisen solely out of strong sympathy for the pupils, and their 'denigration as human beings' (Dick's words), but because it also brought on for him a severe identity crisis. I am reminded of Lemert's analysis (1978) of the identity problems of the check forger (not to be confused with moral career, in which Dick and the check forger have nothing in common):

> In a sense the forger fails because he succeeds; he is able to fend off or evade self-degradation consequences of his actions, but in so doing he rejects forms of interaction necessary to convert his rewards in positive, status-specific self-evaluations. In time he reaches a point at which he can no longer define himself in relation to others on any basis. The self becomes amorphous, without boundaries; the identity substructure is lost. (pp. 459–60)

Dick could only preserve his sense of who he was by leaving. Had he stayed, he would have been a changed man. His one real achievement — the new social studies syllabus — rather significantly perhaps, had been credited to somebody else. In other respects he had gone from experiment to experiment on an ever increasing scale of pervasiveness despite their evident failure. In the circumstances, there could be only one outcome, and it was *he* who made the decision, not the headmaster. It is my guess that leaving solved at a stroke what had become for him an intolerable identity problem.

In other ways, Dick and the headmaster aggravated their identity concerns, and we can see how lack of a certain awareness compounded both their difficulties. Dick disputed not only the head's power, but also his position as 'critical reality definer' (Riseborough, 1981, p. 37). Dick's frequent utterances that some decision or action of the head's was too grotesque to be 'true' carried almost literal significance for him. They lived in different worlds. So did Tom. But, whereas Tom appreciated how those worlds had come into existence and what their social supports were, Dick did not, except in a very hazy way. The core of the projection of those worlds seemed at times within the person, almost in a spiritual sense. At others, it was seen as purely a managerial problem. But always as individualized. I suggest this was why he was so frequently outraged at the head's behaviour, and *vice versa*. They both took it personally, the headmaster who was so traditionalist 'it wasn't true', and the 'bloody anarchist' bent on nihilistic revolution. Having affixed these labels to each other, they seemed determined to make each other live up to them. Tom could have stepped outside these labels. Dick and the headmaster seemed to revel in them. Each saw the other as a 'judgmental dope' (Garfinkel, 1967). But in their outright condemnation of each other, each was reinforcing his own identity. This preoccupation, I would suggest, blunted the edge of awareness.

The starkness of Dick's position is revealed by a consideration of the rest of the staff, Tom included, whose roles and careers hung in the balance because of the forthcoming change in the school's status to comprehensive. There would be more jobs, but who would get them? Would their present positions be guaranteed? Would they need a degree to remain head of department? Who would get the key senior positions? During Dick's solitary year at the school, the rest of the staff, all on a somewhat longer time span, were in a state of unease and uncertainty about their professional careers and identities, and most were playing it safe. 'If I play my cards right', one told me, 'I might get head of department'. It was not the time to rebel; not the time to try to overthrow a ruler when he was on the point of abdicating and a new more democratic constitution had already been agreed.

Riseborough, for example, has shown that in the school of his research, career aspirations were fixed during comprehensivization and the 'old' staff thought these aspirations could and would be realistically fulfilled. Much staffroom conversation was concerned with potential career advancement, and there was an atmosphere of career uncertainty and career expectation. One of the staff remarked, 'The school was at a watershed — and you don't drop bombs in watersheds, not unless you are jettisoning them for waste' (Riseborough, 1981, pp. 18–19). That is exactly what Dick did. He dropped a bomb in a watershed.

Conclusion

The comparison of two teachers professing similar views of teaching and in the same situation, but with different strategical orientations, has suggested further refinements to prevailing models of teacher action.

The categorization of strategies employed by our two teachers on a paradigmatic — pragmatic basis led to the argument that if we are to understand correctly the origin and nature of teacher strategies, then we must investigate their type and range of commitments and their identities. I have suggested that what helps Tom maintain an admittedly precarious teaching existence, but nonetheless ideologically intact one, is a range of commitments, both within the school and in the community at large, among which he can juggle or negotiate his general interests depending on circumstances. He has, too, what I have described as a number of 'bridging devices' which enable him to cross the divide between ideals and practice, such as 'fair procedures', his counselling role, and his subject 'art'. These bridging devices might be compared with the 'partial penetrations' noted by Willis (1977) which enabled a group of 'lads' periodically to break through their conditions of existence.

I have argued that a factor playing a large part in Dick's downfall was the preservation of his own substantial identity, which was becoming increasingly at risk with every day that he remained at the school. Resignation was the final act of self-preservation. This is not to say, of course, that there were no other contributory factors. The headmaster, for example, happened to hold fundamentally different views. If Dick had arrived at the school two or three years later he would have been caught up in the initial excitement of comprehensivization. If he had come four or five years earlier, he might have established himself within a powerful reference group, with strong mutual moral support. The circumstances were not of his making and, as they were, they aggravated his identity problems.

It is in these areas of teacher biography that the individual has most choice, choosing how to distribute commitments over a range of concerns, selecting an identity from a range of roles and testing it reflexively in a continuous process of interactions with others (Brittan, 1973). These choices have implications for strategies and for careers.

I should stress again, that I do not claim to have given anything like a full explanation of Tom's and Dick's intentions and actions. That would require much more material, not only in the areas touched on in this paper, but into a deeper socio-historical dimension, into earlier socialization, class and family background that would reveal more about the development of the self concept and the criteria they used for judging how they 'coped' with the situation (see Pollard, 1982). Rather, I have used the material that was available to me to try to indicate the potential fruitfulness of this area for understanding teacher action, and to suggest lines of future enquiries.

Finally, I have cast the problem in terms of why Tom survived in the system, and Dick did not, and in such a comparison, Dick must appear the loser. But of course it is the educational system that is the real loser, for teachers of his talents, energies and charisma are rare. While the thrust of this chapter has been to focus on his own responsibility in the matter as suggested by his identity concerns, there are questions raised about significant others who may have helped shape those concerns — headteachers, colleagues, teacher educators.

One would also need to appreciate the constraints he was faced with. Dick, in fact, had the whole force of society against him — social structure, moral standards, cultural adaptations. In typically optimistic and energetic fashion he attempted to create his own structural supports from the flotsam and jetsam of an unpopular, but dying regime. In the end, that is all it was, something left on the beach between the flow of the new unknown, forthcoming comprehensivization, and the ebb of the elitist paternalism of the old order. What this study of two teachers has shown, I hope, is not only how the constraints and pressures in this tide impinge on action, but also how they can be recognized and grappled with. The results may not be revolutionary, but where there is recognition, there are possibilities.

Chapter 6

Teacher, Self and Curriculum

Introduction

To what extent does a teacher find self-expression within the curriculum? How far is a 'subject' as practised in the classroom a realization of an individual teacher's self? These questions are overdue for consideration among sociologists of the curriculum.

As conceived by Mead (1934), the self is a process, consisting of continual interaction between the 'I' and the 'me', the former representing the individualized impulsive aspect, the latter the socially regulated aspect, which allows one to regard oneself as object, and stabilizes action (Blumer, 1977). In this way, the self interacts with prevailing social circumstances, now borrowing something from them, now contributing (Berger and Luckmann, 1971). Such a dialectical interplay obtains, I would argue, between teachers and subject specialisms. The proposition is, therefore, that rather in the same way that teachers 'make' rather than 'take' roles (Turner, 1962), they also 'make' the curriculum.

I examined this proposition in a series of interviews with a recently retired teacher. I employed the life history method, the merits of which have been argued by Faraday and Plummer (1979), Goodson (1980) and Bertaux (1981). It seemed important to consider the teacher's total life and career, and to try to identify some of the major strands of development of self, and the important influences upon it. The teacher ('Tom') and I talked in consequence on a number of occasions for a total of some twelve hours, yielding over 500 pages of transcript. I had, too, my fieldnotes and interview transcripts from previous projects in which Tom had figured prominently (Woods, 1979 and 1981 and see Chapter 5). In the course of these discussions, a second proposition suggested itself, namely, that if the curriculum and self are in dialectical interplay, large elements of that self have been formulated in early life.

What follows is a framework for the consideration of these two propositions. First, I abstract from the many hours of interaction with this man what I perceive to be major components of his self. I go on to consider the implications of these elements for his strategical action as a teacher, and for his attitude to the curriculum. I next trace the origins of the elements in his earlier life, including a consideration of macro-influences and mediating factors. Finally, I suggest that the actual degree and quality of self-subject interaction depends on ranges of coordinates that we can specify for any particular teacher.

I must stress again the speculative nature of this framework. It is based on only one teacher, and covers a vast field, some parts of which are inevitably sketched over lightly. My purpose is not to present a comprehensive model or an exhaustive biographical account, but more simply to raise some of the issues in this hitherto unexplored area.

A Brief Overview of Tom's Career

1922	Born in the Borders, Scotland. Father, Scottish, civil engineer; Mother, Irish, Catholic. Tom eldest child in family of six. Goes to Catholic primary school.
1934	Tom wins scholarship and goes to local grammar school. Matriculates 1939.
1939	Joins army on eight-year contract. Trains in Signals.
1939–47	Serves in Europe with BEF and invasion force, and training troops in England; after 1945, in India and Japan; 1947, demobbed; married 1943.
1947–50	First experience of teaching in two primary schools in Lincolnshire as emergency-trained teacher.
1950–52	Teacher training college.
1952	Returns to primary school.
1953–55	Takes up post at all-age school (Catholic) in home town.
1955	Moves to all-age school in Midlands; this becomes a secondary modern in 1957, and a comprehensive in 1978. Tom progresses from teacher of general subjects in all-age school to Head of Design in Secondary Modern. He retired through ill-health in 1979.

Aspects of the Self (Summary)

Prominent among the esteemed values of the preferred self were humanitarianism (love of, and trust and faith in people), pacifism (after the war), tolerance, honesty and independence. Tom also has two major dispositions: (i) a questioning, curious, critical outlook on life and the world, and (ii) an artistic temperament, involving love of beauty, creativity and self-expression.

Yet, at times, certain bi-modal features are apparent, Tom at one time espousing one value or cause, or a certain trait or disposition, at another, its opposite. The main features here were:

Tolerance	Intolerance
'Straightness'	'Deviousness'
Idealism	Pragmatism
Romanticism	Realism
Collectivism	Individualism
Involvement	Detachment
Outgoingness	Reserve
Confidence	Uncertainty

In the tension between these features lies the key to Tom's mode of adjustment in life. It represents the means by which he engages with society, but continues to stay 'at one' with himself (though in some respects there are *two* selves). Thus, he is an 'incurable romantic', yet even in the identification of that fact shows himself to be basically a realist. Much of his teaching ideal is contained within the community philosophy of Neill, professing togetherness, friendship, equality, democracy, and found expression, as well as in school, in local pub, entertaining at home and running the Adult Education Centre. But Tom also feels strongly individualistic, independent, detached, aloof. In some respects, he feels this may be a result of an inherent shyness, but in other respects he cultivates it. It is what he wants — to be a 'loner', even among his own family. One of the great lessons he has learned through life is tolerance, yet here and there he shows an intolerance, at times understandable in the light of other things he holds dear (such as his disdain of certain incompetent teachers), at other times more difficult to comprehend (such is his total condemnation of the French as a nation). Then, too, he is a great admirer of 'straight' behaviour, involving fairness, honesty and directness, without fuss or favour, but considers himself a most 'devious' character in finding ways to achieve his own ends if his more direct approaches are rejected.

Such apparent inconsistencies well illustrate the Meadian notion of self, not as a fixed entity, but as a process, constantly in flux as it encounters different situations and intereacts with different others. It does not discount the possibility of a 'core' self (Berger *et al.*, 1973; Turner, 1976). Tom says his 'real me' is the detached, aloof, individualistic 'loner'. Here he can indulge his idealism and romanticism. But in the outside world, in interaction with others, he has acquired the hard edge of realism. Though a romantic at heart, he is nobody's fool. He can see through humbug, other people's strategies, his own failings. Though he has never lost or tempered his ideals, he has never entertained illusions about their chances of realization.

Implications of the Self for Strategical Action and for Curriculum

Tom's tolerance, humanitarianism and 'straightness' are evident mostly in his day-to-day interactions with pupils and parents. There are no threats, subterfuges, coaxings to get pupils to do what he wants, beyond the provision of a friendly atmosphere and the cultivation of a sense of togetherness. His view of the teacher is as a 'facilitator', and of the subject, 'it is what it does to people, not what it is'.

The 'artistic' line comes through his subject, but also his general approach to teaching and child development. For Tom, art is not a body of knowledge, or a collection of skills and techniques. Nor does a product like examination results matter.

> Technique is totally unimportant, in art, you know. When all is said and done, it's what you achieve, not how you achieve it, and even if I read any simple little manual on 'How to paint in oils' — you can imagine all these things, you can learn all these techniques in one night. You may make mistakes at first, but if you are intelligent this sort of thing is only really a matter of commonsense. . . . You don't need instruction. . . . A boy serves an apprenticeship, he just hangs around a bench where people are doing it and just picks it up. . . .

Art thus is not a subject, but a medium for the expression of the self. And the important outcome is not the painting, but what it does to people. Above all, it should increase their sensitivity.

> I'm concerned with bringing art to the populace, making life a little bit richer for them, making a girl understand that laying a table is a work of art, it can either be pleasant and seductive and complementary to the food, or it can just be a lot of crockery chucked down. That's all. That's the basis of all art in my terms . . . just open their eyes a little, and making them feel more.

It follows that you cannot *teach* art. Tom saw his job as 'to create an environment in which these creative things could flourish . . . and children can only create this environment within themselves. You certainly don't "teach".'

Further, art is only part of, and subservient to, the grander design, which is the whole person. Tom is a convinced child-centred integrationist.

> My kind of teaching depends on integration. . . . I didn't waste time on history sessions drawing little Norman castles, you could do that in art. Everything worked together, when you were doing one subject you were talking about another. . . . These teachers [in his last school] were taught in a discipline — their educational training is nil. They don't know what inter-relationships and coordination is about.

Thus he bemoaned his failure to get links with the woodwork and metalwork teachers, who resisted all his overtures. His best memories of teaching were of a time when, as head of art, he could cover his responsibilities for the subject to the whole school in two days, and had one form only for the other three days of the week. Here he could perpetrate an integrated curriculum and cultivate relationships in the holistic, full-blooded way he liked best.

Tom insists he had to do things 'his way', and his solution to the problem caused by the one school where he was not allowed sufficient rein, was to move on. He said he told his prospective new headmaster, at interview:

> I'm very impressed with the school, but I'd like to point out I don't fit very easily into tramlines. I can guarantee that if I come to this job, I'll try very hard to put the school first and keep everything going, but I can only do it my way. I don't know any other way of teaching except my way. It might at times conflict, but we should be roughly going in the same direction.

What is 'his way'?

> It isn't a way, it's not a religion, I've worked out. It's just that I tend to play things off the cuff you know I work by and from the children. I think about the responses I get and I build on those, and I sense what's happening around me, and if I feel there is a more productive line, I'll drop the other with pleasure, because I don't see any point in flogging dead horses if you've got live ones in the stables. . . . I tend to tack furiously if I'm losing wind on that side, I veer over here. . . . I never worked to a time-table. That's another reason no head liked me very much. I swallowed the time-table, and regurgitated it to suit myself.

In the Borders' Catholic school where he taught, he tried to humanize what he saw as the dogmatic teaching of the church. He aimed to give his 'senior lads a more interesting life, and some freedom'. He got woodwork and cookery going 'with a bit of pushing, twisting and cajoling'. He took on 'the school gardens' and 'the kids loved that — there was a certain sort of freedom. We would talk together outdoors freely and easily . . . and we learned a lot together.' Football, youth club — you name it, Tom did it in those days, and he 'loved it'. His method was built on *trust*. He had trusted people, and children in particular, all his life, and had not often been let down. So he developed close relationships with them, and much of his important 'teaching' he feels took place around the edges of the official timetable. For example, 'walking to the swimming pool, on the way I would talk to the kids . . . about the town, and they knew nothing really about it . . . and then we'd spend some time on the seashore inspecting shells and weed and so forth . . . it's so easy to lead children, I've found. I could get topics going in a million things.' While he had the freedom and opportunities to 'teach' in this particular way, he was happy, but opposition built up among his superiors and he felt forced to leave.

However, if much of this smacks of 'redefinition' (Lacey, 1977), Tom had his periods of 'compliance', notably at the beginning and at the end of his teaching career. The latter had something to do with the 'side-bets' (Becker, 1960) he had made by that time (see below), the former with the animal instinct to survive. In his first (junior) school, he

> really did have a very hard training. I had sixty odd children in one room, and he [the headmaster] sixty odd in the other, with a glass partition between us. For the first six months the partition stayed back all the time, and I taught with his listening to me with his left ear while he listened to his own lot with the other, and every move I made was checked and double-checked. I had to cycle six miles to work, and he insisted on my being there at 8.30 a.m., and by 8.45 I had to show him not only my teaching notes for the day, but my blackboards for the day.

At 8.55, these blackboards were inspected, as was Tom's person and clothing. If all was acceptable, he was given pen, inks and register, and supervised while he completed it. He had a hard training, but never held it against that man, and was able to 'put it into proper perspective later'.

Tom learnt the 'nuts and bolts' of the business from these people (his first two junior school headmasters) — preparation, organization and discipline. He had high ideals, but 'was very tied down by them'. He accepted everything the way they presented it and 'did what he was told'. He had a little bit of fun with the children on the side, but only when the head was not around. He was little more than a monitor in his first school, a 'minireplica' of the head. But

> I thought it wasn't hurting me. His way worked, so let's understand that first. I had big ideas . . . but I didn't know how to implement them. Controlling sixty odd children when you have had no experience is a hairy business, so I found the best thing was if his routine worked, use it, if you've nothing better, and when the time comes, chuck it out of the window . . . but in the first instance, you must have some control. Without that there is no hope in life.

When he remembers the vast numbers of young teachers he has met in his career who just could not cope, he counts himself 'very lucky to have had this monster Welshman to put me right when I started'.

By the time he went to training college, he 'really did know the ropes, and was well trained. I didn't get away with anything like a young teacher might today.' He had served his apprenticeship in practical skills and in 'coping', had a better idea of what was and what was not possible, and in some respects had had his horizons broadened, first by his second headmaster, a man after his own heart, imaginative, caring, progressive, and who gave Tom rather more scope and allowed him to spread his wings a little; secondly, by the educational literature he was always saturating himself in, and the 'emergency' courses for trainee teachers he went on. This early period, therefore, found Tom 'situationally adjusting', acquiring the necessary kit of a teacher practising in the state system, momentarily subordinating his preferred self to the indispensable framework of the role, but finding more scope in his second school for his own personal style of teaching — child-centred, de-institutionalized, relevant, free, exciting, fun. This freedom, however, was gained at some cost to other interests — his own creative painting, for example. But it enabled him to 'rise above' his two-year training course, which, for him, was an in-service one. It gave him justification for some of his ideas.

Eventually, at his second primary school, he felt that he began to exercise a reciprocal influence on the head, as he did with a later one 'rejuvenating them. . . . They had probably been such as I was in their youth, but had got in the doldrums, hadn't kept up with the literature, and had lost the desire to keep it up. So I was like a little refresher course to them. . . .' This is the kind of strategic redefinition identified by Lacey (1977, p. 73) — influencing 'those with formal power to change their interpretation of what is happening in the situation'. But it also indicates a readiness to 'trade' on Tom's behalf, accepting some of their ideas and practices, though they might have a totally different concept of education from his, while they accepted some of his. 'I believe one must compromise on the way to winning — and winning is what it is all about. Sell the chap a record — there is a chance he will buy a record player. In the meantime, tolerate his phonogram.' His criterion for judgment here was results, not examination results, but the effect on the person that he held so dear.

In his last school, a secondary modern, eventually to become a comprehensive, Tom felt caught between a number of intractable forces — an unyielding headmaster, a subject-centred staff, the need to remain where he was for his son's sake, and later, periodic illness. He 'wasn't given enough freedom to develop, and having to justify yourself to idiots — that was very upsetting'. The whole concept of education was different — 'I wanted a lot more freedom, a lot more integration. I wanted everything we did to be meaningful.'

There were satisfactions, however, notably on the social side of his teaching, in the administration of the developing design area, and in relationships in the community at large. While at this school, he deployed the following strategies:

(1) to fight for the things he believed in. He and a colleague spearheaded a major 'complaints' exercise against the head. It achieved little, except, Tom suspects, their non-promotion. He feels he may have had more success with younger teachers, struggling to cope.

(2) to compromise, but only to seem to give way in 'smaller battles in order to win larger wars'. Similarly, to bargain, for example, to offer his services for work above the call of duty in exchange for greater freedom. Thus at one stage he opted to take over the terrors of the school, 3D.

> I became known as Mr 3D. Three-dimensional Tom. But it had one good effect. I could lay down my rules about this — 'if you don't like what I'm proposing for these children, well find somebody else' . . . I got my own way, you see. I could do what I liked . . .

(3) to seek a more conducive situation — perhaps even out of education altogether. For a time, he flirted with the notion of personnel work or the social services. He felt they 'worked in smaller units, and that you could be responsible for your own thing . . . your case load would be your own, rather than this restrictive practice I was going through day by day.' Family commitments (see later) prevented him, and his efforts, in any case, were double-edged. Asking the head weekly for a testimonial was, he thought, one form of pressure.

(4) to cultivate marginality. 'I just lived in a little island within the school, you know. I really did.' Within the art room, he could put into

practice his educational ideas, as far as the situation allowed, secure liaisons with the occasional like-minded member of staff, succour the young, inexperienced teachers, and seek to influence those with power in the school whom he felt he could relate to.

(5) to compartmentalize his self. It was another contradiction within Tom that, although a convinced integrationist with regard to the curriculum and a believer in the whole person of the pupil, he divided his own self between private and public arenas (Berger *et al.*, 1973). He increasingly reserved his 'real' self for home, and felt that his public self as teacher was comparatively unreal. After marriage, and particularly as his son grew up, Tom fell into line to stabilize his career for utilitarian purposes. The ideal Tom thus became even more displaced to the interstices of life. Most of the elements of this ideal self were intensely privatized, but this did facilitate the management of the public self.

(6) to engage in creative strategies. Tom's creativity became displaced from art and teaching to coping. It is worth considering this in a little more detail.

Creative Coping

The first example illustrates the divergent approach to the problem of how to cope with the irrepressible boredom of school turning it to personal advantage. Profiting from misfortune is the ultimate in creative acts. This is no mere 'backs to the wall' coping, or 'making the most' of adversity. Within the context of that situation, it is a victory for the self.

Tom: . . . I used to have this trouble with the fourth year forms I had 'Oh god, . . . sick of going into these places' you know, but I'd say you can enjoy it if you set about it the right way you know. You don't have to be rude, you don't have to be obstreperous, you don't have to ruin it, but you can enjoy it quietly on your own. And I'd explain that every time I had to sit on the stage I took a notepad with me and a pencil and I'd sit and sketch the backs of all the people I didn't like and give them new fronts, and do all sorts of things, but you could fill in your time, and that was the point. You could go through the motions of being there. And I did the same at staff meetings. It was just a big doddle for me, you know, and mark you you didn't miss anything, you could still join in any discussion at any time because you didn't have to keep your brain on the business in hand you know. Anything else would do, but not your brain. But this is what I tried to say to children, you know, you sometimes have to go through these situations, and instead of getting stroppy, and getting violent, take it out in some other way.

Peter: Yes, it's a lesson in how to cope.

Tom: How to cope, this is the way of life. I said have you ever studied bottoms, and in assembly what else is there to study you know, have a good look, come back and make a little analysis you know. How many people have a floppier left cheek than a right cheek. Do significant useful things with your life. Be observant, you know. Look at the backs of ears. I said Freud has a little paper on blushing, and I was fascinated reading that. I realize now that people blush all over the place. Try to discover how many people blush behind their ears. Say little things that might make them blush when there's a lull in the conversation, you know, and see where it happens. Fascinating, and this is what I used to do with my form, these were my . . . assemblies you know, telling them how to cope with assemblies when they got there. Well I don't think that's harmful you know. I think it's helpful in point of fact. I had to find a way of doing it so why shouldn't they.

Peter: I think one's whole life is learning how to cope with life with these particular contingencies. How to live in society. There's no existence outside society.

Tom: Do you ever remember a cartoon, it's the only one I've ever pinned up in my life, that I had in my office and part of the time in the last article in my hand. It came from the Courier and it was called, well the text with it was 'Conform or Else' and all these square-headed people were standing by a wall as though they were in an urinal, each with a square aperture in front of them and they were quite happy. There was one round-headed chappie who was normal and he had a square aperture and couldn't fit in, you know. I must have explained that you know a hundred thousand times to children, and yet it's the most important lesson in the world isn't it, you know.

In similar vein, in the next example, Tom neutralizes the hierarchy in the school, whom he feels are becoming authoritarian and losing sight of what teaching and schools are for. It is not the most obvious thing to do, which is to complain, or oppose. He knows from experience and observation that that will not succeed. So he has to invent something else that will both *seem* to meet what is required of him, yet preserve his sense of self and constitute what he perceives as a legitimate lesson for the pupils.

Tom: I think you can achieve more by doing a *Not the 9 o'clock News* act on it. Show how stupid it is. It's much more damaging than trying to make a big issue of the event. I don't think it's worthy of a big issue nine times out of ten. This is a project of a stupid petty mind as a rule. But I, well I found most of the orders I was getting were of that ilk, you know. So I'd show it as such, laugh at it, and to some degree destroy it instantly. You might go through the motions — I mean if it was said that you must march your troops around the playground, you know, all my analogies are getting mixed up, at 10 each morning, well, OK I can't dispute this, I am here to work. I am being paid for doing this; I am being paid for carrying out orders, you know, but you could all walk around on one leg or something, or raise your hand in the air and shout 'Hi-di-hi', it doesn't matter what you do, but you can conform with the order and make it appear ridiculous at the same time. And that seems a better way of knocking it than having a big issue outside the head's office.

Peter: Does it enable the individuals to rise above the bureaucracy, is that what you are saying?

Tom: I think so. I think you've got to show how petty the whole system is, you know.

Peter: It enables you to distance yourself from the bureaucracy?

Tom: Yes, and it's more effective actually, because there's nothing hurts a head more than to see his orders being carried out so that he can't really get at you, and yet know that you are cocking a snook, and making him look a fool in public, and that's great, I love that, that's superb, you know.

Tom clearly thrives on the incongruities of humour, one of the most useful aids in teaching (Walker and Goodson, 1977; Stebbins, 1980; Woods, 1983).

The following shows Tom's intuitive sociological imagination. It enables him to turn potential disasters to his advantage. 'Critical incidents' (Sikes *et al.*, 1985) require uncommon solutions. Teachers are always being 'tested'. It is tempting to suggest that in order to survive they must provide 'the right answer'. But of course there is no 'right' answer, that is not in the nature of such tests. The better the test, the more unanswerable it appears. How is he or she going to get out of this one? One's credibility as a teacher, one's future career can depend on the reaction to a single instance. In this example we see Goffmanesque theatricals, role-management, a recognition of group dynamics and power, the importance of status, a concern for justice, the ability to take the role of the other, what appears to be an instinctive (but which is almost certainly learned over a lifetime's experiences) recognition that the way out of a tricky situation lay in the incongruities permitted by some form of humour. I include some of the ensuing discussion as an illustration of how teacher and sociologist seek for common ground in interpreting the incidents:

> Once, with a particularly difficult group, Tom arranged to puncture the formality of the teaching act by deliberately pressing too hard on one of the old 'stand–up easel type blackboards' so that it would collapse. Unfortunately, it collapsed on his foot and head, which was not intended. 'My God, I created my point alright, and the kids were on the floor, they were ecstatic. It was the best thing that had ever happened! They loved it'. Now ... I pushed my luck a bit too far and I was the victim. Isn't this what humour is really about? They want a victim, don't they? From that point onwards I realized that if I could be the victim occasionally I was adding to this sort of glow, this feeling we all had, and, I'm terrible about remembering incidents because to me life is just a long ripple, you know, I remember once getting on my knees to apologize to Ruston.

He then described how he had censured Ruston (in another difficult class) for a certain incident, and how 'half a dozen came up to me at the end of the lesson and said "you've made a mistake this time, it wasn't Jimmy, you've got the wrong one". So I said "you are not kidding me, are you, you're quite sure?" He then said he had better apologize. After registration, they were all waiting for his apology 'so I thought I might as well score for making my apology so I did it most dramatically. I got on my knees, and I crawled towards him, and I apologized in a way no Ruston had ever been apologized to before'. I embarrassed the boy so much, he didn't know what to make of it. But the point is I retained face with the children in that I admitted I was wrong etc, and I'd taken their word for it ...

PW: And it also shows that you are able to turn the joke on yourself ...

Tom: I think so, and I think this is very important. I find most of the jokes I tell to this day are against myself ...

PW: It suggests to me that they would see you as one of them. They came to you and told you this and you trusted what they said.

Tom: And I don't think this is a case of courting cheap familiarity or whatever.

PW: The actual kneeling is going from one extreme — here you are the teacher ...

Tom: Mark you, at my height, it is very difficult to say this! (Tom was short in stature.)

PW: No, but in the role of the teacher . . .

Tom: . . . the role of the teacher, yes . . .

PW: You are far superior to them, and you make a mockery of this by going down on your knees and shuffling towards them. But that perhaps enabled you to make the apology?

Tom: I might have found it more difficult to be very formal . . . etc. etc.

All of these examples meet the criteria of creativity discussed in Chapter 1. There is innovation, Tom finding unique solutions to the problems in question. He is the author and perpetrator of it, and controls the processes involved. It is attuned to the pupils and situation in question, and yields results. In each of the examples, Tom intends things to happen in that way. He does not lay plans to the last detail, but rather reacts with the germ of an idea, deriving from his knowledge, experience and values, to the contingency as it arises. The idea then gathers pace of its own, and becomes validated in practice.

Derivations of the Self: Micro

So far, I have considered aspects of Tom's self, and their relationship to his views of teaching and of the curriculum. From whence did this self derive?

Home and Parents

For Tom, his home life, particularly during his adolescent years, was by far the greatest influence. The major aspects were:

(a) *The general ambience* — critical, enquiring, down–to–earth factual, religious (Catholic) but undogmatic. His home was a meeting place for young people in the town, and he spent many evenings during his teens witnessing and joining in discussions and arguments about matters of current concern. Tom says, 'They had a big influence over me . . . I got the impression that I was just a piece of putty floating through this world.' His home became a kind of club for the young people who came to the town — mainly young teachers from the high school, grammar school and convent. (Religion was a unifying feature here, for the area was predominantly Calvinist, and Catholics 'stuck together'.) You didn't stay in a place like that long, so there was a considerable turnover, always young people with their specialities in literature, Greek, Latin, politics and so forth. But they weren't all teachers. He could remember a doctor, a dentist, a lawyer, and a manager of the local gas works coming round. So between the ages of 11 and 14, he 'sat on the fringes of life', when they discussed politics, religion, philosophy, psychology and so on. Occasionally, when he asked a question, he would get drawn in, and they would give him books to read.

In general, Tom liked everybody he met during his childhood. 'They were lovely people because they were straight... Nobody told you lies ... they were dead straight.' In this, too, lay the kernel of a later belief that the medium was more important than the message. He had witnessed so many debates and arguments, he could see all points of view, and agree with all. More important to him was 'the quality of the delivery [which] almost overcomes the message underneath. I love a good argument [like his father], presentation of an argument, I get so enthralled by the way it's presented, I wonder sometimes if I've missed the essence.'

(b) *Father* — possible Tom's strongest influence. '... the more I thought about my father, the more I got to understand him since he died, believe it or not, because I am so similar... Everything I do I see my father in me, you know ... I *am* my father, and I do mean that.'

Tom was the eldest child in a family of six, he had his father's name, he was the one 'carrying on his family'. This was why, he thinks, his father wanted him to know everything he knew. So he taught him many practical skills, but also socialized him into a mode of thinking while he was doing it. The one thing he does remember, very positively, was '... never, never accept anything — question, question, question! Always ask why ...'

> He loved an argument, not just for opposition's sake, but for the quality of argument. He would say, for example, 'We've got to get this damn priest of yours over here one night. I can't get any sense out of you people. There's got to be a better argument than this, you know.'

'And he loved it when these priests came, especially the old one, because he would argue and argue and argue. He just loved arguing, and we grew up in this atmosphere. Dad's at it again, just listen to him!'.

Like Tom, his father was a survivor. A civil engineer, he can never remember his father doing any engineering. Tom's teenage years were during the depression of the 1930s, and his father put his hand to all manner of jobs to keep the family supplied, and to use what talent he'd got for his own personal ends . . . making things for the house, etc. Even so, if he set his mind on something he would achieve it, even as a boy. Tom had a massive confidence in his father's ability to manipulate what were basically unfavourable situations. The classic example of this, perhaps, was his conversion to Catholicism (from atheism) shortly before his death.

There are many minor examples of this optimistic approach to life. All things were possible to his father. As a boy, Tom was 'the most nervous, shy, introverted thing' who perpetually thought himself 'not good enough'. But his father gave him confidence and a defence. He said 'you are better than most around you. There are plenty better than you, but on average, you are above most of them. What you've got to develop is a "brass neck" attitude to this world. Walk into a room and say of course I can do it. That's the attitude in life.' 'Now I remember that, and very distinctly I can remember the room, the occasion, all about it, and that stuck with me.' He was a 'dour, taciturn Scot . . . but always there, as a rock. He had become essentially a "private" man, for he did a hundred jobs, and none of them really possibly matched up to what he was capable of doing. So to overcome his frustration, he worked at home using what talent he'd got for his own personal ends . . . making things for the house, etc.'

Tom already appreciated the distinction between private and public. The 'critical' outlook engendered at home was not suited to school, where they preferred unquestioning obedience. His nonconformity was already well in evidence, and in the latter days he played truant for about two-and-a-half days a week. 'Being a devious little kid I got away with it for a year. I was awfully clever! . . . it's escapism.'

Arguments with teachers led to his giving up at an early stage two of his favourite subjects — maths and art. But his home was his own 'personal university'. They coached him, for example, through the School Certificate after years of non-achievement at school. Also, his father encouraged him, by, for example, taking his drawings to show his friends. One of these friends advised Tom to go in for teaching — that or architecture. In fact, Tom got a place at art college in Edinburgh, but it was too far and too costly to take up. His father got him offers of jobs, one with a petrol company, one in an architect's office, but he chose to go into the army, basically to get away from home. He loved his childhood, but now he wanted independence. But going into the army he regards as a romantic act. He didn't want to be a 'soldier' — that was not the intention.

(c) *Mother.* Tom's mother was the focal point of the family, a clever woman who had wanted to be a teacher, but her family could not afford to sustain her, and she was headed off by marriage. She provided the intellectual drive and climate for the family, and sought to compensate for her frustrations through her children. She was thus always drawing Tom's attention to the benefits and virtues of teaching as a profession. 'I think it's a great profession. I think teaching is a wonderful thing. To be able to pass things on to children ... to learn and understand, themselves, you know.' But more important than this direct lesson, perhaps, was the climate that she created in the home, the people she invited there, the intellectual soirées that she hosted.

She was a 'garrulous, lovely' woman, Irish by birth, whose ancestors were 'all pure Irish, and extreme romantics.... Nothing practical in their world at all.' In this, she contrasted with his father's side, one of dour, almost obstinate practicality. It was her religion that held in the home, but it was a 'very liberal sort of religious house. They were total believers ... but they were free. Most of the people coming into our house, a lot of these youngsters, were agnostics, well, you name it, they were it.'

Tom's parents had faith in their children. They were never shocked by anything he did. And they never took anything for granted. 'Mother would never hear people knocked. She always felt that there could be a reason that we just couldn't know about, and might never know about... Nothing was odd to her really.'

(d) *Grandparents.* Tom feels his mother's Irish parents were a significant influence upon him. He remembers in particular the wild romanticism of his grandfather's stories and his grandmother's generosity, not only to him, but to all comers; also, his grandfather's strong sense of independence, and rejection of any normal career.

> ... He had it made. He retired when he was thirty odd. He didn't like the idea of this bloody work and he just thought it pure farce being used by other people, and he retired. I don't know how he lived, because he didn't draw anything from the government.... But he had talents, and he used them. He used to mend clocks. He didn't get worried about it, it didn't seem important to him.

Tom was also impressed by the degree to which he had his life organized in a series of routines governed by the pub's opening hours.

Running through these accounts are all those aspects of Tom's later self that were to find expression in his teaching — a strong sense of individuality, of critical awareness, of coping almost triumphantly in the face of adversity, of marginality, almost brinkmanship, of freedom, and of love of, and respect for, people.

Books, Literature, Art

Tom has been an avid reader all his life. He remembers in particular, in his early days, a book on the miners' strike of the 1920s, which converted him to socialism (the 'official' politics of the family, represented by his mother, was liberalism). When he read *And Quiet Flows the Don*, he wrote to the Russian Embassy to find out more about Russia and was inundated with communist propaganda.

Later in life, of particular note was his encounter with the writings of Neill — during the war, in fact, before his teaching career had begun. Neill's ideas became the cornerstone of Tom's philosophy about teaching, unsurprisingly, for all the features of his earlier socialization are there — the emphasis on democracy, equality, independence, freedom, open discussion and debate, 'straightness', mutual caring, growth and learning from within. Neill convincingly tied all these ideals to education at a time when Tom was becoming interested in instructing in the Signals Corps.

Teachers, Coaches

In general, teachers at school, he recalls, were more of negative than positive influence, cooling him out of maths and art, and being hidebound by rules and routines, which to him were anathema. One example of this he recalls from his infant days concerned a woman teacher who enthused over a sketch of a cat he had made, and fetched the head to see it. While they were away, Tom noticed he had omitted an important detail — the 'belly button' — so he put it in. On her return, with the head, she flew into a temper and boxed his ears:

> 'You naughty boy, you wicked boy, and I've just brought the headmaster here to see this.' And I can still see his face when he looked at it, as much as to say, Oh God, you know, what's the boy done wrong, but he couldn't say it to her or to us, you know, and honestly that was about the first time I'd got the sort of understanding of dealing with awkward people. You could never be right. And also, that adults didn't necessarily back each other up, except on the surface.

He has often drawn on the moral of this memory in his own teaching of art to children. He would never disparage anything. Anything that somebody produced must have value in it. He remembered once when he was sorting through some pupil folders to decide which to keep and which discard, he recalled that incident when 'that good work had been missed by one mark, which wasn't interpreted artistically but biologically', and wondered who was he to judge. 'Half the stuff in the bin may be more valuable to those children than this other work.'

The immediate result of that kind of teacher attitude was the privatization of those areas of the curriculum most dear to him. His art teacher 'made a snide comment to him about religion... It was an effort to put me down without the right of reply... "Shut up, get out" sort of thing. So I just stopped doing art in school. I attended all lessons, but I never painted any more. I did it all at home, ...' where, needless to say, he was duly encouraged by his father, and his father's friends, among whom there was one in particular with strong artistic leanings and connections.

It is no curiosity, then, that Tom should come to believe that art cannot be taught. Later, 'when I went to college, I deliberately didn't take art. I thought I could deal with that on my own. This is personal development as far as I am concerned. I can read, I can look and ... do it myself, and I went into fields which I thought would be more difficult.'

But he admired the headmaster of the grammar school. He had to cane Tom every Friday because of his habitual transgression of the rules, and it went on so long they developed a strange relationship over the business, the head executing his duty with an understanding and bonhomie that Tom much admired. As with his father, it seems this man practised role distance to good effect. Tom was always impressed with that ability in people, and was to use it himself to good effect in his own teaching.

Side-Bets (Becker, 1960)

Tom married during the war. This immediately influenced where he went after the war and to some degree what he did — to England (Lincolnshire), instead of India where he really wanted to go (his wife did not wish to go to India). On demob, he took up teaching. He says that the first thing he wanted was to get back into the swing of painting again, and

> had I not been married I most certainly wouldn't have taught, because I realized that if you are going to be a full-time teacher, dedicated to his job, you couldn't possibly be an artist as well ... it's time consuming, body consuming, mind consuming. So I think I knew then that in a sense I was giving up art for teaching.... If you are

in education, you have to use your art for other people, and help them along the road, and while you are doing that, you are not developing yourself. . . . And I don't think you can even be a good artist and be married and lead a normal happy married life. That's ridiculous. You've got to be a bit more selfish.

Later in his career, his options within teaching were profoundly affected by family considerations. For example, he certainly would have left his final school because of frustration through the policy of a new headmaster, but for his wife and son, whose education and subsequent career he now put first.

When A was about 13 he used to get petrified when he saw me looking through the back pages of the *Times Ed*. He knew by then this was a danger signal, a man looking for a job somewhere, and he was a very nervous boy, and it had taken him a long time to settle in his school. He was worried sick he'd have to leave his friends and start all over again. It was about that time I thought, well what's the point, I'm not ambitious really. . . . I was as happy here as I would be anywhere. . . .

Here we see Tom surrendering some of his interests as artist and as teacher in return for satisfactions as husband and father.

Derivations of the Self: Macro

Throughout his career, certain structural and macro-considerations appear influential in the formation of the self, notably the following.

Social Class

Tom himself disputes his 'middleclassness'. It is never a term he has used in connection with himself, because he considers he 'came from working-class antecedents . . . We all had to work. Of course we had to do jobs that were very menial.' His father may have been a 'cut above, if you like, the average man in the street, in theory, but in practice he was having to do what they did.' His ancestry was rural — farming figures prominently as far as Tom could remember, his father being the first one to break out of the rural mould and go into a more industrial type of work.

What distinguished Tom's parents from most others in the town was their education, and their aspirations. They could be considered members of the 'service' class. As used by Halsey *et al.* (1980), this consists of those 'exercising power and expertise on behalf of corporate "authorities", plus such elements of the classic bourgeoisie, independent businessmen, and "free" professionals, as are not yet assimilated into this new formation' (Goldthorpe and Llewellyn, 1977, p. 259). His father had been educated and trained to the position of the professional, working on behalf of civil authorities. His mother had been a brilliant pupil at school in Perthshire, had won a County Scholarship, studied as a pupil-teacher, but then the family had moved to the Borders, where there was no transfer of scholarships, and so her aspirations to be a teacher were thwarted. However, she never lost the interest. Tom recalls doing some research for her on the history of the Labour Party shortly before she died, because she wanted to talk to someone's group about it. 'She wanted to tell other people . . . she was trying to keep her intelligence on the boil all the time.'

So, although the actual positions were lacking, the reality of a 'service class' home was there. This applied to material things as well as to status and prestige:

> We were, in a sense, better than others, though I don't like saying these things. We had our own house for one thing, and we lived well, you know, what I mean by everybody else's standards we lived well. By their standards we were bloody well off. We had fruit when nobody else ate fruit. They had bread and dripping, you know, when we had fish, steak, and all the rest. We were well off.

Tom thus had the material advantages of such a home, and the motivational example and desire to become more firmly established in a professional occupation. But none of his family was class conscious. Tom prefers to think of himself as 'classless', and feels more affinity for the working class than any other. Objectively, of course, by virtue of his occupation, he would be classified as middle or 'service' class, firmly settling in to a niche offered but then not opened to either of his parents. He has consolidated the position aspired to by his parents. And the intellectual progression from his parents led him from a very early age into socialism. But it is one tempered with the cult of the individual. There are shades, here, of his mother's brand of liberalism, but more potently, I would suggest the influence of significant others who, in a sense, seemed to stand outside and defy society, living on their own wits and their own terms. His father and grandfather are the two outstanding examples of this. This 'marginality' has become Tom's own style.

Religion

As a member of a Catholic family in a predominantly non-Catholic area.

Tom was conscious of the fact that he was different. 'Very conscious of that, and I remember asking about it, questioning it, why *should* . . . and maybe to some degree that's the trigger to my questioning so much, you know.'

Religion was more clearly an integrator and differentiator than social class. They were in different primary schools for a start, and there was great antagonism between the Roman Catholic school and the rest, 'to a degree that one chose one's time to go along a certain road, or one was prepared for attack'. At the grammar school he was fairly well accepted by the children, though he was conscious of being different from the vast majority of them. But he remembers lots of problems with staff. 'It was always the subtlety . . . in history in particular, and I insisted on going to the lessons which I didn't have to [as a Catholic] because it seemed to me to be important to know what the others were talking about, and I didn't want to be outside it. . . I found most of the teachers couldn't resist the snide comments at my expense.' There was, he says, a partisan business going on in the area at the time, 'rather like the Northern Ireland thing today, in a minor key.' Even then, he says, he could identify it as that, he knew it wasn't him personally they were getting at. Again, he felt he could rise above it as an individual, being '. . . bloody devious and twisted and odd, and I think even then I could use what little knowledge and intelligence I had to escape from most of these situations. And humour, I realized early, was the best "let-off".'

There were many doctrines of the church he could not accept. He remembers being worried about the church's teaching on matters like birth control, transubstantiation, purgatory. He was always questioning. Nonetheless, he came to believe that every person should have a belief, 'no matter whether it's Catholicism, Communism, or whatever. I don't think we're big enough on our own to stand on our own feet, mentally or emotionally. We feel the need for something to support us.' This is the basis of his respect for other people's beliefs. Tom was captivated by the romance, beauty and communality of Catholicism:

> What other Church went in for such colourful displays, you know, everything was beautiful . . . and the Latin, and the Vestments. The fact that there was historical significance to it all . . . and equally important, the word Catholic, universal . . . it was the universality of it I think that intrigued me . . . that, and the sheer romance. . . .
> The church itself was the best little museum in town.

In short, Tom's association with Catholicism sharpened his appreciation of beauty, taught him the values of belief and tolerance, and the virtues of sociation, and provided substance for the exercise of his critical judgment. Where, on occasions, religion acted as a constraint, he sought a new situation where he would be free from it. For example, at one stage in his career he returned to his home town to take up a post in the Catholic school. While many aspects of this were delightful, renewing friendships, dealing with parents who were actually contemporaries of his when he was a schoolchild in the town, and generally enjoying the community relations he values so greatly, he found the religion there oppressive. It dominated the school day. His efforts to liven up the teaching of it were frowned upon. Who was he to set himself up as a radical innovator against centuries of development in the church?

> Needless to say I did it my way, I didn't do it the formal way which would be chattering out the questions and the answers... I did it my way which I thought was more interesting and more humorous, with cartoon strips and the like... I was severely castigated for this ... people don't make inroads into my life like that, not my teaching life you know. I organized my teaching and if they didn't like it, they could say so.

Also, to carry on teaching there, he would have to have the 'Bishop's certificate', but had the bishop any qualifications in teaching? That again illustrates how religion predominated over teaching within the school. It choked his personal style, and was one of the main reasons for his leaving the school after a stay of only two to three years. The other major reason was the headmaster who had been appointed on the strength of his religious rather than teaching qualifications. 'I got more and more frustrated. I had done about all I could do. I needed more freedom ...'

Social, Political and Economic Climate

Tom's career runs parallel with four distinct phases:

> pre-war: marked by the economic crisis of the thirties, and mounting international tension;
> the war of 1939–45;
> post-war: optimism, but economic scarcity; 'secondary education for all; 1960s affluence, and later, comprehensive education.

I select just one of these here — the war — to illustrate the impact on self. The army 'was an important part of my life. If that little bit in my adolescence was an introductory course, this was a postgraduate degree I took in the army. It was a very maturing process.' He has had 'a very enclosed life, like a monastery in a way' and the army got him away from home and stood him on his own feet, where he was able to put into practice his father's precepts. He learnt a trade in the Signals, and quickly learnt that you could get money by educational advancement. This induced him to 'improve', and soon he was training new recruits, most much older than himself. He went with them, with the BEF (British Expeditionary Force) to France, and was driven out with them at Dunkirk. After the BEF it was 'a piece of cake', lots more training and courses.

Again Tom adapts, and not only survives, but enjoys — the horrors of the war apart (such as the relief of two concentration camps in 1945). It gave him what he wanted — 'a place of his own' as head of a small workshop unit. Here he had his first real experience of teaching, savoured the satisfaction of getting across difficult concepts, saw the point himself of much discussion, such as that on the gestalt theory, that had taken place at his mother's soirées. There was experiment and research on things like radios for tanks, in an atmosphere at that time of continual urgency and excitement. As for the horrors of the war, they are burned into his mind, not only the excesses of the enemy but also of troops on his own side, and by the end of the war he was a total pacifist. The best of his army experiences were in India and Japan, countries and people that he learned to love, though initial expectations from propaganda had led him to expect otherwise. He was fascinated by the religions, which were not inhibiting but encouraged a certain way of life; and found them both 'totally amenable people', who accepted you for what you were. These experiences helped him to understand other people, not to pre-judge. His teaching activities also expanded, becoming in charge of the army bureau of current affairs. His 'deviousness' ('it was my middle name') developed apace, advancing the interests of his unit. 'I must have been an awful little bastard but I was out to get what I wanted.' In India, too, he came across many marvellous books, including some by Neill. For the first time he realized how important it was 'to belong to and be living with, and be totally part of the community which one was trying to have an impact on.' Above all, the army injected a strong note of realism and practicality. Old soldiers, later, were not going to be 'pushed around' or take kindly to 'airy fairy' ideas. The army also made him supremely adaptable. 'Thanks to the army, moving around, I've never had any problems settling in. I could settle into a pig-sty tomorrow and be happier than the pigs.'

Thus the army made Tom independent, reinforced in practical terms the values he had learnt theoretically at home, expanded his horizons, giving him a rich experience of the world on which his future career could be based, gave him experience of teaching, and sharpened certain aspects of his personality, such as his critical stance and his 'deviousness'. It also meant that he went into teaching as a mature student 'who wasn't going to be pushed around any more'. When he went to training college three years after demob, he and others like him reacted strongly to expectations of conformity. At one of their first meetings with the Principal, they told him 'please understand we've had our ration of this [being pushed around]. We are reasonable human beings, we want to create a life for ourselves, we want to be trained, but we are not boys who have just come from school . . . we had been forced to conform too long . . . ' In commenting on his creative coping strategies illustrated earlier, and how he managed the 'system', Tom referred to his army experiences:

> I went through the motions and I carried out my orders, sort of thing, but at the same time you take the sting out of the whole. You see, I found in the army exactly the same. I had to do this over and over again. They would have been incensed the fellows I had under me if I'd carried this out in a militaristic fashion. I'm talking about Signals, and the people I dealt with were largely teachers who had never taught, you know, they were straight out of college and people like this. They were there under duress. They were there to use their brains for the benefit of the war effort, you know, and the last thing they wanted was this sort of nonsense, and I felt the same. I think somehow you've got to take the heat out of the situation, and that's really what it's about I think, and if you can do it with a little bit of humour I don't know of a better way of doing it, put it like that, you know, than to be humorous.

Mediating Factors

Between the broad, general developments and structures and the everyday detail of the classroom lie a number of mediatory factors, which may hold keys to personal fulfilment. For Tom, three were of special significance:

(1) the position, role and person of the headteacher;
(2) the reference group; and
(3) the subject.

The Headteacher

The negative repercussions for staff of the decisions and actions of the headteacher as 'critical reality definer' have been vividly portrayed by Riseborough (1981). But there is still considerable room for individual manoeuvre.

During Tom's career as teacher, he served under five headmasters. Two were 'admirable', showing an openness of mind and spirit, a good intelligence, and a dedication to teaching which matched Tom's own aspirations. He was still not allowed free rein. Under the first (at his second primary school), he was still learning the *craft* of teaching. Under the second (at the all-age school in the Midlands), he began well, but after a while became sickened with the 'iron discipline', where 'the kids were flogged for nothing'. He could take the daily inspections of staff, but not the military discipline the pupils were subjected to — he 'had been through all this nonsense in the army'. He was on quite good terms with the head, and one night, after a number of drinks, voiced his objections. There followed an uncomfortable period, during which the head checked the books in Tom's room and raised objections about 'every other one', and an eventual amicable agreement which resulted in compromise on both sides.

> So he made his amends and then well, what he really came up with then was all the worries he had from the beginning when he gave me permission to start this thing [for Tom to do it 'his way']. That's what worried him. He maybe thought he'd given me too much freedom. How could he justify some of the things I was doing when an inspector came around?

But Tom admired this man. 'I take my hat off to that old boy. He worked the kids hard, he was an absolute tyrant, but they had everything when they left, because they'd been stretched. He did a good job within his own lights.'

But if he showed Tom the value of discipline and system, Tom also felt that *he* had an effect on the head, making him 'a little more free, letting him see that he didn't have to go along these narrow routes, that you could have a lot of fun and freedom and get just as far if not further.' In fact, this head did not get the top post at the new secondary modern when it was built, because he 'had become very stroppy and fell out with the authority . . mostly because he demanded so many things for that school.' He took up a post with another authority, where he began with a 'six-month terror campaign clearing out the dead-wood teachers left over from the previous all-age school', a policy Tom thought 'pretty rotten, but in a way, I think, right'.

This headmaster illustrates for Tom the best form of adaptation to the mediatory role. Though a person of very strong views and commitment, who would not brook failure, weakness or idleness, he showed a degree of flexibility which allowed Tom's basically diametrically opposing libertarian style some scope — within reason. If Tom exceeded his bounds, the head would complain, but reasonably, and as a colleague, not as a superior authority. In this way, they gained a sense of 'common cause' though their methods vastly differed.

Not so with Tom's final headmaster. Under him, according to Tom, the school, though a 'new concept in education' at the time, became organized on very rigid and traditional lines, with a heavy emphasis on external appearance, and a sacrifice of more power than was necessary to external agencies. The chances for partial autonomy and individual expression, especially of the kind Tom favoured, were therefore lost, with the result that Tom in his final years as a teacher became more marginalized.

Reference Group

Modelling himself on his parents, grandparents and the coterie of intellectuals who frequented his home when he was a child, Tom became a kind of 'conditioned free-thinker'. In later life the sort of people he related to were firstly those like his early headmasters who taught him the discipline of coping, but chiefly people most like himself — liberal free-thinkers in constraining positions of authority, skilled in the practice of role-distancing. They included, in his later years, a canon, chairman of the school governors, who showed the same breadth of view as the canon of Tom's younger days, an educational adviser, previously a close, like-minded colleague in the last beleaguered situation, and the deputy head in the school, who shared many of Tom's educational ideals.

Throughout his life, Tom, a marginal man, picked out other marginals to relate to in society. At the end of his career, destitute of such companionship on an equal basis, he appeared to occupy the role of mentor or counsellor to other marginals in the school, either those young teachers not yet firmly established, or older teachers, who, for one reason or another, were having difficulties. At slightly more distance, Tom related to the local community of art teachers. He helped form an art teacher's group in the county, and 'this was a great help when we came to set up the secondary moderns you know, because we knew each other, we could share experiences, and could discuss courses and things like that'.

Above all, perhaps, as genuine child-centredness would demand, Tom took his main cue from the pupils and their parents. In all the vagaries and uncertainties, they were the one constant. To Tom, 'they are the only known factor'. When he went back to his home town 'every parent I met was my peer, and my relationships with people were great. We'd been to school together . . . And I loved the kids, because I've got a great feeling for these under-privileged country kids, you know. They're tough, hellishly tough, but by God they're good, they're great and I loved them!' In his final years of teaching, the pupils past (as, now, parents) and present, were his major referent.

Subject

Tom had to systematize his teaching and discipline pupils for O-level and CSE, and, at times, serve another function in 'public display'. He felt cramped by the non-integrated curriculum, but there were opportunities for creativity and freedom along the lines he desired. The external reference group of art teachers helped in strengthening this particular bridge. There were also links with galleries and artists, with other schools, and with the Art College, and the activities that involved him in attending or giving talks and lectures to local bodies, to primary schools, and in holding exhibitions.

However, Tom's prime evaluation of himself as a teacher relates not to art as such, nor to pupils formally assigned to him, but to 'spontaneous interaction', where pupils (many of whom he may not have taught) sought him out 'just to talk'. The 'Art Club' was highly informal, and markedly outside the official curriculum. Pupils came in the evenings, in very casual clothes, they made coffee, talked, had background music; they were self-motivated, governed by their own rules; they could just 'talk' if they wished, or, when they chose to apply themselves to tasks, pursue an 'integrated' curriculum.

So instead of using our art club just for painting, we used to do a bit of research into the county's history — the Mechanics' Institute, and things like that. We put on an exhibition in working-class history in the county.

Tom's whole approach is epitomized by his first ever 'O' level candidate, who had to be fitted into other classes, because he was the only one. He got a grade 1, but for Tom that was not important.

What was important was that in the odd moments in between dealing with all the other children in there, one could talk to him. I remember introducing him to T.S. Eliot. The boy got fascinated by poetry through Eliot, and his pictures improved, because he started to see visions, if you like, in poetry and literature. He's a policeman now, but he hasn't lost his love of poetry and art. Now that to me is success — it's got nothing to do with the 'O' level he got . . . I made a total friend of that boy.

These activities, as Tom noted himself, are remarkably similar to the family soirées of his youth, which he recalls as his most educational experiences as learner, and which he now as teacher sought to perpetuate in as many ways as he could in and around the formal curriculum.

Conclusion

The case of Tom shows that a teacher's self, in part at least, both finds expression in, and gives expression to a curriculum area. The dialectic involves persistent and complex strategies, trade-offs, gains and losses. Tom, for example, finds a disjuncture between his professional and personal development, with his real self ensconced in the latter, but with great satisfactions as well as disappointments in each. His successes as a teacher, though very gratifying to him, were made at a considerable sacrifice, he feels, to his own creativity. Nor is it retrievable. Tom has given his best years to teaching and feels his own creative edge has been blunted. 'Tom the artist' remains an unknown, untried character of another life. But he takes comfort in the facts of his involvement in teaching.

We have seen that the quality and extent of that involvement depended on the conjunction of a number of coordinates. 'Self' coordinates are rooted in Tom's personal history. These are the values, beliefs and dispositions to do with such things as creativity, expressivity, romanticism, love of beauty, freedom, individuality, sociability, independence, questioning, a critical attitude, holism. Then, there are 'subject' coordinates, which permit the integration of those of the self. In the case of art, obviously the subject matter and activity speak to the self coordinates at the beginning of the list. Otherwise, its comparatively low status within the curriculum as a whole, as well as its professed need for creative 'space', means that there is less restraint and less pressure than there is on some mainstream subjects, and hence more room for the individual. As far as Tom is concerned, it is integrational and holistic in its approach to people; yet separatist and interstitial within the overall curriculum of the school. It has distinct social and community aspects which emphasize relationships; and it allows scope for creating the kind of environment and atmosphere the teacher wishes. Of all subjects, art arguably offers more opportunity for achieving the ideals of Neill, Rousseau and Dewey than other subjects within the modern curriculum.

There are institutional coordinates, such as nature and power of the headteacher, teacher culture and sub-cultures and school ethos. There are also macro-considerations to do with socioeconomic and political events and trends, and structural factors, such as social class. There are 'private life' coordinates, deriving from family and leisure interests and commitments. At different times and in different places all these coordinates come together in different ways, presenting the individual with a mixture of opportunities and difficulties in varying proportions. I have attempted to show how one teacher steered a personal course through various conjunctions of these factors, trying to ensure the predominance of the 'self' coordinates, and how the strategies employed in this task themselves have roots deep in his past.

Viewed in this way, a curriculum area is a vibrant, human process lived out in the rough and tumble, give and take, joys and despairs, plots and counter-plots of a teacher's life. It is not simply a body of knowledge or set of skills; nor simply a result of group activity (Goodson, 1983). Tom's case shows that, to some extent at least, individuals can and do chart their own courses, and can engage with the curriculum at a deep personal level. For a full appreciation of this I have argued that we need to take a whole life perspective. Our data have suggested how the formulation of self in the early years may relate to later teaching and handling of a subject area, and the part played in the formulation of that self by such factors as home environment, parents, teachers, marriage and socioeconomic and political factors. We need to give more consideration to this whole life perspective, within which individuals personally engage with the process of a subject area if we are to do the study of the curriculum — and the people involved in it — full justice.

Chapter 7

Stress and the Teacher Role

High risk of stress appears to be an inherent feature of the teacher's job. It is hardly surprising, given its nature. Waller (1932) has described teaching as being basically conflictual; Berlak and Berlak (1981) as dilemma-ridden; and Hargreaves (1988) as constrained by factors beyond an individual teacher's control. There are also tortuous problems connected with the teachers role, that is the position a teacher occupies in a school and the expectations that people (including the teacher) have of what should or should not be done in it. There was at one time quite a trend in studies of teachers and role conflict (for example, Grace, 1972). It might be fruitful to reconsider this in the light of the prevailing interest in teacher stress, and of recent and current developments in education. 'Stress', of course, is a psychological state; but it is precipitated largely, I would argue, by social factors.

A Model of Stress

Kyriacou (1987) has suggested that 'stress' is 'the experience by a teacher of unpleasant emotions, such as tension, frustration, anxiety, anger and depression, resulting from aspects of work as a teacher' (p. 146). There are times, however, when tension, anxiety, even anger can be quite productive, and frustration is part of the cost of living in society. At the very least, we must say that these are no ordinary tensions and anxieties such as would go with our own perceptions of the role. Teachers experiencing stress are ones driven to the limits of their personal resources, where they hover on the brink of breakdown.

If this is the psychological product, the immediate cause in many cases, as I see it, is a disjuncture or maladjustment of two or more factors that normally might be expected to work in harmony. It is not just pressures, therefore, which some may need in order to function; nor problems, which are a necessary part of a professional's job. An alternative view is of the 'ordinary' course of events as one exhibiting a dominant climate of harmony among a number of key variables, such as teacher and pupil interests; government, local, and school policy; school climate; the demands made on teachers, the resources to meet them, and the rewards to be gained from meeting them; and so on. Resolution of the conflicts and dilemmas that are an essential feature of the job is an accepted part of the teacher's professionalism, as outlined in Chapter 2. A potentially stressful situation is set up when a teacher's personal interests, commitment or resources not only gets out of line with one or more of the other factors, but actually pulls against it. The classic case is having too much work, plus a strong moral imperative to do it, and not enough time and energy within which to do it. A variant on this basic theme is being pressed to do more work, given fewer resources with which to do it, and then receiving no reward or recognition when it is nonetheless accomplished. An everyday stress point many teachers face is losing at the last minute a restorative, recharging, idyllic free period and being asked to stand in for an absent colleague with a difficult class. In all of these instances there are elements grating against each other, which compounds the blow to the teacher's sense of well-being. One-off occurrences are to be expected and are probably comparatively easily dealt with. These might serve a useful purpose such as highlighting normal procedures, reminding everybody of the ground-rules, or being therapeutic to those involved. Where, on the other hand, there is a degree of permanence behind the underlying causes that produce these fractures, then I would suggest the drain on the teacher's personal resources exceeds their recharge and he/she becomes, gradually perhaps, over time worn down.

Such a model of stress has strong affinities with role conflict. Take, for example, the kind of role conflict arising from conflicting demands from different people. Headteachers are in a highly vulnerable position in this respect. During the troubles of the mid 1980s, for example, they were charged with keeping their schools running by central government, LEAs and parents, yet confronted by the teacher 'action'. A similar situation arose in the 1960s in a battle over who should do 'dinner duties'. In these power struggles between government, employers and teachers, headteachers have frequently been placed in an impossible position. But to some degree this goes with the job. Standing at the intersection of the school and the outside world, and at the centre of a role-set distinctive for conflicting expectations they have to be dexterous diplomatists with almost superhuman powers if they are to survive *and* meet the responsibilities of their position.

There are indications in the late 1980s and early 1990s that these kinds of conflicts for headteachers are increasing. Mooney (1987) for example, claims that 'headteachers' moral authority has been eroded while their responsibilities have expanded' — a clear recipe for stress going by the model above (p. 130). Industrial unrest in the schools, the erosion of the traditional autonomy of the headteacher by central and local politicians (particularly with regard to discipline in the schools, and the selection of staff), the extent and speed of current change are all factors here. One primary headteacher (Chandler, 1989) gives several examples of classic stress–producers in describing a working week at the height of the reforms of the late 1980s:

Monday: Today the fourth years find out if they have got their first choice secondary school. There are three highly sought after schools locally; all draw from a wide catchment area so the disappointment quotient is high. Great thing this freedom to choose . . . When we have open enrolment, I know who will be dealing with the administration, the anger and the resentment, and it won't be the DES.

Tuesday: The National Curriculum is to be in place in September for the 5–year–olds. We thought the consultation documents would be pretty much the shape of the final papers, given that they came out fairly recently and with a consultative period so truncated that no one seriously believed we were being asked for our considered opinions. But no, sections of the science document have disappeared . . . copies of the final document have yet to arrive in the staffroom.

Wednesday: . . . This term I was planning to be out for one day a week getting input on the National Curriculum. Two weeks after Christmas a supply teacher left, there was no one to cover her and I was in the classroom full time . . . for three weeks.

Thursday: The Deputy Head . . . goes home with a raging temperature. There are no supplies available. A teacher bought from my school allowance to help children with reading difficulties is put in to cover for part of the morning and I do the rest of the day . . .

Friday: . . . Everything has to be changed on all fronts, at a breakneck speed with no time to absorb the implications of one piece of legislation before the next one hits. We are reeling under the impact. I have started to look at advertisements for jobs outside education with more than a passing interest . . .

Deputy headteachers are also in a classically difficult position, being expected to support the head in the running of the school, but also being the spokesperson of the staff. In the not infrequent situation of conflict between a head and the staff, both would expect support. Of course in some respects the seniority of these positions and the status afforded them provides some protection in the form of power and rewards. This does not operate, however, where the conflicts set up on these situations becomes personalized. I recall a head describing to me the 'traitorous' and 'two-faced' action of her deputy after promising her support over the initiation of a certain policy (unpopular amongst the staff, but being pushed by the DES and LEA), and then failing to speak up at the crucial staff meeting. 'I'll never forget that' she said, with some venom, 'and I'll never forgive her for it!'. This well illustrates how a problem that is basically to do with the position and role can be perceived in personal terms, which increases the difficulty and renders it more intractable. Once the conflict invades the private sphere, the role provides little defence.

The Teacher Role and the Production of Conflict

Role conflict among senior staff has been further examined by Dunham (1984). Here, I wish to concentrate more on rank-and-file teachers, for, as Cole and Walker (1989) demonstrate, stress is becoming more endemic among them. Even without some of the more obvious recent stress-producing developments, the teacher role is basically conflictual. Galton (1987), for example, has pointed out that primary school teachers are uncertain about their role in the learning situation. The Plowden Committee (1967) recommended the use of 'informal methods', which, however, can only work insofar as the child can work independently of the teacher. But no guidance is offered on the rules of behaviour within their new situation. Thus teachers tend to take a traditional line with regard to discipline. This may not be particularly stressful in itself, but as the mode of working within primary schools comes to embody a subtle blend of different, and sometimes contradictory elements, so it increases the skill-demand on teachers and puts more of them at risk. In Chapter 2, I argued that there is an inherent conflict within the primary school teacher role deriving from the need to combine functions of teacher (in both instruction and control), parent, and friend. To orchestrate these so that there are no discords might be regarded as one of the high points of the teacher's art. But many find it difficult to handle the contradictions involved, and would stand little chance against pupils like Pollard's (1985), 'gang groups' (p. 70) or Beynon's (1985) 'sussers-out'. If the problem is overcome, however, the rewards are great. There is accrued status (Denscombe, 1985) and the satisfaction of overcoming a formidable hurdle.

However, the roots of pupil opposition or non-cooperation run deeper than 'testing' or 'sussing' the teacher out. These lie, some would argue, in the structure of society, in social class, gender and ethnic differences, in socioeconomic circumstances, and the way the educational system is geared towards these, for example, compulsory education 5–16, the curriculum, and selection (Ashton and Webb, 1986; Freedman, 1987; Hargreaves, 1988). For alienated pupils, teachers are the agents of a system that is failing them. In contrast to a previous example where the role afforded protection and difficulty escalated when interpretations shifted to the personal level, the problem here is aggravated the more stringently the role is followed and the more it shifts from the personal. It is susceptible to personal redemption, but it is difficult to keep this up against deep-rooted opposition. A teacher might find that she wins over some recalcitrant pupils one day, only to find she is back where she started the next. The kind of behaviour I have in mind is that of Willis' (1977) 'lads' with their in-built cultural opposition to authority and conformity. Their attitude mirrors those of their parents on the factory shop-floor, and is seen as being similarly related to social structure. Another example is the counter-cultures described by Hargreaves (1967) and Lacey (1970), thrown up in part by the organization of the school into streams (with the counter-culture forming in the lower streams), but also related to social class. Cultures of 'resistance' have been noted among groups of black children who have felt themselves victimized, not only by individual teachers, but by the whole school system (Furlong, 1984; Wright, 1986).

There are several factors involved in this kind of cultural conflict, not least one of different intepretations of the situation by teachers and pupils. Consider this statement from a metalwork teacher in Wright's study (1986, p. 174):

> . . . I had a black girl in my class. She did something or another. I said to her, if you're not careful I'll send you back to the chocolate factory . . . It was only said in good fun, nothing malicious.

Such a remark might have been 'good fun' for the teacher, but the pupils concerned and their parents clearly thought otherwise. Another teacher was observed to 'pick on' selectively a group of Afro-Caribbean girls and thus to promote confrontation, blaming the girls for her inability to establish conducive learning conditions. In general, black pupils were far more likely than any other group to be placed in ability bands and sets well below their actual academic ability. Cultural opposition was driven further in, and pupils defended themselves by berating a teacher with a stream of Jamaican patois, which of course only confirmed the teacher's fears and sense of opposition. Afro-Caribbean boys also rallied into a strong sub-cultural group which took a delight in baiting the teachers.

There is a kind of downward spiral here, with teachers and pupils pulling each other further and further under. Teachers often appear to be the villains in these scenarios with their racist taunts and selection injustices. But it is not easy for them. Developing an alternative definition of the situation requires time for reflection, which teachers do not have in great quantity. On the contrary, their working conditions are most alien to self–reflection, and the opportunities for inservice training and sabbaticals are meagre. The pressures and constraints of work either anchor them to current views, attitudes, and practices or to very limited reform, and the downward spiral continues.

Are teachers too tied here to official expectations of the role? Why is it so difficult to establish channels of communication? Consider the following testimony from an English teacher who resigned at 28 years of age after only three-and-a-half years teaching. At her last school, a comprehensive,

> . . . A lot of the staff were scared and apprehensive. One woman teacher spent her lunch hours and breaks hiding in a lavatory. She was really frightened of the kids. She had to do the job — presumably for financial reasons — but she was petrified of it.

She herself had a totally uncooperative class, and 'if you told them off it was you who was in the wrong'. A group of boys in another class

> were determined to give me a hard time . . . On one occasion I had hennaed my hair. I heard comments about this, and somebody asked in a loud stage whisper, whether I'd had enough left over to do my pubic hair. Then they called me a slag. I thought Christ, I don't need this. I told those I thought were responsible to stay behind after class. When I tackled them about the rude remarks they appeared quite shamefaced. But next day the abuse started all over again.

On Fridays she took a class nicknamed 'The Wild Animals'. She remembers on one occasion 'standing there with twenty minutes to go before the bell thinking: Just get in the cupboard and come out in twenty minutes. But I knew I had to stay with them . . .'. Others suffered to: 'A lot of hardened teachers were quietly battling on. They talked about their problems — and the fact that nobody in authority seemed able to do anything to solve them. The teachers were left impotent. There was nothing they could do to make the children work.' She remained committed to the job however, putting in twenty hours preparation work at home every week, with occasional weekend work added; and providing her own cassette players as a teaching aid as none were available at school. But she began to suffer from 'depression and stress' and to feel 'increasingly undervalued.'

In the end 'the children forced her out'. Now 'when I see schoolkids in the street I think Thank God I got out' (Lock, 1986).

> I was earning £7,500 as a scale 1 English teacher. A girl I knew at that time was working as a general receptionist and dogsbody for

> a local firm and getting £10,000 plus a car. I was slogging my guts
> out for next to nothing. I began to wonder why. Eventually, I reached
> the end of my tether. I couldn't face the prospect of carrying on any
> longer. I didn't believe in caning. I didn't want the kids to do work
> for me because they were scared of me but because they wanted
> to do to. But there was nobody to deal effectively with pupils who
> stepped out of line.

This vividly illustrates the kind of sexual harassment women teachers might
be subjected to (see also Walkerdine, 1981; Mahoney, 1985); the feeling of
impotence and hopelessness; the physical and emotional investment; and
competing definitions of the situation, which includes different expectations
of the teacher by the pupil. It was she who was 'in the wrong'. We are familiar
with how rules of classroom procedure are 'negotiated' between teacher and
pupil (Werthmann, 1963; Rosser and Harre, 1976). In this case, clearly, no
common ground could be found.

   This kind of behaviour by pupils can force teachers to behave in ways
inconsistent with their interpretation of the role, even if they are experts
at orchestration. Richard Perrins (1986) resigned after ten years at a London
comprehensive. He saw the school 'decay in front of his eyes':

> Some of the buildings had not been decorated for fifteen years. Leaks
> in the roof were not repaired, mainly because of the privatization
> of the caretaking staff. Chairs and tables were falling to bits and
> there were never enough of them. I'd sometimes have to send the
> kids round to filch chairs from other classes before we could start
> a lesson . . . Over the years, due to the lack of routine maintenance,
> the school ended up looking like a disaster area.

Walls were covered in graffiti, blackboards scored with obscenities, books
in hopelessly short supply. 'There was never a complete set of anything and
the kids often had to share one book between two.' His cash allocation for
books had remained the same for six or seven years. This 'decay' sapped
morale and enthusiasm of staff and pupils alike. Perrins could 'spend long
hours preparing lessons — only to find them consumed without appreciation
or even interest'. The amount of personal investment was enormous, with,
in addition to lesson preparation the school play, ferrying pupils to rugby
matches at his own expense, school trips, parents' evenings. Even so, it might
have been worth it had he felt the pupils would benefit. He came to the
conclusion that all these factors were the product of the system, and this
was fundamentally at odds with his conception of what education should
be. He increasingly came to see 'the secondary school system as a paradigm
of society's hierarchical structure' 'a means of teaching people to accept
authority without question and know their place in society . . .'. He started

to feel less like a teacher, more like a prison warder, alternately conning and bullying his young charges . . . 'I ended up doing ridiculous things I'd never do outside school — threatening, cajoling, yelling at people. I just didn't want to do it. Finally I realized I was policing a system I no longer believed in.' Disillusioned, underpaid, undervalued, unappreciated, overworked, Perrins resigned shortly after reaching 30 years of age — a notable 'stock-taking' stage of life (see Sikes *et al.*, 1985). He remains committed to education, but not 'within the structures of the existing secondary education system'.

The Teacher Role and the Teacher Person

This raises another question. If a teacher is forced to be a police officer or drill-sergeant or welfare-officer; or to be traditional when progressivism is the aim, or to shout at and be nasty to pupils on occasions when it is not in one's character to do so, what is it doing to the teacher as a person? Here is another source of conflict, therefore, between teacher as teacher, and teacher as person. At the heart of this in many instances is the struggle of the individual with bureaucracy, the problem being to make it work for us with its coordination, rules and regulations, its certainty and security; and not against us with its impersonality, hierarchy, resistance to reform, and devotion to extrinsic rewards. Schools and teachers, therefore, have a difficult relationship with bureaucracy. A teacher can become submerged as a person in the role. Penny Blackie (1980), for example, describes how she was seen by her pupils as 'not quite proper'. Asked if they would not be embarrassed to talk about sex with a teacher they knew, during a discussion about sex education, one boy replied, 'Well, yes, maybe, but perhaps we need not have a teacher — perhaps we could have a proper person'. (p. 279) On another occasion when they discovered she went to pubs, they were amazed: 'You mean to say . . . you mean . . . that you go to pubs . . . with your friends . . . to pubs . . .just like ordinary people?' (p. 280).

Blackie's school had less of the problems of those of Lock's and Perrins'. Teaching was hard work, but enjoyable. However, she was coming under strain through 'the built-in schizophrenia of the job'. This arises from the 'number of different and often explicitly contradictory roles teachers have to fulfil.' Blackie (like Perrin) draws attention to the 'management roles' teachers have to take on 'towards students who do not necessarily choose to be at school, who are not paid to be there, and who are not free to go somewhere else'. Stress arises from the pressure on the person in adjusting between these roles. Blackie does not believe, for example, that she has the right to tell people what clothes to wear. As a teacher, therefore, in a school that has a school uniform, enforcing the rules about it brings on a 'conflict of personal integrity' (p. 281). Teaching involves so much and so frequent role-change, it is no wonder that pupils consider teachers somewhat less than human. Notice, however, the 'double-bind' that teachers are in here, for if they try to break down these barriers, achieve more consistency and appear too human, they will run the risk of being considered 'not proper teachers' (see Chapter 5).

How a teacher can be submerged under the bureaucracy is illustrated by Andrew Bethell (1980), who gave up his head of department post after ten years because he 'needed a break', 'space to recoup', yet his LEA would not allow him unpaid leave of absence. 'A faint aura of moral disapproval hung over their judgment' (p. 22). Probably they thought that there were sufficient opportunities for secondment. But Bethell points out 'those lucky enough to get seconded have to commit themselves to a course of professional improvement, when what many of them need is a chance for personal enrichment' (p. 23). Looking back he reflects on another stress-inducing feature of teaching:

> As a teacher, and I do not think I was unique in this respect, my every action was tainted by guilt. Not because I did not work hard and not because I was failing, but because however much I did there was always more to be done. I was conditioned, so that the uneasiness would set in at five o'clock on a Sunday afternoon, and not leave hold until the next Saturday morning. Sitting down in front of the television at nine o'clock was always less of an event because of the report I *should* have written, the Chaucer I *should* have prepared, the teacher I *should* phone or the parent I *should* have contacted. It was not that I had not done enough already; it was merely that the more you did the more there was to do. (p. 23)

This case illustrates why leaving teaching is so difficult. People see in careers the best chances of realizing their aims for themselves, be they vocational or instrumental, and even though they may be constrained. There are, too, the more mundane reasons of security, and other forms of cushioning. As Bethell wistfully remarks, 'you can fail in education and never be confronted with the blunt implications of your failure.' But he points to other reasons within teaching — the general ethic 'which keeps the rest of them at it', 'the constant pressure of immediate demands', which he had 'internalized', so that attendance day after day was 'not just a routine, it was a deep-seated imperative'. These routines were so ingrained that he had to force himself to construct similar ones during his year off. At school he had a strong sense of moral obligation. His 'every action' as a teacher 'was tainted by guilt'. However much he did, there was more to do, and a strong feeling that he should do it. But it was these very pressures which, in the long run, caused him to resign. He was increasingly feeling that his job was stunting his growth rather than promoting it — unlike Tom, as described in Chapter 5 and 6, who, despite the problems and vicissitudes he encountered in teaching, found sufficient opportunities for self development to enable him to keep going. Taking time off from teaching, therefore, offered to provide Bethell with those opportunities of finding out what he was best at, giving him the personal control of his time and activities, the flexibility, and ultimately the discovery of 'whole areas of his life, which his job, while giving him much else, had denied him'. The crucial point for Bethell was that this was a quest for 'personal enrichment' and not simply 'professional improvement.' Again it illustrates the disjuncture that can occur in bureaucracies between the role and the person.

Such is the character of 'the greedy institution' (Coser, 1974). It devours the person, always wants more, is never satisfied, the more it consumes the more it needs. One does not have the personal resources for this. Nor are the traditional compensations of bureaucracy in great abundance — the acquisition of status, monetary rewards, career advancement. 'Poor career structure' was, in fact, one of the major sources of stress among Kyriacou and Sutcliffe's (1978) sample, and things have worsened considerably since then (see Roy, 1983; Ozga, 1988). This is particularly hard on teachers in mid-career. When they first entered the profession in the 1960s, education was undergoing expansion. There were growing opportunities to advance through the Burnham scales and onward to head of department, deputy head and headteacher. When it seemed as if they were losing ground they were given a boost by the Houghton award (1974). Many of these teachers are now experiencing career-blockage and are having to rethink their career models. Some have been cooled out of the system, through, for example, early retirement. Others have been redeployed, often a trying, and potentially degrading experience. Many more have worked in the shadow of these trends, and some have themselves found something better than teaching.

This can take a surprising form. Doyle (1987) reports on two technically unemployed sisters, one of whom boosts her income with housework, the other with 'patient-sitting', dog-walking and child-minding. These are both trained teachers with four-five years' experience in primary schools:

> They make it quite clear that not till hell freezes over would they go back to teaching. They have left behind forever the playground duty, the dinner duty and the endless reorganization and shuffling of timetables due to falling rolls and children in bed and breakfast accommodation for the homeless.

Of course, as Doyle points out, the two sisters might not have been suited to teaching. But a high incidence of such behaviour points away from the individual and towards social factors. This is a point apparently not fully appreciated by the DES and HMI. As noted in the Introduction, in a series of reports, such as *The New Teacher in School* (1982), *Teaching Quality* (1983), *Better Schools* (1985) and *Education Observed 3 - Good Teachers* (1985), they build up a model of teaching which puts the major emphasis on the personal qualities of teachers. In other words, if teachers were not succeeding, the chances were that there was something deficient in them as teachers. The policy that follows from such a diagnosis is one of repair (for example, by better training) removal of those judged beyond repair, or redeployment to 'suitable' situations. The sense of threat to existing teachers from such an interpretation, especially when coupled with a programme of teacher appraisal, is clear (see Walsh, 1988).

It adds to the menace that it rests on such weak foundations. As noted earlier the reports have been criticized for not making explicit their underlying, pre-existing criteria for 'good teaching'; for not showing how 'personal qualities' arose as a key variable during the research, nor considering how they relate to effective teaching; for categorizing teachers and thus encouraging 'labelling', the counter-productive effects of which have been well demonstrated in respect of pupils (see Hargreaves *et al.*, 1975); for reducing the 'real life' of the classroom to a set of prescriptions (which have their own problems over definition, operationalization and evaluation); and for not giving due weight to other factors that lie beyond the teacher's control (see McNamara, 1986; Broadhead, 1987; and the Introduction). This book has outlined an alternative framework, one that pays due attention to teacher subjectivities and to social factors. Such a model has vastly different policy implications — including the allocation of improved resources to education, and improving systems of staff development and colleagial support. It has been argued that this would stand a better chance of improving teaching quality. It would certainly reduce teacher stress — perhaps the two are not unconnected.

Survival and Non-Survival

The DES/HMI model on the contrary adds to the teacher's problems. The three traditional ways of handling such problems are retreatism (for example, leaving teaching as with some earlier examples), redefinition of the situation (for example, revising one's views of what teaching is about, or readjusting one's notion of teacher career to a more personally subjective orientation, or updating one's knowledge), and adaptation. With regard to the latter, I have suggested in Chapter 4 how 'survival strategies' come into being.

I argue that teachers are subject to a number of pressures and constraints, as already outlined. In recent years these have become more severe. Now there would appear to be two options open to teachers: (i) to try to change the situation; and (ii) to leave it. The first is very difficult since teachers have little power to influence policy. The second is even more difficult though apparently on the increase. It is difficult, as described earlier, because teachers are committed to their job. They are professionals who tie their energies, and loyalties, and identities to the system they work in. Self, career, achievement, prospects are all identified with the institution. They are highly qualified, and the more they become so, the more committed they become, and the more other options recede. It is a cumulative investment process from which they expect due rewards, not increased pressure. Here we have the classic recipe for stress as defined earlier in the chapter, for these two factors — increased pressures and growing commitment — are on a collison course. Something has to give. It could be their commitment. One might expect, for example, a trend from vocational, professional and total to more instrumental and partial commitment (Sikes *et al.*, 1985). This would not be a complete remedy, for the instrumental prospects have also shrunk, as we have seen. But at least there is less of the self invested in the system, less emotional involvement, less complete dedication to all aspects of the job. The problems thus have less impact. An alternative, possibly associated course is to adjust one's teaching. I argued in Chapter 4 that in that instance it was *teaching* that suffered as teachers were forced into the prior consideration of surviving, and developed a range of 'survival strategies' (such as 'domination', 'fraternization', 'absence', 'therapy').

I am less concerned here with those who do not survive, than with those who are in between, those for whom redefinition or adaptation for some reason or other, is difficult, painful or impossible. Among these, I would suggest, are those teachers who are highly committed, vocationally oriented and 'caring', for there is no escape route open to them. They will not compromise or adulterate their teaching; nor will they change or weaken their commitment. There is nothing left to give way but themselves. The best teachers, arguably, are the most vulnerable. Mike Vernon (1986) was one of these. A successful teacher for twenty years, he suddenly broke down:

> It was a Thursday afternoon and I was teaching a fairly bottom-heavy CSE group. I had a good relationship with them and they were behaving no better or worse than they had done before, but you know, there was a constant level of chatter, and one had to work very hard to keep their concentration. I had every confidence in them and I am sure they would have done reasonably well at the end of the course, but I remember thinking to myself 'you can't go on putting in this amount of effort, year after year'. Earlier that afternoon

I had taken the sixth form, one of the brightest and nicest I have ever known. They were very demanding and I enjoyed the lesson, but by the end of the day I was in a dreadful state, utterly exhausted. I was in the habit of marking books after tea, but on this occasion I just fell into bed. I awoke about nine o'clock sweating like a pig and trembling. I was in a panic about the marking and started getting the files out, but my wife who is also a teacher, took one look at me and said 'you simply can't go on like this, it's bloody silly'. I think I made a conscious decision then, not to return to teaching. (p. 21)

Here clearly is a conscientious teacher cracked by the pincer-grip of pressures and commitment. He compares a group of his ex-colleagues who are just as vulnerable as him with teachers who have adjusted their teaching and commitment in the manner discussed above, which he understands but could never countenance himself:

... Many of them would like to do what I have done, because they are under stress, but for various reasons they are afraid to leave teaching. I have seen them work day in and day out, year after year with love, and yes, compassion, as the kids come up with one problem after another. It's like parenthood, you can't distance yourself if you are a really caring teacher and want to create a warm and receptive atmosphere. There has been much debate lately about what teachers should and shouldn't be doing, and implicit in it is the suggestion that they should be in tune with the children, listening to them, and caring about their needs. Yet the way to survive in the present school situation is the reverse. Many teachers build great walls of defence around themselves, teaching subjects in a cold and formal way, year after year, and distancing themselves from the children. They 'survive' and one is tempted to admire them in an awful twisted sort of way. But the thought of becoming like them brings you to your senses. There is not doubt at all that it is the caring teacher who is most vulnerable to stress.

The pressures in Vernon's case derived from a series of radical organizational changes with the accompanying political struggles — not the best scenario for 'education'. If a change leads to better conditions for education, the destabilization is regarded as temporary and acknowledged as necessary. If it is followed by yet further change, the destabilization itself becomes the norm.

The school I left was a very energetic and thrusting comprehensive, in which there were some hard-working and lively-minded individuals, but we had all been caught up in the comprehensive debate and long drawn-out sagas of reorganization and the battle to implement it and justify it to parents and others.

Although we eventually became fully comprehensive and developed a flourishing sixth form, we were then told to prepare for yet another policy change — the sixth form which we had built up was to be disbanded and the pupils were to attend a sixth form college. Not only were we to lose our brightest children, but we actually had to help with the plans for their removal.

I don't believe that people are generally aware of just how much effort, planning and organization goes into building up a sixth form. So many teachers behaved unselfishly over plans for the dispersal, but I know that it left them emotionally exhausted. All these things add up to stress, and in my own case I would add to it the unsympathetic remarks that some parents and others make such as 'well you have longer holidays than anyone else, and you only work from nine to four'.

Vernon receives an invalidity pension, and while he feels 'fortunate' in some respects, he is concerned that some people will consider him 'inefficient' because he dropped out, thus re-emphasizing the pyschological pressure that keep many others similar to him grinding away at the job. He concludes:

I feel desperately angry that society and the government don't understand what the present demands are doing to teachers. I want my children to go to a school where the teachers are fairly happy and ready to work and where they are not under exceptional stress and have the time and resources to do the job properly.

The experience of Dick, described in Chapter 5, is another example of non-survival through a clash of strong commitment impacting against intolerable pressures, but one possibly where a strong personal factor does contribute. Dick's commitment knew no compromise, and, indeed, I argue that it was bound up with his identity. His aims and methods were ill-adapted to the situations he found himself in, with the consequence that teaching was one long series of stressful incidents for him. His colleagues thought his problems were largely of his own making. Dick might reply that they were 'journeymen' teachers, like those described by Vernon above, or those using survival strategies as described in Chapter 4.

Conclusion

I have argued that stress arises when elements grate against each other and thus produce a special kind of difficulty which puts an excessive strain on a teacher's personal resources. These elements on their own and when not related together in direct opposition are handled with more equanimity. This is not to say they are easily dealt with, for teaching is a demanding job at the best of times.

From this point of view the teacher role is a potential source of considerable stress, for it produces conflicts of such a nature. There are conflicts caused by different people's different expectations of the teacher (for example, where the pupils considered the teacher to be 'in the wrong'); there are within-role conflicts (for example between teacher as instructor/controller and teacher as parent/friend); and conflicts set up by tension between the person and the role (such as experienced by the teacher who felt the need of 'personal enrichment' rather than 'professional enhancement'). The teachers most at risk here would seem to be: (i) probationary and inexperienced teachers, for they have not yet learned how to cope with the dilemmas and contradictions; (ii) teachers who lack knowledge and understanding, perhaps through no fault of their own, of such things as pupil cultures (some of these matters are not well understood by anybody, and teachers are given little time for reflection and/or in-service training; see also Dunham 1984); (iii) teachers who find it difficult, for whatever reason, to 'orchestrate' their teaching; and (iv) senior teachers, such as heads and deputies, who are in the positions of greatest role conflict. There is, in addition, another group of teachers for whom circumstances and recent developments have made the management of role-conflict and satisfactory role performance exceptionally difficult. These include (v) career-aspiring teachers, especially those in mid-career, who face career blockage, for they lose the main reward that helps balance out the increased pressures, and experience instead profound frustration; and (vi) the caring and highly committed teachers who refuse to compromise their high ideals, and who are faced with increased physical and emotional strain on the one hand and less self-fulfilling performance of the role with less investment of the self on the other.

Personal qualities must come into consideration somewhere, but only, I would argue, as a local factor. One teacher might manage better than another in a given situation, all other things being equal. However, the growing incidence of stress across the profession points strongly to other factors, which, I have suggested aggravate the teacher's perennial problem of role conflict. There is no doubt that many teachers are experiencing serious problems, and that the morale of the profession as a whole is low — a conributory factor to stress in itself (Coverdale, 1973). The root cause of all this, I would argue, lies mainly outside the schools and is to do with the kind of educational system envisaged and how it is resourced.

So far we have considered the effects of stress on individuals. But what are the effects of a rising incidence of stress among teachers on the educational system as a whole? In terms of the earlier portrayal of teacher skills in Chapter 1–3, we could expect, first of all, less creative teaching. The essential criteria mentioned of time, resources, control, ownership and relevance do not seem in the ascendancy in such circumstances. Further, role-conflict has become increasingly problematic, making it even more difficult, even for experienced teachers, to 'orchestrate' their activities. Stress and burnout are the opposite of orchestration, for they indicate discord and disharmony. When this begins to affect a number of teachers in any one school, the general ethos also inevitably suffers, possibly becoming less holistic, splintering, and exhibiting crisis management as one of its main features.

By the same token, one might expect to see more survival-oriented teaching, a decrease in vocational and an increase in instrumental commitment. The primary teacher interests of 'maintaining health and avoiding stress' and 'controlling workload' will become all-consuming. The opportunities for teachers to find self-expression in their teaching and in their subject will be limited. Teaching thus becomes a mechanical, technical exercise.

One would also expect a certain turn-round in staff as increased numbers leave the profession. This is not easy for them to do, for reasons made clear earlier and in Chapter 4. Any change in incidence, therefore, can be regarded as significant. Here, research by Smithers (1989), carried out in 430 schools in ten LEAs, points to a worsening crisis. Summarizing this, Smithers said

> Our research has revealed a deeply discontented profession, but many of them don't have the alternative of getting other jobs. The people with numerical and language skills, which are in demand, are leaving. They are the ones who are creating the shortage. Others, who do not have the option of leaving, feel they are trapped.

The proportion of those feeling 'trapped' is as high as one in three. The extent of change and the accompanying administration were the main grievances, rather than matters concerning pay or status. One teacher, leaving to become a trainee manager, said,

> I feel I am not teaching, partly because of behaviour and standards of the kids, and partly because of the administrative work that now goes with teaching. For GCSE (General Certificate of Secondary Education), in the final year, we worked something in the region of 200 hours extra in three months which was one hell of a lot of work. I did five or six hours a night, break times, dinner times, for which we were paid 40p a script.
> The salary bears no relation to what teachers have to do. The

stress is intolerable — I go home and shake a bit for the first couple of hours. The particular problem is the kids: you spend 80 per cent of the time controlling them.

He and some colleagues who met on Sunday nights formed themselves into an 'escape committee', a new phenomenon in British education. All this illustrates the model of stress that I have outlined, where aspects of the teacher role, grinding away against each other instead of acting together in unison, grind the teacher down between them in the process. The number feeling 'trapped' support the view of teaching outlined at the beginning of Chapter 4, but in this case many appear unable to accommodate through 'survival strategies.' Such is the extent of the entrapment that 'escape committees' have to be formed in places to aid their easement out of the profession. We have thus come full circle from the almost idyllic teacher creativity discussed in Chapter 1, where teachers were comparatively free to exercise their professional abilities.

Having said this, it must be acknowledged that there are many successful, and indeed contented, teachers. This is testimony to their ingenuity and dedication, to their ability to use the role for their purposes, and/or to find alternative career patterns within teaching; to many schools for developing climates that are supportive of their staff; to LEAs, heads and deputies who work constructively and creatively together and with their staffs. They are coping, as most teachers will. Also, the current crisis in the late 1980s and early 1990s has been induced by the changes culminating in the Education Reform Act of 1988, which purports to be the most radical change in British education since 1944. All such change inevitably brings disturbance of many kinds. When the dust settles, will things be worse than they were before — or better? I give my views on this in the next chapter.

Chapter 8

Teaching in Crisis? Classroom Practice and the Education Reform Act of 1988

Teaching in Crisis

A student in a recent examination concluded that 'while the National Curriculum is going to determine the education of school pupils, it is not going to change the way teachers teach or pupils learn'. Some, however, are not so sanguine, believing that such a major change 'cannot fail to have a considerable impact on the way teachers see their task and the way they do their work' (Broadfoot and Osborn, 1988). This view is strengthened when taking into account the general drift of events leading up to the 1988 Education Act.

The last five years have seen a pronounced decline in teacher morale following the unsuccessful 'action' of 1986–87, the loss of salary negotiating rights, the imposition of conditions of service, weakening control, greater direction and increased demands on the service. This depressed view of themselves is mirrored in, and aggravated by, the views of the rest of society. A survey, for example, of British Social Attitudes, carried out in 1987 with a sample of 3000, found that 71 per cent of parents had less respect for teachers than they did ten years previously; 88 per cent felt that pupils were not similarly disrespectful, while 86 per cent thought that classroom behaviour was much worse now than in the 1970s (Jowell, 1988). Sixty per cent thought that teachers were less dedicated than ten years ago, though 62 per cent thought that the job of a state secondary school teacher is much more difficult. Even so, accountability being the order of the day, teachers personally are held by many to be the main contributory factor to educational standards. As noted in the Introduction a number of DES reports placed 'personal qualities' of teachers at the top of the list of contributory factors. On the whole, these personal qualities do not seem to have been working to best effect. An HMI report, for example, announced that, in 1987, a quarter of all lessons given by new teachers in England and Wales in their first year were unsatisfactory, and only 6 per cent were excellent. 'Could do better' is the implied summary report on our teachers. Yet some have been trying *too* hard, for there have been several accounts of increased levels of stress and burnout in the profession in recent years (see Chapter 7). Summarizing the research on this an AMMA report concluded that the main causes were 'problem pupils and indiscipline, lack of support and failings in leadership, poor working conditions both physical and psychological, lack of communication, and role ambiguity and role conflict' (1985, p. 6). None of this is good news for those contemplating a career in teaching, and this is reflected in the inadequate numbers of those choosing to join the profession, and in the quantity of those changing their minds after joining it. In 1986, for example, four out of ten teachers who qualified (about 5500 in all) failed to take up a post (see also Smithers, 1989).

Capping all these trends and events is the Education Reform Act of 1988. Avowedly designed to rectify some of the deficiencies in the system and to arrest the supposed decline in standards, it appears to some to run contrary to many prevailing educational principles, such as modular, multidisciplinary curricular, constructivist learning theory, imaginative teaching and learning with local and individual initiative, formative assessment, comprehensive schooling, integration, equality, partnership. As far as teaching is concerned, to some, 'the spectre is raised of an inevitable return to such anti-educational practices as cramming, teaching to the test, rote learning and regurgitation of inert knowledge, didactic teaching styles and streaming' (Haviland, 1988, p. 85). The 'flair and initiative' of teachers, such as outlined in Chapter 1, will be curtailed; oral work and other learning opportunities restricted. One teacher of young children argued that, 'Once we accept and perform the role of deliverer of pre-packaged and prescribed knowledge we are on the way to losing our teacher expertise . . . .Anyone can supervise worried and nervous little children doing their tests, and anyone can mark and grade with the aid of answer books, league tables and lists of established national standards. To go down this road is to end up qualified to be only one thing, "the idiot teacher"' (Whitehead, 1988, p. 71). Elsewhere, it has been reported that 'teachers . . . are intelligentsia no longer. They are not technocrats, not thinkers but quality control operatives . . . Who needs ideas when we have performance indicators?' (*Times Educational Supplement*, 2 September 1988).

In some ways, however, the projected effects all these developments are likely to have on teachers and teaching is nothing new. There always seems to have been an element of alienation, a subjugation of the self, a suppression of individual initiative in what teaching does to teachers. In his classic depiction of the teacher, first published in 1932 and still a set text on many courses, Willard Waller paints a gloomy picture: 'The authoritative manner, the flat, assured tones of voice that go with them, are bred in the teacher by his (sic)dealings in the school room, where he rules over the petty concerns of the children as a Jehovah none too sure of himself . . . That inflexibility or unbendingness of personality which (characterize) the school teacher flows naturally out of his relations with his students . . . The teacher must not accept the definitions of situations which students work out, but must impose his own definition upon students' (pp. 382–6). The teacher role thus becomes formalized, the teacher's personality becomes partly 'paralysed', and enthusiasm is suppressed. As noted in Chapter 1, Waller speaks of the 'peculiar blight which affects the teacher mind . . . and devours its creative resources'; of the 'gradual deadening of the intellect'; of being shut off 'from all the subtler kinds of personal interchange with their fellows' (pp. 391–7). Waller's teachers are well represented in English literature. Amongst Somerset Maugham's teachers,

> Enthusiasm was ill-bred. Enthusiasm was ungentlemanly. They thought of the Salvation Army with its braying trumpets and its drums. Enthusiasm meant change. They had goose-flesh when they thought of all the pleasant old habits which stood in imminent danger. They hardly dared to look forward to the future (1917, pp. 58–9)

In Ursula Brangwen's case there were so many pupils, so few resources, such large cultural differences. School was not 'a definite reality' to her at first. She came to the children full of 'love and kindnesss', but before long she was beating her pupils, as soundly as her colleagues. She had learnt that she too must learn to subdue them to her will. For it was her duty . . . Never more would she give herself as individual to her class. Never would she, the person she was, come into contact with those boys. She would be standard five teacher, as far away personally from her class as if she had never set foot in St. Philip's School' (Lawrence, 1915).

To this conception of the alienated, authoritarian teacher role, we might add the religion of the 'fact', as enunciated by one of its arch-priests, Gradgrind (Dickens, 1907, p. 2):

> Now, what I want is, Facts. Teach these boys and girls nothing but Facts. Facts alone are wanted in life. Plant nothing else, and root out everything else. You can only form the minds of reasoning animals upon Facts: nothing else will ever be of any service to them. This is the principle on which I bring up my own children, and this is the principle on which I bring up these children. Stick to Facts, Sir!

Later, a representative of the Department of Practical Art illustrated the application of the theory to his subject — no flowers on carpets, foreign birds or butterflies on crockery, quadrupeds on wallpaper. Such are matters of 'fancy' — which is to be discarded altogether.

Are those 'Hard Times' about to return? Is the Education Act of 1988 promoting this model of teacher? Is there to be a new lease of authoritarianism, alienation, deskilling, traditionalism? One headteacher, after a tirade against the Act concluded more optimistically, 'But it is too early to despair. A long experience of teachers and teaching has taught me that no body of people is better equipped to circumvent the dictates of authority, nor is there one more practised in the art' (Spooner, 1988, p. 299). Once we start thinking in these terms, it is not long before other possibilities begin to emerge. This is not to say that in some of its clauses, particularly with respect to opting out and open enrolment, the Act is not an educationally retrogressive measure. In an open market, those with material and cultural capital will always be at an advantage (Bourdieu, 1971). However, the consequences for classroom practice itself are not so clear. Undoubtedly for some, especially in situations of low resource, it will contribute towards the effects described in Chapters 4 and 7. Elsewhere, however, it could conceivably enhance teaching practice, and help boost the skills outlined in Chapters 1–3.

Opportunities to Teach and Learn

My starting point is to contest the rather simplistic and stereotypical portrayal of teaching given above. It is both true and untrue. True of some teachers, some schools, not others. It is the part that is produced by constraint, not by opportunity. A comprehensive view, has to take account of both factors in an 'opportunities to teach and learn' model (OTAL) such as described in the Introduction. Pupils need 'opportunities to learn', particularly with regard to time allocated particular tasks, and the extent to which tasks match pupils' abilities (Bennett *et al.*, 1984) and cultures. The teacher also needs time, resources, rewards. However, while a certain base-line of external resource and facilitative structure is necessary, much of these things are provided by teacher commitment. The opportunities here, therefore, are bound up with teachers' identification with the job.

The nature of the job also requires a certain latitude, in order to adjust to local circumstances, to particular pupils, and to variable and sometimes unpredictable developments. To exploit the latitude to educational advantage involves considerable practical knowledge on the part of teachers — knowledge of pupils' backgrounds, abilities, life-histories, relationships, development; of their own strengths and limitations as teachers; of their teaching area; of what works in what circumstances, with whom, and when.

They have to be skilled orchestrators, able to play different roles, from instructor to enabler, from parent/friend to controller, and to switch amongst them almost instinctively (see Chapter 2). They do not stand outside the process like some objective arbiter, nor do they occupy simply one position within it, that is as teacher, for they also learn. One 12-year-old student, considering the attributes of a good teacher, told me recently: 'The teacher also learns from the pupils, the teacher is more educated but even when she's old she's got something to learn ... the pupils give her ideas, they may be only little ideas but she uses them. You learn together'. Waller also saw this as a quality of what he considered to be the best teachers. Speaking of G. Stanley Hall, he said he was 'one of those rare teachers who keep the learner's attitude to the extent of being anxious to learn from their own students, and this was surely not unconnected with the creativeness of his intelligence' (p. 394, see also Shulman, 1987). The teacher's command of her knowledge, therefore, is matched by a democratic openness to new input.

Teachers' personal involvement in, and control of, teaching is matched in this model by pupils' involvement in, and control of *their* own learning. Pupils appropriate knowledge and reconstruct it in relating to their own concerns. An alternative mode of learning is the 'receive and deliver' type, probably more educational in the strategies for coping to which it has given rise than in its substance. The two models permeate our entire system, from nursery school to university. This can be illustrated by comparing two approaches to a very similar activity which on the surface appears very open and democratic. The first concerns the session in primary schools where children are encouraged to give their 'news'. This, typically, comes at the beginning of a day, and children are freely invited to tell the rest of the class anything interesting that has occurred to them or that they have been doing out of school; an expedition, a visit, shopping, loss of teeth, acquisition of new skills like riding a bicycle, or new items in a collection — anything they like. The atmosphere is relaxed, the teacher herself may join in with her news, and the whole activity seems very person- and community-oriented. Ostensibly it is a pupil-centred exercise in encouraging the art of speaking in public, in confidence-boosting, in breaking down formal barriers, learning about each other, and promoting a sense of togetherness, while giving individuals a chance to excel.

A recent study of news sessions, in some Australian classrooms however, came to a different conclusion, arguing, from a detailed study of transcripts, that far from this being an example of pupils owning, and appropriating knowledge to their own concerns, the reverse is the case, that is that they are occasions for the initiation of pupils into aspects of *school* knowledge and culture (Baker and Perrott, 1988). The events, typically, are stage-managed by the teacher who 'to varying degrees, appropriates the questioning, asks curriculum-talk questions and reformulates the content into that common in the school culture' (*ibid*, p. 35). The competencies the pupil learns in consequence are the same as in other lessons — learning what the teacher wants, and how to be an appropriate pupil. To take part successfully, the authors conclude, pupils require 'advanced judgement and fine tuning on both "form" and "content" criteria' (p. 36). This is certainly not pupil-centred. Nor is it teacher-centred in the sense I have advocated, for it is dubious to what extent teachers genuinely own and control such transactions, or to what extent they are working to formulae laid down by others.

Contrast this with 'forum' sessions that are currently operating in some of our schools. Here, a class will choose a topic to discuss. They will select some main speakers to introduce and chair the discussion, they will research and prepare their own input, and all will be encouraged — by their peers — to take part on the day. The teacher sits on the sidelines. She does not input, control or suggest, other than to see that the democratic base is established and functions for example, by advising the chair on procedures that will help ensure everyone who wishes has an opportunity to speak. Here the teacher is facilitator, rather than central operator. The exercise, it is claimed, develops initiative and confidence, the formulation of views, ability to discuss, appreciation of others' points of view, identification of prejudice, critical awareness. Moreover, this is not the kind of bland 'progressivism' that advocates individual, child-centred learning without reference to the social groups to which individual children belong, as boys or girls, black or white, middle or working class. For in the 'forum' debate, they are exposed to the views of others both as individuals and as representatives of other social groups. We need to monitor carefully the outcomes of these sessions, but elsewhere, in similar work, others have noted that young 'children are able to operate powerful social concepts and can articulate their own perspectives' (Lee, V. and J., 1987). This example illustrates some of the most important opportunities to learn, what we might call 'pupil-friendliness', the construction of the learning situation within the pupils' own relevancies, to some extent under their control and under their direction.

Teacher-friendliness is also important. This is well illustrated in the 'exchange' project described in Chapter 1, which meets all the requirements of an 'opportunities to teach and learn' model. Its most notable feature was the inspiration for teaching and learning that it provided. The motive-force for this inspiration was the relationships concerned — between the teachers involved, who were friends, and between the two sets of pupils, who in the preparations for, and follow-ups to, the meetings, as well as the meetings themselves, established close contacts with each other. The learning outcomes affecting the whole curriculum appeared considerable (see Woods, 1989a).

Apart from the usual areas of English, with considerable advances in vocabulary, and mathematics, with estimating times, distances and bus fares, and so on, there were great gains in personal and social development. A hitherto friendless child (because of age differences) found some new friends, a shy and timid boy was inspired to join in the public greetings with his peers; and collectively there was a coming together of the two groups with a strong community spirit. As described earlier, the motive-force for this project was the teachers' inspiration, and an essential condition was having the freedom in which it could flourish. This need is echoed by other research. For example, a teacher who had done some particularly creative work with pupils on crystal radios told Nias (1988b): 'the work could *only* have matured within an atmosphere of freedom — without intervention or restriction from headteacher, timetable or the DES' (p. 147).

An interesting feature of the exchange project is that it involved teachers who might have been thought otherwise very traditional in their classroom teaching. Freedom is not just a prerequisite for so-called 'progressive' teaching. In fact, we know that traditional/progressive is not a fruitful way of regarding classroom practice. Nor can teachers be brilliant, exciting, pedagogical pioneers *all* the time. They don't need to be, for the learning, the motivation, the insights involved in creative activities like the 'Exchange' illuminate and are consolidated by more formal and routine activities and areas of the curriculum. Exciting possibilities, therefore, lie in ringing the changes among various techniques of both traditional and progressive nature. The key factors are the teacher's skills in campanology and freedom to practise it.

Such examples suggest that too heavy direction of teachers, and too heavy pupil direction are anti-educational. They foreclose on the opportunities. Yet this, many fear, will be a consequence of the Act. A possible strategy to help offset this is to celebrate and advertise teaching that extends opportunities. But if foreclosure is to be the case in some areas, the converse may well be true in others. In other words, the Act may *open up* opportunities in some areas. For example, there is a trend at the moment in the teaching of modern languages towards encouraging communicative competence in real, practical situations. There is much active learning, role-play, variety and interaction, backed up by quiet periods for reflection and consolidation.

The question is — shall we be allowed to continue with and develop this kind of teaching in the new system? Some would argue that we must try to continue to develop methods like this *because* of the legislation. In the first place, the national criteria for the GCSE (General Certificate of Education) have as their first aim, 'to develop the ability to use the foreign language effectively for purposes of practical communication'. Secondly, the National Curriculum means that everybody between the ages of 11 and 16 must take a foreign language. Hitherto, the vast majority of students opted out of language at age 14, if not earlier. It was assumed that they either lacked the ability or the aptitude, two of the watchwords of the 1944 Act. We now know these both to be largely a function of culture, not innate personality. The Act provides some of the structural conditions for progress in languages. Teaching methods must move to meet the challenge.

Consider the extreme alternative — methods employed by a representative of the 'traditional' teacher model outlined earlier. He was 'one of the finest Latin masters in the country' ... a brilliant teacher of Latin ... well known for the number of scholarships he had obtained at top public schools. His methods may now appear somewhat crude, for although they were staggeringly successful in implanting an indelible knowledge of Latin grammar, they achieved no success at all in teaching Latin as a history or a literature or a culture. He was concerned solely with North and Hillard and Kennedy's 'Revised Latin Primer', the contents of which books he rammed into us by the sternest discipline and with unremitting and brainwashing repetition. This 'brilliant' teacher made his pupils 'learn Kennedy's grammar by heart. Particularly the rules of syntax at the back, the prepositional phrases and the gender rhymes. We learned definitions, examples and exceptions till we could say them in our sleep. They had no reference outside the pages of grammar, however, and I can recall no conscious attempt to interpret them in any kind of living context. They were learned like the parts of a play; sentences, titles, quotations and tags with no apparent relevance at all ... We learned the gender rhymes as a piece of end-of-term light relief. They were never of much use because the words involved were mostly too rare to be encountered in even the most advanced 'unseen' or prose exercise unless one happened to have to translate such sentences as 'The dropsy-stricken husband met the fornicator by the Adriatic Sea' (Marshall, 1982, pp. 71–3). Heinrich Heine observed that the Romans would never have had time to conquer the world if they had been obliged to learn Latin first of all. Perhaps he had that sort of method in mind, rather than those currently being promoted by the Joint Association of Classical Teachers, which are much more in line with the OTAL model, and which are promoting something of a revival of the subject.

One might expect a pedagogical boost in other curriculum areas. For example, large numbers of pupils, and particularly girls, have opted out of science at age 14, possibly to their later disadvantage. However, making them do it up to age 16, as the Act how requires, does not mean they will enjoy it, do well at it, and go on to develop careers in it. It doesn't mean that many girls will feel they do not possess the analytical skills, feel revulsion at the smells, take feminine exception to wearing safety goggles, and so on. Part of the problem lies rather, in what Kelly (1985) has called the construction of masculine science — the whole concept of it as a male subject, which has a long history of development and consequently a considerable culture attached to it. Forcing girls to take science in the same subject-centred mould without attention to process thus carries dangers of increased alienation on the part of both pupils and teachers. The same argument, of course, applies to languages, and any other subject all pupils now have to take. If, however, this structural opportunity being offered to pupils is matched by opportunities being given to teachers to revise their conception of the subject and their methods of teaching it, an enormous advance could be made. In this respect, it is not unlike the raising of the school leaving age and the institution of comprehensive schools and mixed–ability classes. Intrinsically beneficial reforms, they posed enormous problems for teachers in areas and schools where resources and other kinds of support did not match the demands being made. It might, however, be argued that the first, structural move has been made. The National Curriculum establishes a general entitlement.

It will be apparent that the examples I have given come from different stages in the system. It may be that the Act, and other developments, particularly the institution of the GCSE (despite problems of implementation which caused stress for some), offer more OTAL at secondary rather than at primary level. In fact, it could be one of the curious consequences of the Act, that while it helps bring new meaning to teaching in secondary schools, for years hidebound by final examinations and tradition, it threatens to constrain primary school teaching, especially that creative integrative, holistic work that has come to be the distinctive and internationally acclaimed mark of that sector, some examples of which were given in Chapter 1.

Again, a pair of contrasting examples might help provide substance to the speculations. The first is the creative mathematics project described in Chapter 1, that grew to involve the whole school and the whole curriculum. This appeared to be an excellent example of 'education for all' (DES, 1985). We might compare this project to one in another school (Grugeon and Woods, 1990). This was a whole-school, term-long project occupying a third of the curriculum and infused with a 'multicultural perspective', in response to the LEA's *aide-mémoire* promoting such activity. This was an honest endeavour by an all–white Church (Church of England) school to meet the spirit of the Swann report (DES, 1985). However, the project was devised within a factual — rather than person-based framework. This was evident from the worksheets. These took the form of asking factual questions for pupils to research. In a report to the teachers the question was raised whether a factual mode of writing was the most appropriate for thinking about people and the way they live. The use of the present tense and the generalizing pronoun 'they' allow the writer to state unquestionable facts. Using the same model in writing about human beings seems to produce statements which could easily become stereotypes and the basis for the sort of over-simplified points of view which give rise to all kinds of prejudice:

They do not have houses like we have.

The bushmen go around practically naked.

This project had clear objectives, a tight schedule and involved a great amount of work for both teachers and pupils. There was no time for the teachers to step outside the parameters, not even to avail themselves of an evening television programme about the Kalahari bushmen which most of the children had seen and been absorbed by, and which had clearly given them much more understanding of their lives and culture than many of their school activities. The teachers, therefore, seemed locked within a mode of teaching which frustrated their intentions. However, there were some gains. There were some instances, for example, where, from the style of writing or discourse, pupil knowledge appeared to be more clearly *theirs*. Also, the project had delineated the problems in sharp relief. In future projects, the teachers would be better equipped to formulate strategies to meet those problems.

However, this is where the 1988 Education Act poses a threat. The teachers in the former school can hardly fail to continue to experiment. They have developed a school ethos that maximizes the opportunities for teaching and learning in their particular situation whether operating under the 1944 or the 1988 Act. Their creative experiments are already yielding results in forms generally recognized. The other school would appear to be at greater risk, for their attempted innovation did not bear fruit, and the lessons learnt from it are likely to be lost. This is because the pressures will undoubtedly be to concentrate upon what they already do very well, and to avoid risk-taking experimentation, which 'might not work'.

I was in a primary school recently observing a class of 7-year-olds. The register was being called. After the teacher had called out the first six names, she suddenly lost her voice. But the answers went on, unprompted . . . 'Yes, Miss Jackson . . . Yes, Miss Jackson' . . . Yes, Miss Jackson . . . all the way through without hestitation, in alphabetical order, boys first. The teacher looked across at me afterwards, and said, 'I sometimes wonder why we bother to come'. I had a vision of a regulated school, wound up at the beginning of the day, and unfolding to precision – an omen perhaps.

Rallying Resistance

If we wanted to take this line, certainly, as I have said, there would be much in the Act to criticize and this has been well catalogued. To some (for example,

Simon, 1988), a whole generation's educational achievements stand to be abolished at a stroke. At this extreme, if these predictions come to fruition, we might see the coming years as a kind of educational 'Dark Ages'. Here, barbarian technicists and bureaucrats hold sway. 'Real' education and learning will be suppressed, trodden under the feet of the entrepreneurial hordes. In this situation, teachers might recall the monks of the middle ages, who against similiar odds, applied themselves diligently to their manuscripts and preserved learning, knowledge and civilization. This is not all teachers have in common with the monks. They also had a vocational calling ('Laborare est orare'); they worked long hours; they had trouble with the government; and they took a vow of poverty. Teachers might consider an alternative to union activity based on the technique of the Egyptian solitary who, 'perched upon a pillar or tree, exhibited the charms of his pious emaciation and squalor to the admiring pilgrim' (Fisher, 1936, p. 175).

On the other hand, teachers may choose to be a little more politically active than the monks. They are not without resources here. First they have their own professionalism. Though there have been many ways in which their political position has been assailed in recent years, educationally many have made considerable strides towards becoming 'extended professionals' (Hoyle, 1980). According to Hoyle, these are 'concerned with locating their classroom teaching in a broader educational context, comparing their work with that of other teachers, evaluating their work systematically, and collaborating with other teachers'. The extended professional is theory-friendly, concerned about educational and teacher development, and sees 'teaching as a rational activity amenable to improvement on the basis of research and development'.

'Extended professionality' has found expression in the 'teacher-researcher' and the 'action research' movement. Stenhouse (1985, p. 117) has set out the epistemological grounds for his belief in 'research-based teaching'. He argued that the knowledge we have to offer teachers is not warranted without the teacher knowing something about how that knowledge was come by. Its warrant rests in evidence, not the expertise or authority of persons. Research-based teaching, conceived as enquiry-based teaching, shifts the balance of power towards the student for it concedes 'the importance of the right of the learner to speculate, to learn autonomously, to criticize and correct . . .' (pp. 120–1). The means of acquiring knowledge are thus democratized. The emphasis is placed not on facts or extant bodies of knowledge, but on powers of critical scrutiny'. Teachers, Stenhouse argued, 'must be educated to develop their art'. They can never 'master' it, for 'teaching is not to be regarded as a static accomplishment like riding a bicycle or keeping a ledger; it is, like all arts of high ambition, a strategy in the face of an impossible task' (p. 124). For Stenhouse then, the best prospect for the improvement of teaching and learning in schools lay in the development of the critical and creative powers of teachers.

This model of the curious, open-minded, enquiring teacher contrasts strongly with the dull, constrained authoritative teacher described by Waller, Lawrence and Maugham. As yet, however, many of the gains have remained where they primarily belong — in practice — and have been unrecorded and unpublicized. We have, as yet, no archive on teacher practice (Shulman, 1987). Nonetheless, the advances made in individual teacher knowledge and expertise are gradually becoming documented (see, for example, Nixon, 1981; Burgess, 1985; Hustler *et al.*, 1986; Woods, 1989b). Some noteworthy examples here are the identification and illustration of the professional, personal and social skills, initiative and dedication of primary school teachers embodied in the minutiae of their everyday work, as revealed, for example, in the research of Nias and her associates (1989). In a number of closely-observed studies, she has shown how teachers aid their own and each other's professionalism, thus providing evidence to support their firm conviction that they themselves are the best equipped to promote, organize and measure such change. A head and her deputy are like 'one finger, one thumb' in their administration of school affairs. Elsewhere, in 'Russian Dolls' a teacher who was having problems identifying with children's concerns — rather as in the 'news' example given earlier — was brought to recognition by a senior teacher over a series of weeks (Simmonds and Nias, 1989). The success of this appeared to rest on the counselling teacher's *own* development as she sought to encourage a radical rather than just a superficial change — hence the Russian dolls analogy. Much of this kind of activity must be second nature to many practising teachers. They do it, but do not record it. Perhaps this kind of research work can help accumulate a record of practice which can provide impetus for the development of others.

Crucial to its success is what Nias *et al.* (1989) describe as a 'culture of collaboration' within the school, where there are 'few status differentials', where teachers accepted and fostered their interdependence while valuing individuality, in an atmosphere of openness tempered by security. This research is putting flesh on the bones of the school 'ethos' and 'climate' work (Rutter *et al.*, 1979; Mortimore *et al.*, 1988). It might be thought more likely to develop in the primary school where the staff are comparatively small in number, and can thus more easily identify as a group — as with the teachers in the mathematics' project discussed earlier. And that large comprehensive schools are more likely to show more ideological divisions which work against such unitary cultures. However, this is not necessarily the case, especially where the school has a distinctive ideology of its own, as in the school described in Chapter 3. Such is the case also at Stantonbury. In so many ways, Stantonbury offers illustrations of teachers breaking the mould of the image conjured up by Waller, Lawrence, Maugham, and Gradgrind. A recent initiative, supported by GRIST funding, was the 'Mutual Support and Observation' programme, the central thrust of which is to observe a colleague teach, have that colleague observe you and subsequently spend a time debriefing and reflecting on the lessons (Gates, 1989). Such a mode contrasts strongly with the ingrained 'classroom isolation' and jealously guarded teacher autonomy identified by some as one of the chief barriers to educational progress (Hargreaves, 1988). Gates (1989) argues that this kind of activity has a firm epistemological basis in the formal recognition of the role of the practitioner in the development of knowledge. The MSO model offers to enhance teachers' professional integrity by 'valuing the ordinary' through 'critical reflection'.

So many of these issues at the moment seem to hang on a knife-edge. As Hewton (1988, p. 143) says of the similar School Focused Staff Development scheme in East Sussex, 'the fact that SFSD has taken root in these circumstances (i.e. a paring down of the educational budget, increasing demands on the service, shifting control to the centre) is a credit to the dedication and perspicacity of teachers. But it could easily grind to a halt. If it is seen, not as a positive step towards greater professional autonomy, but as a management strategy to increase control and accountability and possibly a back door to introduce appraisal, then it will be discarded or sabotaged; and rightly so'. Hewton thinks that the essential spirit of SFSD will survive in East Sussex, but clearly vigilance is necessary.

In this endeavour, teachers will be aided by the academic community. There have, of course, been notable contributions here, and these possibly might increase. One development here is the growing identification of academics in the disciplines with educational issues, policy and practice, teacher development and collaborative research with teachers. This is well illustrated in the sociology of education. During the early years of its appearance in this country — in the 1950s and 60s — the typically macro approach was concerned to relate output factors — pupil achievement — to input factors, such as social class background. In terms of political impact, this has been, arguably, the discipline's most successful period. But the whole of the educational *process* that lies in between input and output had, as yet, been largely unstudied. During the 1970s, sociologists researched these processes, and in most studies, teachers were part of the situation being researched. Teachers found themselves being represented in sociological theories often in ways completely at odds with their own understandings. In one prevailing line, teachers emerged as either the active agents of an evil system, or passive dupes, unaware of the implications of what they were doing. It was the era of 'cut-and-run' research in the interests of preserving independence and autonomy, which were seen as essential if there were to be a genuine advancement of knowledge. This has been described as 'the rape model' because it takes rather than gives (Lather, 1986). There were some exceptions, of course, but that was the general trend. A contrasting trend is gathering pace today, one of sociologists and teachers working together (Burgess, 1985; Hustler *et al.*, 1986; Whyte, 1986; Woods and Pollard, 1988; Arnot, 1989). There are several factors that have brought this about. First, there is greater understanding among sociologists of the teacher's role and job and of teacher skill in 'managing' it. On the other hand, there is greater critical awareness among teachers, a feature of the 'extended professional'. An openness, and willingness (often desire) to engage with the academic issues, as long as they could be shown to be directed toward enriching or enhancing the job, has replaced the defensiveness more typical of the profession during the earlier period. In some ways this is a commentary on the developing professionalism of the teacher.

Secondly, there has been increasing recognition among sociologists and teachers that they are engaged in the same enterprise — the improvement of education. The advancement of sociological theory is a worthy endeavour, and should not get lost through political disfavour (a few monasteries for sociologists might be set up in the coming years!). But the implications of sociological theory for the practice of teaching has been largely unexplored. More attention is now being focused upon these connections, as sociologists come to address policy and practice more squarely, and as they do so, to feel increasingly that any change must come *through* the teacher rather than *in spite of* the teacher (Hargreaves, 1984). This in turn has increased interest in teacher's 'practical knowledge' (Schon, 1983; Connelly and Clandinin, 1985; Ben-Peretz *et al.*, 1986; Smyth, 1987). Further, whilst sociology should not lose its critical edge, it could add its strength of depiction and analysis to the positive experience, in other words it could contribute to the preservation and furtherance of those elements of classroom practice which have been shown to be educationally productive, and which now seem under threat. Sociologists and teachers, thus, are political allies. In the assault that has been made on education recently, both have come under attack. The challenge to teacher professionalism is seen as a threat to educational advance; the attempts to delimit their practical knowledge counter-productive; and to curtail their power and influence ill-advised, educationally. The situation of the late 1980s and 1990s, contrasted with that of the 1950s and 60s, calls for a rallying to the teacher cause.

This collaboration is not without its problems. It does represent quite a fundamental shift in research model. There are new psychologies involved in the move from academic-directed research to participatory research, to which academics and teachers contribute on an *equal* basis. There are new roles, with the teacher as co-research worker, inputting practical knowledge;

the academic contributing specialist knowledge of theory and method and a more generalized overview, acting as 'critical friend', liaison person, and co-analyst and -writer. There is a new language to be invented, or at least an old one re-discovered as sociologists tackle the problem of 'researcher-speak'. Perhaps that will take care of itself as the new reference groups involved consisting of mixed, as opposed to separate, groups of teachers and researchers come to develop their own cultures.

There are forces militating against collaboration — institutional separateness, occupational cultures and their boundedness, the fact that the school is part of an intricate social structure, with its hierarchies, statuses, micropolitics, power relationships. Relating theory to practice is also not without difficulties (Chisholm and Holland, 1987). In some ways, collaboration runs against sociological sense. Where it works, it is a tribute to the professionalism of both sides, reflected in their ability to recognize these structures and their own relationship to them, and to rise above them. Only then can the critical edge of sociology, wherein lies its radical promise, become formative, that is, part of the teacher's own constructions rather than being seen as undermining them. It helps if there is a common prior commitment. One example of this is the group of teachers, advisers and academics working with Arnot (1989) on developing anti-sexist approaches in London schools. Part of the underlying philosophy was the need to move away from LEA-based courses to school-focused projects on equal opportunities undertaken by school working parties or individual teachers. These projects in turn took girls, their biographies and experiences, as their focus, working outwards towards theory rather than the other way round. This teacher- and pupil-centredness was thought to have been the major factor behind the success of the initiative. But of course the support of the authority and headteachers is indispensable. Sadly, this is not always the case (see, for example, Deem, 1987).

However, in similar ways, teachers will at times find support from LEAs, but also pupils, parents, and employers. Elliot (1988), for example, who sees the Reform Act as anti-educational in almost every respect, pins his hopes for educational recovery on teachers initiating a 'real dialogue with parents and employers' (p. 61). Hitherto, he claims, the relationship has not been active and empathic. The professionals have defended their autonomy, not really listened to parents or promoted school-industry links in numbers and with enthusiasm. The responsibility of the professionals in any new and real dialogue, in Elliot's view, 'should be to clarify and articulate a coherent view of education, in response to the concerns expressed by (parents, employers, school governors and elected members) . . .' (p. 61). In this way, the national curriculum might be reconstructed 'in a form which reflects both authentic educational values and parental concerns' (p. 62). This would be not only recovery, therefore, but progress, in a new form of partnership that maximized strength at the seat of teaching and learning, forming a useful counterweight to the power of the centre.

There are other ways in which such a partnership could be productive. Anderson (1988, p. 35), for example, argues that with the additional powers and responsibilities given to parents and governors, 'without their cooperation equal opportunities policies may well flounder, if indeed they are not strangled at birth'. Non-sexist and non-racist programmes could be undermined unless schools reach out and include parents within the discussions and debate instituting such programmes. Anderson suggests, 'Workshop sessions, talks, videos, open days, special events focusing on equality', and, as reaching-out activities, 'leaflets, home-visits, phone-ins on local radio, community slots on regional television . . .' (pp. 35–6). Here, then, is another challenge, that can be met by a redisposition of forces and the forging of another new alliance to produce an *educational* advance.

Pupils might be included in these new alliances. Much has been made of the conflict side of classroom activity. Military analogies abound — battles, warfare, siege, outflanking, attrition, sides, drill. Waller (1932, p. 195) was of the view that, 'Teacher and pupil confront each other in the school with an original conflict of desires, and however much that conflict may be reduced in amount, or however much it may be hidden, it still remains'. On the other hand, pupils are the main source of teachers' intrinsic rewards. The 'caring' function was prominent among the teachers interviewed by Nias (1988a), some even expressing 'love' for their pupils. 'I used to get very close to them', said one. 'At the end of the summer term I used to be sad at losing them and having to pass them on to someone else' (p. 190). A factor working in the teachers' favour here is pupils' basic desire to learn. One boy told me recently, 'I want to educate my brain more' — and that sums it up for many pupils. Even some of those who appear to be in deepest opposition would like to do well at school, as shown in several studies of supposedly deviant pupils (for example, Fuller, 1980; Furlong, 1984; Wright, 1986).

Some approaches are being advocated here that may radically restructure teacher-pupil relationships. Troyna and Carrington (1989), for example, urge that these be based on democratic principles where each are respected, and the transactions between them collaborative and cooperative. Young people should be 'encouraged to take a critical stance towards political information; be open minded and show respect for evidence; act in an empathetic manner; extend their appreciation of how power is exercised (and by whom); and explore fundamental questions relating to social justice and equality' (p. 2). Kemmis (1983) has urged something similar in what he calls the 'socially critical school.' Hargreaves' (1984) ILEA report also argued for more student involvement in educational decision-making (see also Hull, 1985). In some respects Dick (see Chapter 5) would have been a model teacher in this kind of scenario.

Regression Towards the Norm

The teacher, then, is not without resource in the coming struggle, and there are sound educational reasons and impetus for certain alliances being fostered and strengthened. But the struggle itself may not be quite as polar as it first appears. For it will be tempered by a well-known phenomenon in education — the regression toward the norm. The norm, that is the way we do things, has evolved gradually over the years in response to many different factors, legal measures being only one particular set of them. Factors helping to preserve the norm are, at one level, resources, teacher supply, and teacher-pupil ratio; at another, the kind of society in which we live, and the cultures and traditions to which it has given rise. Usually, these hold back progress. For example, the 1944 Act, the raising of the school leaving age, and the comprehensive movement, though egalitarian in character, and distinct advances, did not radically alter the basic divisions and inequalities in society. However, there were certain gains from these things, which have become inbuilt into practice where they chime with, rather than challenge, existing conditions.

Just as this norm checks progress in one direction, it will check it in another. It is completely apolitical in this sense. Strongly political measures, therefore, such as the 1988 Act, put together and passed very largely in the face of educational advice, are particularly susceptible to 'norm pull', for the Act is incapable of being implemented in the form passed. Points of consensus have to be found, and on those, compromise will be built (McLean, 1988). Much is made of the centralizing features in the Act. But there is a difference between formal and effective centralization (Archer, 1989). Controlling what goes on in the classroom is rather difficult for politicians and governments. Holt (1988) observes that attempts to do so 'generate either counter-movements, or they prove in practice to be wildly unworkable' (p. 4). He cites a similar attempt to seize control of the curriculum in Texas, reported by O.L. Davis, who concludes: 'Now that "reform" is "in place", most educational professionals believe they can get back to doing what they enjoy — teaching'. Far from pre-empting local curriculum work, the drive for state control 'created both the opportunity and the legitimacy for local curriculum work' (Davis, 1987, pp. 35–6). The UK is not Texas, but already there are signs of redemption. Even before the Bill became an Act, there was a certain amount of 'softening up' on its journey through Parliament. For example, the diagnostic role of assessment came to be emphasized more;

attainment targets were to reflect different levels of ability; and socioeconomic factors were to be taken into account in the publication of school results.

However, things may go further than this kind of modest modification. For the working groups on the new curriculum, at the time of writing, have made some interesting recommendations. The report of the working group on English, for example, chaired by Professor Brian Cox, himself a prominent figure in the Black Papers on education, the right-wing answer to Plowdenesque progressivism, steers a judicious course between the two. This is not just tact, or political expediency — it is what the educational sense of the moment seems to demand. Thus, the report recommends that all pupils be taught to write standard English, whatever their ethnic, social and regional origins. Since this is a key factor in future life-chances, this must be correct. They should only be taught to *speak* it if motivated to do so, and should be able to choose when and where to use it if they wish. Teachers, thus, must respect pupils' native language or dialect. This is not just a strategic matter for their intrinsic value is recognized. Creole varieties of English, for example, 'are highly complex . . . governed by rules in their own right, and it is a political/ideological question as to whether they are dialects or languages in their own right'. The report recommends that schools should develop their own coherent policies, which are sensitive to local circumstances and the needs of the individual child on exactly how and when Standard English should be taught. The balance recommended by the Kingman Report (1988), which had been unpopular in powerful government circles favouring traditional teaching of grammar, is thus preserved.

The Cox working group strikes a further balance between creative work in English and the need for enjoyment on the one hand, and traditional standards of spelling, punctuation, parts of speech and structure on the other. The latter, again, are only appropriate when children need it. It is to be done in 'context' — a major theme of the report. I wonder where this places a request I had recently from a 7-year-old boy, writing a story about a holiday abroad, to spell 'aeroplane'. I wrote it out for him, 'A-E-R-O etc'. He studied it, then gave it back. 'No, that's not the word I asked for. I want "erraplane"', presumably spelt 'E-R-R-A etc'. This illustrates the dilemma between coaching correct English and encouraging creative writing. The compromise that many primary teachers employ of not obstructing the creative flow, but helping to build up successive drafts seem to work quite well. I came across a superb example of this recently, a book no less, written by primary school pupils under the guidance of their headteacher, and of an experienced author of children's fiction.

Reflecting on this work, this author commended the head's teaching methods, which 'were all aimed toward drawing out, rather than cramming in, and he laid great stress on getting each child to talk out his or her ideas freely. Classes made their own exercise books in their own designs, learning techniques of decorating, lettering, marbling, lino-cutting and so on in the process, not as separate "art lessons". The head and his staff encouraged pupils to combine on any activity whatever disciplines seemed relevant. He also read aloud with them an astonishing range of the best imaginative books . . .'. The author found these children 'not at all passive; they came to meet any idea I put forward. They talked, easily, confidently and expressively. They listened intently and remembered very accurately. They were also far less shy than most school children of revealing private and romantic feelings in front of their peers. There was a welcome absence of a pecking-order of seniority . . .' (Whistler, 1988, p. 162).

Here we have a profusion of opportunity, which will be preserved if the Cox working group has its way. Further, the requirements of the National Curriculum might not cause the problems for integration that were first thought. For heads and teachers will have freedom to organize timetables so that compulsory 'attainment targets' and programmes of study can reach across subjects. Cross-curricular work will thus be encouraged (*The Guardian*, 29 December 1988). In any event, a school of such inventiveness, strongly supported as it is within the community and the authority, is well equipped to find a way around any problems the Act may cause, like the school of the mathematics' project discussed earlier.

In sum, the report confirms and celebrates what many teachers already do. As Cox observed, getting a National Curriculum in place for all schools 'can't be done without enthusiasm from the teachers so it must relate to what they already do'. This, therefore, could be a stimulus to considerable advances in English teaching which make the most of previous apparently oppositional developments in a new constructive balance. Perhaps this is to be the keynote of the next decade.

Other working group reports, though also not without controversy, are broadly in line with recognized educational developments. For many teachers, however, the main threat to practice is in the new forms of assessment, which for some may undo any good emerging from the National Curriculum. Here, again, the situation may not be quite as desperate as it seems. To some extent the proposals are once more a reflection of current practice. As Whitehead (1988) points out, with regard to younger children, 'Teachers already find sensible and non-threatening ways of testing children's competence in the more formalized and traditional curriculum areas. Reading assessments are made and profiles of children's understanding and achievements in literacy and mathematical thinking are kept . . . the best defence against testers' panic is better teaching records . . . for these are far more comprehensive, detailed and predictive than many existing tests at 7'. (p. 69). Only the tests nationally of specific curriculum areas is new. 'The processes of constant monitoring, assessing and diagnosing of difficulties have always been central features of teaching and learning in schools'. Whitehead argues that teachers must adapt to the tests, incorporating them within their current practice, 'playing the testing game' so as to 'produce the statistics while protecting the young learners from the stress of early competition and failure' . . . 'taking children into our confidence about any meaningless test items which we are required to impose on them and make it clear that the tasks have little to do with daily reading, writing or mathematical and scientific investigations' (p. 71).

Professor Black's Task Group on Assessment and Testing (TGAT) report is a superb example of compromise. It has been described as 'extremely skilful' (Maclure, 1988) a 'miracle' no less (Davies, 1988) though not everybody agrees (Gipps, 1988). Produced in the whirlwind time of five months, it seemed to meet the requirements of the Act for a system of national assessment, while calming the fears of many teachers and educationists who had been sceptical of such a system. The report is replete with safeguards. The first condition is teacher commitment. Paragraph 224 notes that 'the strategy will fail if teachers do not come to have confidence in, and commitment to, the new system as a positive part of their teaching'. The scheme envisages the full involvement of teachers, close interdependence between curriculum, teaching and assessment, varied forms of assessment, including assessment via tasks which form a normal part of classroom activity, assessment at the primary level which is compatible with good primary practice and public identification of school attainment only in the light of appropriate data about school inputs. The report also called for widespread consultation and discussion before proposals are put into effect, and adequate resources, including inservice provision. The government in turn, sought to remodify these proposals in the Act more in accordance with their initial intentions. For example, they ignored Black's recommendation that results should only be published within the context of a report on the work of a school as a whole. Black had also advised against the publication of results at age 7, but while this was not made compulsory in the Act, strong recommendations for publication were made. The main principles of the TGAT Report still hold, however, as we move, at the time of writing, into the phase of the development of the standard assessment tasks, with the groups concerned making appropriate TGAT noises.

Negotiation goes on, therefore, and no doubt will continue over the five-year phase-in period. There are of course other significant developments in assessment which could have considerable influence on teaching. Records of achievement are seeking to provide more comprehensive cover, though some (for example, Nuttall, 1988) fear they may be a cover for national assessment rather than liberating and enabling. The GCSE, the launch of which was described in one report as an unmitigated disaster, seems to be offering more scope for varied teaching at secondary level, and perhaps in terms of classroom practice is the more significant reform. One GCSE student wrote, 'In the second and third years we were mostly working out of books and everybody ended up with the same piece of work. Now I have to depend on myself a lot. My work I do is original'. Another student surprised himself by 'doing work he didn't think he was capable of'. An English teacher felt that, 'the emphasis on collaboration, drafting and individuality are helping create confident students far more capable of handling a far wider variety of language forms' (*Times Educational Supplement*, 1988). HMI who visited 500 schools awarded the examination a 'good pass' in their first report, in that it raised pupils' motivations and led to improved tuition. Children's enthusiasms in response to wider opportunities to gain and display competence 'contrasts markedly with the boredom present in some lessons which were observed, such as one which consisted solely of copying from the blackboard and another in which pupils did nothing other than complete seemingly endless and repetitive exercises'. They noted however that the problems of implementation were exacerbated in schools where there was a shortage of accommodation and teachers in some subjects. Wragg (*The Guardian*, 14 June 1988) reports, 'In foreign languages the emphasis on oral and written communication in topics such as the family, travel, employment, recreation and leisure, is significantly different from the translation and essay paper of yesteryear. In music, the interweaving of listening to, composing and performing music has led to some brilliantly creative music making'. This is all very compatible with the pedagogical styles mentioned earlier in relation to the OTAL model.

This encouraging progress has been kept within limits by the government's refusal to accept the Higginson Report's recommendation for a broader-based 'A' level to relieve overcrowded syllabuses, to avoid straining, instead of developing pupils' memories, and passive learning. Higginson asked for five subjects instead of three, with more emphasis on understanding and process as compared with content (DES, 1988). One opinion has it that influential members of the government were concerned about what they saw as a threat to standards. Another argument might be that the norm was coming under too great attack. However, the principle of gradual evolution was supported by the government's suggestion that schools adopt a modular approach to 'A' and 'AS' levels, and to use alternative methods of assessment, such as credits, which build up to a final grade. This is not altogether out of keeping with what is happening on either side of 'A' levels in GCSE, and in higher education, where some continuous assessment and modular, flexible degrees are common.

Regression to the norm occurs from all sides, therefore. Where the Act, and related contemporary developments appear to challenge educational principles proven in practice and held dear by the majority of the educational community, they will be held in check by the purchase those principles have already gained on the system. Where, on the other hand, those principles seem to be being furthered, movement in that direction is also restrained. Where this is not done at source, where something has escaped the net, we might anticipate a clawing back. The rejection of the Higginson Report is an example of this. Another is the adjustment made to some of the working group's reports. Science is perhaps the most obvious example here to date. The original working group had recommended that all fourth and fifth year pupils should spend 20 per cent of their school time on 'broad and balanced' science, of which there should be four weighted components: (i) knowledge and understanding; (ii) exploration and investigation; (iii) communication; and (iv) science in action. The Secretary of State was not happy with this for two main reasons. Firstly, he thought it over-ambitious (it is difficult to staff science teaching adequately as it is!); secondly, he wanted to reassert the supremacy of facts over interpretation. The National Curriculum Council duly obliged, and recommended a two-tier syllabus in science, in which some spend 20 per cent of their time leading to a double GCSE, some 12½ per cent, leading to a single GCSE. One might expect to find a disproportionate number of girls in the second group. Much of the good promised in this respect, therefore, is undone. There simply are not enough teachers to implement the National Curriculum. The select committee on education investigating teacher shortage, projects a shortfall of about 30 per cent by 1995 in key subjects. The core subjects in particular may have to be diluted as science, above — or class sizes increased. This, in itself, will promote widespread use of recitation, chalk and talk methods. This will be aided by the restored emphasis on facts. In science, for example, instead of the original four profile components, we now have two (i) knowledge and understanding; and (ii) exploration of science. And so the bargaining goes on.

Conclusion

Supporters of the Act see it as a great reform, comparable to 1944, 1902 and 1870. Not for nothing was it known in its formative stages as the 'Great Education Reform Bill' (GERBIL). Already there are reports of significant developments within the teacher occupational culture, as groups of what Mac An Ghaill (1988a) calls 'new entrepreneurs' become established. These support the enterprise culture and the marketing of schooling. To these, with their increased supervisory and administrative responsibilities, their use of new techniques, and of new abilities acquired through courses, teachers are being reskilled, rather than deskilled. To others, and particularly those who support comprehensive education and egalitarianism, the Act is a disaster. Clearly, to say the least, the legislation is not good for those interests. But in terms of classroom pedagogies, the student who began this chapter may not be too wide of the mark. The pace already generated in all points and at all levels of the system in teacher-, study-, and school-based techniques in the OTAL model I have outlined will gather strength from the more favourable aspects of the Act, and of other current developments. Where they come under attack, they will be shorn up by new alliances and forces of resistance, who will have their senses sharpened about what needs to be preserved. For once, also, the conservative pull of the basic system, which this Act does nothing to alter, may operate to educational advantage. Even Brian Simon, one of the most outspoken critics of the Act, sees it in the longer term as only a temporary interruption in the 'slow but steady march towards a decent education for all children', going so far as to recognize that 'from the present crisis positive outcomes may be achieved' (1988, p. 185). The Dark Ages did come to an end. The monks were successful in their work of preservation, and some of them are known to have secured some material possessions and enjoyed some worldly comforts. Even Gradgrind was converted. Wittgenstein apparently always expected the worst, hence one of his favourite quotations: 'Always remember, when things are going well, they don't have to'. But the converse also surely applies, and for those who see the Act as signalling the death of education as we know it, perhaps this 'Tanka' on 'Death' from a 13-year old philosopher might provide some comfort:

Death

A gruesome word which
Unnecessarily drills
Fear in mortal souls.
In reality, the end
Is only the true beginning.

References

ABBOTT, B., GILBERT, S. and LAWSON, R. (1989) 'Towards anti-racist awareness: Confessions of some teacher converts' in WOODS, P. (Ed.) *Working for Teacher Development*, Cambridge, Peter Francis.

ACTON, T.A. (1980) 'Educational criteria of success: Some problems in the work of Rutter, Maughan, Mortimore and Ouston', *Educational Research*, 22, 3, pp. 163–73.

AMES, V.M. (1973) 'No separate self' in CORTI, W.R. (Ed.) *The Philosophy of George Herbert Mead*, Amiswiler Bucherie, Winterhur, Switzerland, pp. 43–58.

ANDERSON, B. (1988) 'Equal opportunities and the National Curriculum — a challenge to educators' in SIMONS, H. (Ed.) *The National Curriculum*, London, British Educational Research Association, pp. 27–37.

ANDERSON, C.S. (1982) 'The search for school climate: A review of the research', *Review of Educational Research*, 52, 3, pp. 368–420.

ANON (1988) 'Confessions of a sociologist', *Times Educational Supplement*, 15 January, p. 26.

APPLE, M. (1982) *Education and Power*, London, Routledge and Kegan Paul.

APPLE. M. and TEITELBAUM, K. (1986) 'Are teachers losing control of their skills and curriculum?' *Journal of Curriculum Studies*, 18, 2, pp. 177–84.

ARCHER, M. (1989) Audio-Cassette 2, Course E208, *Exploring Educational Issues*, Milton Keynes, Open University Press.

ARNOT, M. (1989) 'The challenge of equal opportunities: Personal and professional development for secondary teachers' in WOODS, P. (Ed.) *Working for Teacher Development*, Cambridge, Peter Francis.

ASHTON, P.T. and WEBB, R.B. (1986) *Making a Difference: Teachers' Sense of Efficacy and Student Achievement*, London, Longman.

ASPINWALL, K. (1989) '"A bit of the sun": Teacher development through an LEA curriculum initiative' in WOODS, P. (Ed.) *Working for Teacher Development*, Cambridge, Peter Francis.

ASSISTANT MASTERS AND MISTRESSES ASSOCIATION (AMMA) (1986) *A Review of the Research into Primary Causes of Stress Among Teachers*, London, AMMA.

BAKER, C. and PERROTT, C. (1988) 'The news session in infants and primary school classrooms', *British Journal of Sociology of Education*, 9, 1, pp. 19–38.

BALL, D. (1972) 'Self and identity in the context of deviance: The case of criminal abortion' in SCOTT, R.A. and DOUGLAS, J.D. (Eds) *Theoretical Perspectives on Deviance*, New York, Basic Books..

References

BALL, S.J. (1987) *The Micro-Politics of the School: Towards a Theory of School Organizations*, London, Methuen.

BARKER, B. (1987) 'Visions are off the agenda', *The Times Educational Supplement*, 3 December, p. 4.

BARNES, D., BRITTEN, J. and ROSEN, H. (1969) *Language, the Learner and the School*, Harmondsworth, Penguin.

BECKER, H.S. (1960) 'Notes on the concept of commitment', *American Journal of Sociology*, 66, July, pp. 32–40.

BECKER, H.S. (1964) 'Personal change in adult life', *Sociometry*, 27, 1, pp. 40–53.

BECKER, H.S. (1976) 'The career of the Chicago public schoolteacher' in HAMMERSLEY, M. and WOODS, P. (Eds) *The Process of Schooling*, London, Routledge and Kegan Paul.

BECKER, H.S. (1977) 'Personal change in adult life' in COSIN, B. *et al.* (Ed.) *School and Society*, (2nd edn), London, Routledge and Kegan Paul.

BELL, R.E. (1981) Approaches to Teaching, Unit 15 of Course E200 *Contemporary Issues in Education*, Milton Keynes, Open University Press.

BENNETT, N. (1976) *Teaching Styles and Pupil Progress*, London, Open Books.

BENNETT, N. (1987) 'The search for the effective primary school teacher' in DELAMONT, S. (Ed.) *The Primary School Teacher*, Lewes, Falmer Press.

BENNETT, N., ANDREAE, J., HEGARY, P. and WADE, B. (1980) *Open Plan Schools: Teaching, Curriculum, Design*, Windsor, NFER.

BENNETT, N., DESFORGES, C., COCKBURN, A. and WILKINSON, B. (1984) *The Quality of Pupil Learning Experiences*, London, Lawrence Erlbaum.

BEN-PERETZ, M., BROMME, R. and HALKER, R. (Eds) (1986) *Advances of Research on Teacher Thinking*, Berwyn/Lisse, ISATT/Swets and Zeitlinger.

BERGER, P.L. (1963) *An Invitation to Sociology*, Harmondsworth, Penguin.

BERGER, P.L., BERGER, B., and KELLNER, H. (1973) *The Homeless Mind*, Harmondsworth, Penguin.

BERGER, P.L. and LUCKMANN, T. (1967) *The Social Construction of Reality: A Treatise in the Sociology of Knowledge*, Harmondsworth, Penguin.

BERLAK, A. and BERLAK, H. (1981) *The Dilemmas of Schooling*, London, Methuen.

BERNSTEIN, B. (1977a) 'On the classification and framing of educational knowledge' in *Class, Codes and Control*, Vol. 3, London, Routledge and Kegan Paul.

BERNSTEIN, B. (1977b), 'Ritual in education' in *Class, Codes and Control Vol. 3*, London, Routledge and Kegan Paul.

BERNSTEIN, B. (1977c) 'The sociology of education: A brief account' in *Class, Codes and Control Vol. 3*, London, Routledge and Kegan Paul.

BERTAUX, D. (Ed.) (1981) *Biography and Society*, Beverly Hills, CA, Sage.

BETHELL, A. (1980) 'Getting away from it all', *Times Educational Supplement*, 21 March, pp. 22–3.

BEYNON, J. (1985) *Initial Encounters in the Secondary School*, Lewes, Falmer Press.

BLACKIE, P. (1980) 'Not quite proper' in REEDY, S. and WOODHEAD, M. (Eds) *Family, Work and Education*, London, Hodder and Stoughton.

BLUMER, H. (1966) 'Sociological implications of the thought of G.H. Mead', *American Journal of Sociology*, 71, March, pp. 535–44.

BOURDIEU, P. (1971) 'Systems of education and systems of thought' in YOUNG, M.F.D. (Ed.) *Knowledge and Control*, London, Collier-Macmillan.

BRIGHOUSE, T. (1987) 'Goodbye to the head and the history man', *Guardian*, 21 July, p. 11.

BRITTAN, A. (1973) *Meanings and Situations*, London, Routledge and Kegan Paul.

BRITTON, J. (1975) 'The development of writing abilities, 11–18', *Schools Council Research*, London, Macmillan.

BROADFOOT, P. and OSBORN, M. (1988) 'What professional responsibility means to teachers: National contexts and classroom constraints', *British Journal of Sociology of Education*, 9, 3, pp. 265–87.'

BROADHEAD, P. (1987) 'A blueprint for the good teacher? The HMI/DES model of good primary practice', *British Journal of Educational Studies*, XXXV, 1, pp. 57–72.

BRUNER, J.S. (1962) 'The creative surprise' in GRUBBER, H.E., TERRELL, G. and WORTHEIMER, M. (Eds) *Contemporary Approaches to Creative Thinking*, New York, Atherton Press.

BRUNER, J. (1986) *Actual Minds, Possible Worlds*, Harvard, MA, Harvard University Press.

BURGESS, R.G. (1985) *Issues in Educational Research*, Lewes, Falmer Press.

CAMILLERI, C. (1986) *Cultural Anthropology and Education*, Paris, Logan Page/UNESCO.

CARROLL, J.B. (1963) 'A model for school learning', *Teachers College Record*, 64, pp. 723–33.

CARR, W. and KEMMIS, S. (1986) *Becoming Critical*, Lewes, Falmer Press.

CENTRAL ADVISORY COUNCIL FOR EDUCATION (ENGLAND) (1963) *Half Our Future* (The Newsom Report), London, HMSO.

CHANDLER, L. (1989) 'Running to stand still', *Guardian*, 30 May, p. 21.

CHISHOLM, L.A. and HOLLAND, J. (1986) 'Girls and occupational choice: Antisexism in action in a curriculum development project', *British Journal of Sociology of Education*, 7, 4, pp. 353–65.

CLARK, C.M. and YINGER, R.J. (1987) 'Teacher planning' in CALDERHEAD, J. (Ed.) *Exploring Teachers' Thinking*, London, Cassell.

COHEN, A. (1976) 'The elasticity of evil: Changes in the social definition of deviance' in HAMMERSLEY, M. and WOODS, P. (Eds) *The Process of Schooling*, London, Routledge and Kegan Paul.

COLE, M. and WALKER, S. (Eds) (1989) *Teaching and Stress*, Milton Keynes, Open University Press.

CONNELL, R.W. (1985) *Teachers' Work*, London, Allen and Unwin.

CONNELLY, M.F. (1972) 'The functions of curriculum development', *Interchange*, 3, 2–3, pp. 161–77.

CONNELLY, M. and CLANDININ, J. (1985) 'Personal practical knowledge and the modes of knowing: Relevance for teching and learning', *NSSE Yearbook*, 84, 2, pp. 174–98.

COOLEY, C.H. (1902) *Human Nature and the Social Order*, New York, Charles Scribner's Sons.

COSER. L.A. (1974) *Greedy Institutions*, New York, Free Press.

COVERDALE, G.M. (1973) 'Some determinants of teacher morale', *Educational Review*, 26, 1, pp. 30–8.

CROPLEY, A.J. (1967) *Creativity*, London, Longmans.

DALE, I.R. (1978) 'From endorsement to disintegration: Progressive education from the golden age to the green paper', *Conference of the Standing Committee for Studies in Education*, King's College, London, December.

DAVIES, B. (1982) *Life in the Classroom and Playground: The Accounts of Primary School Children*, London, Routledge and Kegan Paul.

DAVIES, B. (1988) 'Destroying teacher motivation? The impact of nationalising the curriculum on the education process', *Working Papers in Urban Education No. 3*, Centre for Educational Studies, King's College, London.

DAVIS, F. (1972) *Illness, Interaction and the Self,* Belmont, CA, Wadsworth.

DAVIS, O.L. Jr (1987) 'Some notes on the persistence of the myth of local control of the curriculum: A Texas case,' *Curriculum*, 8, 2, pp. 33–6.

DEEM, R. (1987) 'Bringing gender equality into schools' in WALKER, S. and BARTON, L. (Eds) *Changing Policies, Changing Teachers*, Milton Keynes, Open University Press.

DENSCOMBE, M. (1980) '"Keeping 'em quiet"': The significance of noise for the practical activity of teaching' in WOODS. P. (Ed.) *Teacher Strategies*, London, Croom Helm.

DENSCOMBE, M. (1985) *Classroom Control: A Sociological Perspective*, London, Allen and Unwin.

DENZIN, N. (1978) *The Research Act in Sociology: A Theoretical Introduction to Sociological Methods*, London, Butterworths.

DEPARTMENT OF EDUCATION AND SCIENCE (1982) *The New Teacher in School*, London, HMSO.

DEPARTMENT OF EDUCATION AND SCIENCE (1983) *Teaching Quality*, London, HMSO.

DEPARTMENT OF EDUCATION AND SCIENCE (1985a) *Better Schools*, London, HMSO.

DEPARTMENT OF EDUCATION AND SCIENCE (1985b) *Education Observed 3 – Good Teachers*, London, HMSO.

DEPARTMENT OF EDUCATION AND SCIENCE (1985c) *Education 8–12 in Combined and Middle Schools*, London, HMSO.

DEPARTMENT OF EDUCATION AND SCIENCE (1985d) *Education for All* (The Swann Report), London, HMSO.

DEPARTMENT OF EDUCATION AND SCIENCE (1988) *Advancing A Levels* (The Higginson Report), London, HMSO.

DESFORGES, C. (1985) 'Matching tasks to children' in BENNETT, N. and DESFORGES, C. (Eds) *Recent Advances in Classroom Research*, Edinburgh, Scottish Academic Press.

DEUTSCHER, I. (1969) 'Evil companions and naughty behaviour: Some thoughts and evidence bearing on a folk hypothesis', mimeo, Case Western Reserve University.

DICKENS, C. (1839) *Nicholas Nickleby*, London, Nelson.

DICKENS, C. (1907) *Hard Times*, London, Dent.

DONALDSON, M. (1978) *Children's Minds*, London, Fontana.

DOYLE, V. (1987) 'When school is very definitely out', *Guardian,* 11 August.

DUNHAM, J. (1984) *Stress in Teaching*, London, Croom Helm.

EDWARDS, D. and MERCER, N. (1978) *Common Knowledge: The Development of Understanding in the Classroom*, London, Methuen.

EISNER, E.W. (1979) *The Educational Imagination*, London, Collier Macmillan.

EISNER, E.W. (1985) *The Art of Educational Evaluation: A Personal View*, Lewes, Falmer Press.

ELBAZ, F. (1981) 'The teacher's "practical knowledge": Report of a case study', *Curriculum Inquiry*, 11, 1, pp. 43–71.

ELBAZ, F. (1983) *Teacher Thinking: A Study of Practical Knowledge*, London, Croom Helm.

ELLIOT, J. (1988) 'The state v education: The challenge for teachers' in SIMON, H. (Ed.) *The National Curriculum*, London, British Educational Research Association, pp. 46–63.

FARADAY, A. and PLUMMER, K. (1979) 'Doing life histories', *Sociological Review*, 27, 4, pp. 773–98.

FISHER, H.A.L. (1936) *A History of Europe*, London, Arnold.

FONTANA, D. (1986) *Teaching and Personality*, London, Blackwell.

FRASER, B.J. (1989) 'Twenty years of classroom climate work: Progress and prospect', *Journal of Curriculum Studies*, 21, 4, pp. 307–28.

FREEDMAN, S. (1987) 'Burntout or beached: Weeding women out of women's true profession' in WALKER, S. and BARTON, L. (Eds) *Changing Policies, Changing Teachers: New Directions for Schooling*, Milton Keynes, Open University Press.

FREIRE, P. (1972) *Pedagogy of the Oppressed*, Harmondsworth, Penguin.

FULLER, M. (1980) 'Black girls in a London comprehensive school' in DEEM, R. (Ed.) *Schooling for Women's Work*, London, Routledge and Kegan Paul.

FURLONG, V.J. (1976) 'Interaction sets in the classroom: Towards a study of pupil knowledge', in HAMMERSLEY, M. and WOODS, P. (Eds) *The Process of Schooling*, London, Routledge and Kegan Paul.

FURLONG, V.J. (1984) 'Black resistance in the liberal comprehensive' in DELAMONT, S. (Ed.) *Readings and Interaction in the Classrooms*, London, Methuen.

GALTON, M. (1983) 'Classroom research and the teacher' in GALTON, M. and MOON, B. (Eds) *Changing Schools . . . Changing Curriculum*, London, Harper and Row.

GALTON, M. (1987) 'An ORACLE chronicle: A decade of classroom research' in DELAMONT, S. (Ed.) *The Primary School Teacher*, Lewes, Falmer Press.

GALTON, M. and SIMON, B. (Eds) (1980) *Progress and Performance in the Primary Classroom*, London, Routledge and Kegan Paul.

GALTON, M., SIMON, B., and CROLL, P. (1980) *Inside the Primary Classroom*, London, Routledge and Kegan Paul.

GARFINKEL, H. (1967) *Studies in Ethnomethodology*, Englewood Cliffs, NJ, Prentice-Hall.

GATES, P. (1989) 'Developing consciousness and pedagogical knowledge through mutual observation' in WOODS, P. (Ed.) *Working for Teacher Development*, Cambridge, Peter Francis.

GIPPS, C. (1988) 'The TGAT Report: trick or treat?' *Forum*, 31, 1, pp. 4–6.

GLASER, B.G. and STRAUSS, A.L. (1967) *The Discovery of Grounded Theory*, London, Weidenfeld and Nicolson.

GOFFMAN, E. (1961) *Encounters*, New York, Bobbs-Merrill.

GOFFMAN, E. (1967) *Interaction Ritual*, New York, Doubleday Anchor.

GOFFMAN, E. (1968) *Asylums*, Harmondsworth, Penguin.

GOFFMAN, E. (1971) *The Presentation of Self in Everyday Life*, Harmondsworth, Penguin.

GOLDTHORPE, J., LOCKWOOD, D., BECHHOFFER, F. and PLATT, J. (1971) *The Affluent Worker in the Class Structure*, Cambridge, Cambridge University Press.

GOLDTHORPE, J.H. and LLEWELLYN, C. (1977) 'Class mobility in modern Britain: Three theses examined', *Sociology*, 11, 2, pp. 257–87.

GOODSON, I. (1980) 'Life histories and the study of schooling', *Interchange*, 11, 4, pp. 62–76.

GOODSON, I. (1987) *School Subjects and Curriculum Change*, Lewes, Falmer Press.

GRACE, G. (1972) *Role Conflict and the Teacher*, London, Routledge and Kegan Paul.

GRACE, G. (1978) *Teachers, Ideology and Control*, London, Routledge and Kegan Paul.

GRACEY, H. (1972) *Curriculum or Craftsmanship: Elementary School Teachers in a Bureaucratic System*, Chicago, IL, University of Chicago Press.

GREEN, A. (1977) 'Structural features of the classroom' in WOODS, P. and HAMMERSLEY, M. (Eds) *School Experience*, London, Croom Helm.

GRUGEON, E. and WOODS, P. (1990) *Educating All: Multicultural Perspectives in the Primary School*, London, Routledge.

GUMP, P. (1971) 'What's happening in the elementary school classroom' in WESTOBY, J. and BELLOCK, A.A. (Eds) *Research into Classroom Processes*, New York, Teachers College Press.

HALSEY, A.H., HEATH, A.F. and RIDGE, J.N. (1980) *Origins and Destinations*, Oxford, Oxford University Press.

HAMBLIN, D.H. (1978) *The Teacher and Pastoral Care*, Oxford, Blackwell.

HAMMERSLEY, M. (1977) 'Teacher Perspectives', Units 9–10 of Course E202, *Schooling and Society*, Open University Press, Milton Keynes.

HANSON, D. and HERRINGTON, M. (1976) *From College to Classroom: The Probationary Year*, London, Routledge and Kegan Paul.

HARGREAVES, A. (1977) 'Progressivism and pupil autonomy', *Sociological Review*, 25, 3, pp. 585–621.

HARGREAVES, A. (1978) 'Towards a theory of classroom coping strategies' in BARTON, L. and MEIGHAN, R. (Eds) *Sociological Interpretations of Schooling and Classrooms*, Driffield, Nafferton Books.

HARGREAVES, A. (1979) 'Strategies, decisions and control: Interaction in a middle school classroom' in EGGLESTON, J. (Ed.) *Teacher Decision-Making in the Classroom*, London, Routledge and Kegan Paul.

HARGREAVES, A. (1981) 'Teaching and Control', Unit 10 (Part I) of *Course E200, Contemporary Issues in Education*, Milton Keynes, Open University Press.

HARGREAVES, A. (1984) 'The significance of classroom coping strategies' in HARGREAVES, A. and WOODS, P. (Eds) *Classrooms and Staffrooms*, Milton Keynes, Open University Press.

HARGREAVES, A. (1988) 'Teaching quality: A sociological analysis', *Journal of Curriculum Studies*, 20, 3, pp. 211–31.

HARGREAVES, D.H. (1967) *Social Relations in a Secondary School*, London, Routledge and Kegan Paul.

HARGREAVES, D.H. (1972) *Interpersonal Relations and Education*, London, Routledge and Kegan Paul.

HARGREAVES, D.H. (1984) *Improving Secondary Schools*, London, ILEA.

HARGREAVES, D.H., HESTER, S.K. and MELLOR, F.J. (1975) *Deviance in Classrooms*, London, Routledge and Kegan Paul.

HARRIS, A. (1976) 'Intuition and the arts of teaching', Unit 18 of course E203 *Curriculum Design and Development*, Milton Keynes, Open University Press.

HARTLEY, D. (1985) *Understanding the Primary School: A Sociological Analysis*, London, Croom Helm.

HAVILAND, J. (Eds) (1988) *Take Care, Mr Baker!*, London, Fourth Estate.

HEWTON, E. (1988) *School Focused Staff Development*, Lewes, Falmer Press.

HIRST, P.H. (1971) 'What is teaching?', *Journal of Curriculum Studies*, 3, 1, pp. 9–10.

HOLLIES, A. (1988) '*Coping with change: An examination of the extent of stress among further education lecturers*', MA dissertation, Milton Keynes, Open University.

HOLLY, D. (1973) *Beyond Curriculum*, London, Hart-Davis, MacGibbon.

HOLT, M. (1988) 'The whole curriculum: prospect', *Cambridge Journal of Education*, 18, 2, pp. 155–66.

HOWARD, J. (1989) 'On teaching, knowledge and "middle ground"', *Harvard*

Educational Review, 59, 2, pp. 226–39.

HOYLE, E. (1969) *The Role of the Teacher*, London, Routledge and Kegan Paul.

HOYLE, E. (1980) 'Professionalization and deprofessionalization in education' in HOYLE, E. and MEGARRY, J. (Eds) *World Yearbook of Education 1980: professional development of teachers*, London, Kogan Page, pp. 42–54.

HULL, C. (1985) 'Pupils and teacher educators', *Cambridge Journal of Education*, 15, 1, pp. 1–8.

HUNTER, C. and HEIGHWAY, P. (1980) 'Morale, motivation and management in middle schools' in BUSH, T., GLATTER, R., GOODEY, J. and RICHES, C. (Eds) *Approaches to School Management*, Milton Keynes, Open University Press.

HUSTLER, D., CASSIDY, A., and CUFF, E.C. (Eds) (1986) *Action Research in Classroom and Schools*, London, Allen and Unwin.

ILLICH, I. (1973) *Deschooling Society*, Harmondsworth, Penguin Books.

JACKSON, P.W. (1968) *Life in Classrooms*, New York, Rinehart and Winston.

JACKSON, P.W. (1977) 'The way teachers think' in GLIDEWELL, J.C. (Ed.) *The Social Context of Learning and Development*, New York, Gardner Press.

JACKSON, P.W. and MESSICK, S. (1965) 'The person, the product and the response: Conceptual problems in the assessment of creativity', *Journal of Personality*, 33, pp. 309–29.

JENKS, C. (1971) *'A question of control: A case study of interaction in a junior school'*, Unpublished M.Sc. thesis, University of London Institute of Education.

JOWELL, R. (Ed.) (1988) *British Social Attitudes*, Aldershot, Gower.

JUDGE, H. (1976) *School Is Not Yet Dead*, London, Longmans.

KANTER, R.M. (1974) 'Commitment and social organization' in FIELD, D. (Ed.) *Social Psychology for Sociologists*, London, Nelson.

KELLY, A. (1981) (Ed.) *The Missing Half: Girls and Science Education*, Manchester, Manchester University Press.

KELLY, A. (1985) 'The construction of masculine science', *British Journal of Sociology of Education*, 6, 2, pp. 133–54.

KEMMIS, S., COLE, P. and SUGGET, D. (1983) *Towards the Socially Critical School*, Australia, Victorian Institute of Secondary Education.

KING, R.A. (1978) *All Things Bright and Beautiful*, Chichester, Wiley.

KOUNIN, J.S. (1970) *Discipline and Group Management in Classrooms*, New York, Holt, Rinehart and Winston.

KUHN, M.H. (1964) 'The reference group reconsidered', *Sociological Quarterly*, 5, pp. 6–21.

KYRIACOU, C. (1987) 'Teacher stress and burnout: An international review', *Educational Research*, 29, 2, pp. 146–52.

KYRIACOU, C. and SUTCLIFFE, J. (1978) 'Teacher stress and satisfaction', *Educational Research*, 21, 2, pp. 89–109.

LACEY, C. (1976) 'Problems of sociological fieldwork: A review of the methodology of "Hightown Grammar"' in HAMMERSLEY, M. and WOODS, P. (Eds) *The Process of Schooling*, London, Routledge and Kegan Paul.

LACEY, C. (1977) *The Socialization of Teachers*, London, Methuen.

LATHER, P. (1986) 'Research as praxis', *Harvard Educational Review*, 56, 3, pp. 257–77.

LAWN. M. and OZGA, J. (1981) 'The educational worker: A reassessment of teachers' in BARTON, L. and WALKER, S. (Eds) *Schools, Teachers and Teaching*, Lewes, Falmer Press.

LAWRENCE, D.H. (1915) *The Rainbow*, London, Heinemann.

LAWTON, D. (1987) 'Teaching quality, quality teaching and the culture of the school: The 1986 SERA lecture', *Scottish Educational Review*, 19, 1, pp. 3–13.

LEE, V. and J. (1987) 'Stories children tell' in POLLARD, A. (Ed.) *Children and Their Primary Schools*, Lewes, Falmer Press.

LEMERT, E. (1978) 'The check forger and his identity' in RUBINGTON, E. and WEINBERG, M.S. (Eds) *Deviance: The Interactionist Perspective*, New York, Macmillan.

LINDESMITH, A.R. (1947) *Opiate Addiction*, Bloomington, IN, Principia Press.

LISTER, I. (1974) 'Drifting into more and more trouble', *Times Educational Supplement*, 1 November.

LOCK, L. (1986) in GODFREY, M. 'Telling tales out of school', *Guardian*, 12 March, p. 22.

LORTIE, D.C. (1973) 'Observations on teaching as work' in TRAVERS, R.M.W. (Ed.) *Second Handbook on Research on Teaching*, Chicago, IL, Rand McNally.

LORTIE, D.C. (1975) *Schoolteacher*, Chicago, IL University of Chicago Press.

MAC AN GHAILL, M. (1988a) 'Teachers' work: Culture and power', paper presented at Conference on *Histories and Ethnographies of Teachers' at Work*, Oxford, St Hilda's College.

MAC AN GHAILL, M. (1988b) *Young, Gifted and Black*, Milton Keynes, Open University Press.

MACDIARMID, H. (1969) *Selected Essays of Hugh MacDiarmid*, (ed. Duncan Glen), London, Cape.

MCKELLAR, P. (1957) *Imagination and Thinking*, London, Cohen and West.

MACKINNON, D.W. (1975) 'IPAR's contribution to the conceptualization and study of creativity' in TAYLOR, I.A. and GETZELS, J.W. (Eds) *Perspectives in Creativity*, Chicago, IL, Aldine.

MCLEAN, M. (1988) 'The Conservative education policy in comparative perspective: Return to an English golden age or harbinger of international policy change?', *British Journal of Educational Studies*, 36, 3, pp. 200–17.

MACLURE, S. (1988) *Education Re-Formed*, London, Hodder and Stoughton.

MCNAMARA, D. (1986) 'The personal qualities of the teacher and educational policy: A critique', *British Educational Research Journal*, 12, 1, pp. 29–36.

MAHONEY, P. (1985) *Schools for the Boys*, London, Hutchinson.

MANNHEIM, K. (1952) 'The problem of generations' in *Essays on the Sociology of Knowledge*, London, Routledge and Kegan Paul.

MARDLE, G. and WALKER, M. (1980) 'Strategies and structure: Some critical notes on teacher socialization' in WOODS, P. (Ed.) *Teacher Strategies*, London, Croom Helm.

MARSHALL, A. (1982) *Whimpering in the Rhododendrons: The Splendours and Miseries of the English Prep School*, London, Fontana.

MASLOW, A.H. (1943) 'A theory of human motivation', *Psychological Review*, 50, pp. 370–96.

MAY, N. and RUDDUCK, J. (1983) *Sex-Stereotyping and the Early Years of Schooling*, Norwich, Centre for Applied Research in Education.

MAY, R. (1976) *The Courage to Create*, London, Collins.

MEAD, G.H. (1934) *Mind, Self and Society*, Chicago, IL, University of Chicago Press.

MEASOR, L. (1983) 'Gender and the sciences: Pupils' gender-based conceptions of school subjects' in HAMMERSLEY, M. and HARGREAVES, A. (Eds) *Curriculum Practice: Some Sociological Case Studies*, Lewes, Falmer Press.

MEASOR, L. and WOODS, P. (1984) *Changing Schools: Pupils Perspectives on Transfer to a Comprehensive*, Milton Keynes, Open University Press.

MILLER, C. and PARLETT, M. (1974) *Up to the Mark*, London, Society for Research into Higher Education.

MOONEY, T. (1987) 'A morale boost for heads is long overdue', *Education*, 14 August, p. 130.

MORRISON, A. and MCINTYRE, D. (1969) *Teachers and Teaching*, Harmondsworth, Penguin.

MORTIMORE, P., SAMMONS, P., LEWIS, L. and ECOB, R. (1988) *School Matters: The Junior Years*, London, Open Books.

MUSGROVE, F. (1974a) 'Education of teachers for a changing role' in TURNER, J.D. and RUSHTON, J. (Eds) *The Teacher in a Changing Society*, Manchester, Manchester University Press.

MUSGROVE, F. (1974b) *Ectsasy and Holiness*, London, Methuen.

MUSGROVE, F. and TAYLOR, P. (1974) *Society and the Teacher's Role*, London, Routledge and Kegan Paul.

NATIONAL CURRICULUM COUNCIL (1988) *English for Ages 5 to 11* (The Cox Report), London, HMSO.

NEILL, A.S. (1968) *Summerhill*, Harmondsworth, Penguin.

NIAS, J. (1981) 'Commitment and motivation in primary school teachers', *Educational Review*, 33, 3, pp. 181–90.

NIAS, J. (1984) 'The definition and maintenance of self in primary teaching', *British Journal of Sociology in Education*, 5, 3, pp. 267–80.

NIAS, J. (1987) 'One finger, one thumb: A case-study of the partnership between the head and deputy of a nursery/infant school', paper presented at *British Educational Research Conference*, Bristol.

NIAS, J. (1988a) 'What it means to "feel like a teacher": The subjective reality of primary school teaching' in OZGA, J. (Ed.) *Schoolwork: Approaches to the Labour Process of Teaching*, Milton Keynes, Open University Press.

NIAS, J. (1988b) 'Informal education in action. Teachers' accounts' in BLYTH, W.A.L. (Ed.) *Informal Primary Education Today*, Lewes, Falmer Press.

NIAS, J. (1989) *Teachers and Their Work*, London, Methuen.

NIAS, J., SOUTHWORTH, G. and YEOMANS, R. (1989) *Staff Relationships in the Primary School: A Study of Organizational Cultures*, London, Cassell.

NIXON, J. (1981) *A Teacher's Guide to Action Research*, London, Grant McIntyre.

NUTTALL, D. (1988) 'The assessment of learning', Unit 13 in Course E208 *Exploring Educational Issues*, Milton Keynes, Open University Press.

OZGA, J. (1988) 'Teachers' work and careers', Unit W1 in Course EP228 *Frameworks for Teaching*, Milton Keynes, Open University Press.

PARLETT, M. and HAMILTON, D. (1976) 'Evaluation as illumination' in TAWNEY, D. (Ed.) *Curriculum Evaluation Today: trends and implications*, London, Macmillan.

PERINBANAYAGAM, R. (1975) 'The significance of others in the thought of Alfred Schutz, G. H. Mead and C.H. Cooley', *The Sociological Quarterly*, XVI, autumn, pp. 500–21.

PERRINS, R. (1968) in GODFREY, M. 'Telling tales out of school', *Guardian*, 12 March, p. 22.

PLOWDEN REPORT (1967) *Children and Their Primary Schools*, Report of the Central Advisory Council for Education in England, London, HMSO.

POLLARD, A. (1980) 'Teacher interests and changing situations of survival threat in primary school classrooms' in WOODS, P. (Ed.) *Teacher Strategies*, London, Croom Helm.

POLLARD, A. (1982) 'A model of coping strategies', *British Journal of Sociology of Education*, 3, 2, pp. 19–37.

POLLARD, A. (1985) *The Social World of the Primary School*, London, Holt Rinehart and Winston.

POLLARD, A. (1987) *Children and their Primary Schools*, Lewes, Falmer Press.

POWER, M. (1972) 'Neighbourhood, school and juveniles before the courts', *British Journal of Criminology*, 12, pp. 111–32.

PRIBRAM, K.H. (1964) 'Neurological notes on the art of educating' in HILGARD, E.R. (Ed.) *NSSE Yearbook*, Vol. LXIII, Chicago, IL, University of Chicago Press.

REID, W.A. and WALKER, D. (Eds) (1975) *Case Studies in Curriculum Change*, London, Routledge and Kegan Paul.

REYNOLDS, D. (1976) 'The delinquent school' in HAMMERSLEY, M. and WOODS, P. (Eds) *The Process of Schooling*, London, Routledge and Kegan Paul.

RISEBOROUGH, G.F. (1981) 'Teacher careers and comprehensive schooling: An empirical study', *Sociology*, 15, 3, pp. 352–81.

RISEBOROUGH, G.F. (1985) 'Pupils, teachers' careers and schooling: An empirical study' in BALL, S.J. and GOODSON, I.F. (Eds) *Teachers' Lives and Careers*, Lewes, Falmer Press.

ROSSER, E. and HARRÉ, R. (1976) 'The meaning of disorder' in HAMMERSLEY, M. and WOODS, P. (Eds) *The Process of Schooling*, London, Routledge and Kegan Paul.

ROWLAND, S. (1984) *The Enquiring Classroom*, Lewes, Falmer Press.

ROY, W. (1983) *Teaching Under Attack*, London, Croom Helm.

RUBINGTON, E. and WEINBERG, M.S. (Eds) *Deviance: The Interactionist Perspective*, New York, Macmillan.

RUTTER. M., MAUGHAM. B., MORTIMER, P. and OUSTON, J. (1979) *Fifteen Thousand Hours*, London, Open Books.

SCARTH, J. (1987) 'Teacher strategies: A review and a critique', *British Journal of Sociology of Education*, 8, 3, pp. 245–62.

SCHÖN, D.A. (1983) *The Reflective Practitioner: How Professionals Think in Action*, London, Temple Smith.

SCHOSTAK, J.F. and LOGAN, T. (Eds) (1984) *Pupil Experience*, London, Croom Helm.

SCHUTZ, A. (1970) *On Phenomenology and Social Relations: Selected Writings* (Ed. WAGNER, H.R.), Chicago, IL, University of Chicago Press.

SHARP, R. and GREEN, A. (1975) *Education and Social Control*, London, Routledge and Kegan Paul.

SHULMAN. L. (1987) 'Knowledge and teaching: Foundations of the new reform', *Harvard Educational Review*, 57, 1, pp. 1–22.

SIKES, P., MEASOR, L. and WOODS, P. (1985) *Teachers Careers: Crises and Continuities*, Lewes, Falmer Press.

SIMMONDS, G. and NIAS, J. (1989) 'Russian dolls: An account of teachers' professional learning' in WOODS, P. (Ed.) *Working for Teacher Development*, Cambridge, Peter Francis.

SIMON, B. (1988) *Bending the Rules: The Baker 'Reform' of Education*, London, Lawrence and Wishart.

SMITHERS, A. (1989) 'Where have all the teachers gone', *Times Educational Supplement*, 12 May, p. A17.

SMYTH, J. (1987) *Educating Teachers: Changing the Nature of Pedagogical Knowledge*,

Lewes, Falmer Press.

SPOONER, R. (1988) 'The classroom's tainted future', *Education*, 8 April, p. 299.

SPRECHER, T.B. (1959) 'Committee report on criteria of creativity' in TAYLOR, C.W. (Ed.) *The Third University of Utah Research Conference on the Identification of Creative Scientific Talent*, Salt Lake City, UT, University of Utah Press.

STEBBINS, R. (1980) 'The role of humour in teaching' in WOODS, P. (Ed.) *Teacher Strategies*, London, Croom Helm.

STENHOUSE, L. (1985) *Research as a Basis for Teaching*, London, Heinemann.

STONE, G.P. (1962) 'Appearance and the self' in ROSE, A.M. (Ed.) *Human Behaviour and Social Processes*, London, Routledge and Kegan Paul.

STUBBS, M. (1976) *Language, Schools and Classrooms*, London, Methuen.

TAYLOR, W. (1969) *Society and the Education of Teachers*, London, Faber.

TODD, F. (1984) 'Learning and work: Directions for continuing professional and vocational education', *International Journal of Lifelong Education*, 3, pp. 89–104.

TODD, F. (Ed.) (1987) *Planning Continuing Professional Development*, London, Croom Helm.

TROYNA, B. and CARRINGTON, B. (1989) 'Whose side are we on? Ethical dilemmas in research on "race" and education' in BURGESS, R. (Ed.) *The Ethics of Educational Research*, Lewes, Falmer Press.

TURNER, R.H. (1962) 'Role-taking: process versus conformity' in ROSE, A.M. (Ed.) *Human Behaviour and Social Processes*, London, Routledge and Kegan Paul.

TURNER, R.H. (1976) 'The real self: From institution to impulse', *American Journal of Sociology*, 81, 5, pp. 989–1016.

VERNON. M. (1986) 'A burnt out case', *Times Educational Supplement*, 31 January.

WAGNER, A.C. (1987) '"Knots" in teachers' thinking' in CALDERHEAD, J. (Ed.) *Exploring Teachers' Thinking*, London, Cassell.

WALKER, R. and ADELMAN, C. (1976) 'Strawberries' in STUBBS, M. and DELAMONT, S. (Eds) *Explanations in Classroom Observation*, Chichester, Wiley.

WALKER, R. and GOODSON, I. (1977) 'Humour in the Classroom' in WOODS, P. and HAMMERSLEY, M. (Eds) *School Experience*, London, Croom Helm.

WALKERDINE, V. (1981) 'Sex, power and pedagogy', *Screen Education*, 38, pp. 14–24.

WALLER, W. (1932) *The Sociology of Teaching*, New York, Wiley.

WALSH, K. (1988) 'Appraising the teachers: Professionalism and control' in DALE, R., FERGUSSON, R. and ROBINSON, A. (Eds) *Frameworks for Teaching: Readings for the Intending Secondary Teacher*, London, Hodder and Stoughton.

WEBB, J. (1962) 'The sociology of a school', *British Journal of Sociology*, 13, 3, pp. 264–72.

WELTON, J. (1973) 'Comprehensive education and the egalitarian dream', mimeo, University of Bristol.

WERTHMAN, C. (1963) 'Delinquents in schools: A test for the legitimacy of authority', *Berkeley Journal of Sociology*, 8, 2, pp. 39–60.

WESTBURY, I. (1973) 'Conventional classrooms "open" classrooms and the technology of teaching', *Journal of Curriculum Studies*, 5, 2, pp. 91–121.

WHISTLER, T. (1988) *Rushavenn Time*, Brixworth V.C. Primary School, Northants.

WHITEHEAD, M. (1988) 'Testing . . . testing . . . . Can a broadly-based early years curriculum survive the introduction of testing for seven-year-olds?', *Curriculum*, 9, 2, pp. 69–73.

WHYTE, J., DEEM, R., KANT, L. and CRUICKSHANK, M. (Eds) (1985) *Girl Friendly Schooling*, London, Methuen.

WILLIAMS, R. (1968) *Culture and Society*, Harmondsworth, Penguin.

WILLIS, P. (1977) *Learning to Labour*, Farnborough, Saxon House.

WILSON, B.R. (1962) 'The teacher's role: A sociological analysis', *British Journal of Sociology*, 13, 1, pp. 15–32.

WOODS, P. (1978) 'Negotiating the demands of schoolwork', *Journal of Curriculum Studies*, 10, 4, pp. 309–27.

WOODS, P. (1979a) *The Divided School*, Routledge and Kegan Paul.

WOODS, P. (1979b) 'The language of order' in HAIG, G. (Ed.) *On Our Side*, London, Temple-Smith.

WOODS, P. (Ed.) (1980) *Teacher Strategies*, London, Croom Helm.

WOODS, P. (1983a) *Sociology and the School*, London, Routledge and Kegan Paul.

WOODS, P. (1983b) 'Coping at school through humour', *British Journal of Sociology of Education*, 4, 2, pp. 111–24.

WOODS, P. (1986) *Inside Schools: Ethnography in Educational Research*, London, Routledge and Kegan Paul.

WOODS, P. (1987) 'Becoming a junior: Pupil development following transfer from infants' in POLLARD, A. (Ed.) *Children and Their Primary Schools*, Lewes, Falmer Press.

WOODS, P. (1989a) 'Learning through friendship: Teaching and learning opportunities in primary school' in BURGESS, H. (Ed.) *Teaching in the Primary School: Careers, Management and Curricula*, London, Croom Helm.

WOODS, P. (Ed.) (1989b) *Working for Teacher Development*, Cambridge, Peter Francis.

WOODS, P. and POLLARD, A. (Eds) (1988) *Sociology and Teaching*, London, Croom Helm.

WRIGHT, C. (1986) 'School processes – an ethnographic study' in EGGLESTON, J., DUNN, D. and ANJALI, M. (Eds) *Education for Some: The Educational and Vocational Experiences of 15–18 year old Members of Minority Ethnic Groups*, Stoke on Trent, Trentham Books.

YEOMANS, R. (1989) 'Primary school staff relationships', *Forum*, 31, 3, pp. 67–8.

ZEICHNER, K. (1983) 'Alternative paradigms of teacher education', *Journal of Teacher Education*, 31, pp. 3–9.

Author Index

Subject Index